Shoot the
Piano Player

Shoot the Piano Player

François Truffaut, director

Peter Brunette, editor

Rutgers University Press

New Brunswick, New Jersey

Shoot the Piano Player is volume 18 in the Rutgers Films in Print series

Copyright © 1993 by Rutgers, The State University

Library of Congress Cataloging-in-Publication Data

Shoot the piano player: François Truffaut, director /
  Peter Brunette, editor.

    p.   cm.—(Rutgers films in print; v. 18)
  "Truffaut filmography, 1954–1983": p.
  Includes bibliographical references.
  ISBN 0-8135-1941-1 (cloth)
  ISBN 0-8135-1942-X (pbk.)
  1. Tirez sur le pianiste. 2. Truffaut, François—
Criticism and interpretation. I. Truffaut,
François. II. Brunette, Peter. III. Series.
PN1997.T533S5   1993
791.43′72—dc20   92-32702
                                                 CIP

The film *Shoot the Piano Player* is based on the novel *Down There* by David Goodis. The English-language version of the continuity script is used by virtue of an agreement between Hélène Laroche Davis and the Estate of David Goodis, dated December 16, 1979.

Illustrations on pages 4, 12, 70, 89, 90, 106, 107, 110, 124, and 143 are reproduced courtesy of the Museum of Modern Art/ Film Stills Archive. Stills on pages 92 and 225 are used courtesy of Les Films du Carrosse.

We wish to thank Hélène Laroche Davis for the following materials, some of which were provided to her by François Truffaut and which Ms. Davis translated: "An Interview with François Truffaut," with a one-page introduction; budget page for the film.

Interviews: "I Wanted to Treat *Shoot the Piano Player* like a Tale by Perrault: An Interview with François Truffaut," by Yvonne Baby, originally published as "J'ai voulu traiter *Tirez sur le pianiste* à la manière d'un conte de Perrault," *Le Monde,* November 24, 1960; copyright © 1960 by *Le Monde;* reprinted by permission of the publisher. François Truffaut, "Adapting *Shoot the Piano Player,*" adapted and excerpted from "Ce qu'a dit François Truffaut," *Cinéma 67* 112 (January 1967): 41–44; reprinted by permission of *Cinéma 67.* François Truffaut, "Should Films Be Politically Committed?" from "Questions à l'auteur," *Cinéma 61* 52 (January 1961): 7–11; copyright © 1961 by La Fédération Française des Ciné-Clubs, reprinted by permission of *Cinéma 61.* "From an Interview with François Truffaut," by Michel Chion, originally published in *Cahiers du Cinéma* 138 (December 1962): 50–51; copyright © by Les Editions de l'Etoile; reprinted by permission of Les Editions de l'Etoile and Grove Press, Inc.

Reviews: Alain Vargas, *Cinéma 60* (March 1960): 31–35, copyright © 1960 by *Cinéma 60;* reprinted by permission of the publishers. Marcel Martin, "*Le Pianiste* de Truffaut," *Cinema 61* 52 (January 1961): 5–7, copyright © 1961 by *Cinéma 61;* reprinted by permission of the publishers. Edith Oliver, "In Perfect Tune," *The New Yorker,* August 4, 1962, reprinted by permission; copyright © 1962, 1990, originally in *The New Yorker.* "Tirez sur le pianiste," *Variety,* August 31, 1960; reprinted with permission from *Variety.* Peter John Dyer, *Sight and Sound* 30, no. 1 (Winter 1960–1961), reprinted by permission. Pauline Kael, "Shoot the Piano Player," originally appeared in *Film Culture;* reprinted from *I Lost It at the Movies* (Boston: Atlantic–Little, Brown, 1965): 189–194; copyright © 1954, 1955, 1961, 1962, 1963, 1964, 1965 by Pauline Kael; reprinted by permission of Pauline Kael. Andrew Sarris, "Shoot the Piano Player," *The Village Voice,* July 26, 1962; reprinted by permission of the author and *The Village Voice.* Bosley Crowther, *The New York Times,* July 24, 1962; copyright © 1962 by The New York Times Company; reprinted by permission. Dwight Macdonald, *Esquire,* March 1961; copyright © 1961 by Dwight Macdonald; reprinted by permission of the author, *Esquire,* and the Hearst Corporation.

Commentaries: Gabriel Pearson and Eric Rhode, "Cinema of Appearance," *Sight and Sound* 30, no. 4 (Autumn 1961); reprinted by permision. Annette Insdorf, excerpt from "Are Women Magic?" from *François Truffaut* by Annette Insdorf (New York: Touchstone, 1989); copyright © 1978 by Annette Insdorf, reprinted by permission of Georges Borchardt, Inc., for the author. Allen Thiher, "The Existential Play in Truffaut's Early Films, " *Literature/Film Quarterly* 5 (Summer 1977): 183–197; copyright © 1977 by Salisbury State University. Leo Braudy, "Truffaut, Godard, and the Genre Film as Self-Conscious Art," from *The World in a Frame* by Leo Braudy; copyright © 1976 by Leo Braudy; used by permission of Doubleday, a division of Bantam Doubleday Dell Publishing Group, Inc. James Monaco, "The Statement of Genres, " from *The New Wave: Truffaut, Godard, Chabrol, Rohmer, Rivette* by James Monaco; copyright © 1976 by James Monaco, reprinted by permission of Oxford University Press, Inc. C. G. Crisp, "*Tirez sur le Pianiste,*" from *François Truffaut* by C. G. Crisp; reprinted courtesy of Henry Holt & Company and November Books. Don Allen, "*Tirez sur le Pianiste,*" from *Finally Truffaut* by Don Allen; copyright © 1985 by Beaufort Books. Jean-Paul Török, "The Sensitive Spot," originally published as "Le Point Sensible," *Positif* 38 (March 1961): 39–47; copyright © 1961 by Editions du Terrain Vague, reprinted by permission of *Positif.* Graham Petrie, "On *Shoot the Piano Player*" from *The Cinema of François Truffaut* by Graham Petrie (New York: A. S. Barnes, 1970); copyright © 1970 by A. S. Barnes & Co.; reprinted by permission of the Tantivy Press, Ltd. Roger Greenspun, "Through the Looking Glass," *Moviegoer* 1 (Winter 1964): 3–11; copyright © 1964 by Roger Greenspun; reprinted by permission of the author. Karel Reisz and Gavin Millar, "The Technique of *Shoot the Piano Player,*" from *The Technique of Film Editing* by Karel Reisz and Gavin Millar, 2nd rev. ed. (London: Focal Press, 1968), pp. 330–344; copyright © 1968 by Focal Press, Ltd.; reprinted by permission of Butterworth-Heinemann Ltd.

The following translations by Leo Braudy are copyright © 1972 by Leo Braudy and reprinted courtesy of the translator: Interviews: "I Wanted to Treat *Shoot the Piano Player* like a Tale by Perrault: An Interview with François Truffaut," by Yvonne Baby; François Truffaut, "Adapting *Shoot the Piano Player*"; François Truffaut, "Should Films Be Politically Committed?"; "From an Interview with François Truffaut," by Michel Chion. Reviews: Alain Vargas, *Cinéma 1960;* Marcel Martin, "*Le Pianiste* de Truffaut." Commentary: Jean-Paul Török, "The Sensitive Spot."

Acknowledgments

Several people have been helpful in the creation of this book. Hélène Laroche Davis supplied—in addition to her unpublished interview with Truffaut, which is included in this volume—a great deal of other information on *Shoot the Piano Player* that has been useful to me. The film's budget sheet also came from her collection. Thanks are due to Leo Braudy for many past kindnesses and for the excellent example of his *Focus on "Shoot the Piano Player,"* now unfortunately out of print, upon which the present volume to a large extent depends. Many of the pieces that make up the "Interviews, Reviews, and Commentaries" section originally appeared more than twenty years ago in Professor Braudy's book; the editing of these articles and many of their titles were supplied by him, as were the English translations of those reviews and essays that originally appeared in French. Donie Durieu, in Pittsburgh and Puygiron, helped me with the linguistic nuances of the film's famous song, "Avanie et Framboise."

Dean Kingsley Haynes and the Graduate School of George Mason University provided some welcome funds to pay for permissions, and Scott Breivold, the audiovisual librarian at George Mason's Fenwick Library, provided important technical assistance during the early phases of work on the volume. I am grateful to Pat Loughney at the Library of Congress, who made the frame enlargements on short notice, and to Madeline F. Matz, a librarian at the same institution, dear to my heart for nearly twenty years, who cheerfully and efficiently helped me locate material on the film. I am also grateful to my editor, Leslie Mitchner, for her enthusiasm and drive, legendary in the field of film studies, without which this project would never have been completed. Finally, as always, thanks are due to my wife, Lynne Johnson, who smilingly put up with the manifold, if thankfully minor, obsessions that seem to attend all acts of writing, however modest.

Contents

Introduction

Shoot the Piano Player as Postmodern Text

Peter Brunette

François Truffaut's *Tirez sur le pianiste* (*Shoot the Piano Player*, 1960) is, more than anything else, a film about its own *insouciance,* that French word that, like the film, has never gotten more than partway into English. It is about youth, about thumbing one's nose at all the life-denying rules and regulations (even the rules of the movies), always an attractive stance for each new generation. Life is tragic, it tells us, but it is a tragedy that cannot and should not, finally, be taken very seriously. As Pauline Kael has said of the film, it "is both nihilistic in attitude and, at the same time, in its wit and good spirits, totally involved in life and fun."[1] Supremely self-confident, *Shoot the Piano Player* succeeds by flaunting its madeness. Unlike the American films it simultaneously emulates and discards, it never ceases to push its authorship—the delightful fact that some very clever young man must have made it—in the viewer's face.

Concerned as it is with its own manufacture, it is a modernist text, and stands, not unworthily, in the self-reflexive tradition of the great modernists of literature like James Joyce, Marcel Proust, Virginia Woolf, and Samuel Beckett. (And, as with their work, the political quotient of this modernist self-reflexivity is quite low; for all the film's brash, self-aware nose-thumbing, the politics of *Shoot the Piano Player* is always aesthetic rather than direct or practical.[2]) Yet Truffaut's self-reflexive gestures in this film go beyond the merely modernist toward what has come, many years after the film was made, to be called the postmodernist.

1. Pauline Kael, "*Shoot the Piano Player*," in *I Lost It At The Movies* (New York: Atlantic–Little, Brown & Co., 1965), p. 211, reprinted in this volume.
2. It is important to distinguish between, on the one hand, what Truffaut is doing, in this film and others, and, on the other, what the German playwright and theorist Bertolt Brecht and his cinematic disciple, Jean-Luc Godard, are doing. In his later films, at any rate, Godard's self-reflexivity is almost always meant to make the viewer aware that he or she is watching a spectacle, so as to insure an intellectual and thus political freedom from control by the spectacle. Truffaut, however, is always more than willing to opt for the playful for its own sake.

François Truffaut, Charles Aznavour, and Marie Dubois

Like other postmodernist artifacts, it is a film made of fragments from both the past and the present that comment ironically upon one another—self-contradictory elements that, by calling attention to their difference from each other and insisting on remaining dispersed, never harmonize or let themselves be brought together into some overall meaning.

Some thirty years ago, Truffaut said of *Shoot the Piano Player:*

> In spite of the burlesque side to certain scenes, it's never a parody (because I detest parody except when it begins to rival the beauty of what it's parodying). For me it's something very precise that I would call a *respectful pastiche* of the Hollywood B films from which I learned so much.[3]

What is interesting here is that, in contrasting pastiche and parody, Truffaut is using the very terms used many years later by the Marxist theoretician Fredric Jameson to define postmodernism. In "Postmodernism and Consumer Society," Jameson described postmodernism as pastiche and claimed that

> Pastiche is, like parody, the imitation of a peculiar or unique style, the wearing of a stylistic mask, speech in a dead language: but it is a neutral practice of such mimicry, without parody's ulterior motive, without the satirical impulse, without laughter, without that still latent feeling that there exists something *normal* compared to which what is being imitated is rather comic. Pastiche is blank parody.[4]

For Jameson, of course, this affinity with pastiche, its very quality of being unmoored, is precisely what makes postmodernism suspect, and thus the apoliticism of *Shoot the Piano Player* accords well with later postmodern works. Furthermore, Jameson explicitly connects the postmodern fascination for pastiche with a nostalgia for long-gone forms of popular culture—such as the "Saturday afternoon serial of the Buck Rogers type"—a fascination that is also manifestly in evidence in Truffaut's nostalgic relation to the Hollywood genre films of his youth. What complicates things, though, is that, if Truffaut is, in *Shoot the Piano Player,* uncannily providing an example of Jameson's definition of postmodernism some twenty-five years before the fact, Jameson's association of pastiche with the "death of the subject" or "the end of individualism"—ongoing themes of postmodernism and its theoretical sibling poststructuralism—could not be further

---

3. François Truffaut, "Should Films Be Politically Committed?" translated from "Questions à l'auteur," *Cinéma 61* 52 (January 1971): 7–11, reprinted in this volume. It should also be pointed out, however, that, in keeping with Truffaut's penchant for inconsistency in his film, he elsewhere says "I systematically practiced a mélange of genres and sometimes I didn't hesitate to parody." (Yvonne Baby, "I Wanted to Treat *Shoot the Piano Player* like a Tale by Perrault: An Interview with François Truffaut," *Le Monde,* November 24, 1960, reprinted in this volume.)

4. "Postmodernism and Consumer Society," in *The Anti-Aesthetic: Essays on Postmodern Culture,* ed. Hal Foster (Port Townsend, Wash.: Bay Press, 1983), p. 114.

from Truffaut's constant assertion of his own distinct personality in all of his films. For Jameson, it is *modernism,* not postmodernism, that was "predicated on the invention of a personal, private style, as unmistakable as your fingerprint." *Shoot the Piano Player* works this rich paradox, becoming, in a sense, a modernist, even romantic, assertion of a postmodernist sensibility.

In any case, it is clear that Truffaut's film is a kind of exemplification or enactment of many theoretical issues that have arisen in contemporary post-modern theory. One particularly noteworthy theme is the manner in which the film systematically confounds and dismantles binary oppositions, the (shaky) structure for so much of our thinking, and perhaps for logic itself. One way this challenge is accomplished in the film is through a persistent, critical examination of *borders,* especially the border between inside and outside, and the idea of context or frame that gives a border its sense. Another important postmodernist theme with which the film deals concerns the coherence and unity of the individual self.

After all these years, Truffaut's film has managed to retain to some extent a sense, common to much of postmodernism, of bursting energy and of fascination with surfaces, primarily in the breathlessness of its dialogue and extra-quick cuts and in its often-mentioned mélange of tone and genre. At the same time, however, its zestful spirit has, perhaps inevitably, grown somewhat dim since it first appeared more than thirty years ago. Truffaut, even more than most innovative directors, has been both beneficiary and victim of extensive imitation, proverbially the sincerest form of flattery, but in reality a decidedly mixed blessing. Thus, for example, the stunning freeze-frame ending of his first film, *The 400 Blows*—a freeze-frame that, in the context of the film, is filled with thematic and emotional resonance—has become one of the most tired clichés of television advertising. So, too, with *Shoot the Piano Player,* in the wake of subsequent films in which generic conventions are playfully explored and willfully confused, we can have little idea of the initial impact of the startling and attractive mix of styles that Truffaut's film offered to its audience in 1960.

By way of beginning to think about this film, then, it may be useful to try to recreate its reception when it first appeared. This is, naturally, an impossible task, and one worth attempting, if at all, only with the obstacles firmly in mind. The first problem, of course, is posed by the question, Reception by whom? Even in 1960, different members of the audience presumably constructed meanings of the film, as recent film and television theory has taught us, that were unique and useful in one way or another to themselves. Too much in film studies is dependent upon the positing of some mythically uniform and—in a more sinister light—normative or "standard" response that is in actuality more fiction than fact. Of course, there are also problems of an opposite sort that arise when one tries to take account of this problem—for one thing, basing a reading upon a totally impressionistic, solipsistic view of things is clearly an even more fruitless process. To some extent, though, this eternal problem—what constitutes a true or even "permissible" interpretation—can be circumvented if we avoid seeking the "meaning" of the film and instead concentrate on the field of multiple meanings it triggers and on its (self-)placement in the history of the genres in which it indulges and, in a larger sense, on its placement in the history of cinema itself.

One useful place to begin might be to examine the terms in which the film presented itself (that is, how the film's distributor presented it) to the American audience back in 1960, in the form of a trailer shown in all the "art film" theaters of the era (then, as now, pitifully few in number).[5] A deep, mellifluous male voiceover begins by immediately highlighting *Shoot the Piano Player*'s difference from other films: "a fascinating new film that plays in many keys—all of them delightful, all of them different." This accent on *difference,* once again an important theme in postmodernism, is continued in the written titles: "AN UNUSUAL TITLE ... AN UNUSUAL FILM!" The voiceover continues:

> *Shoot the Piano Player:* A unique combination of melodrama and comedy, of cynicism and sentimentality, of fantasy and fact. . . . *Shoot the Piano Player* is *definitely* an unusual film. It defies classification. In spite of its melodramatic overtones, it is delightfully amusing throughout. Like life itself, a montage of various moods, a potpourri of contrasting emotions. You may call it a modern fairy tale, an improvised pipedream; you may call it an irreverent tribute to Hollywood gangster pictures. But above all, you'll call it great for, above all, *Shoot the Piano Player is* an outstanding motion picture.

The film's contradictory dynamics can be seen clearly embodied in the trailer, for all its brevity. Obviously, even in 1960, its complicated—and funny—playing with genres separated the film from almost everything that had gone before. (Yet, because it so blatantly quotes from film history, and is so preoccupied about its place in that history, the "pastness" that it on one level rejects—and on another level celebrates—is, paradoxically, ever present.) *Shoot the Piano Player* claims to be unrelated to any specific genre, and revels in the fact. At the same time, however, the film is, before anything else, placed within the context or frame of the *other* art films its distributor, Astor Pictures, had already released in the United States. Thus, the trailer begins like this:

> Astor Pictures—the company that gave you *La Dolce Vita,* and François Truffaut, the brilliant young director whose first motion picture, *The 400 Blows,* won the Academy Award and the New York Film Critics award, proudly present *Shoot the Piano Player,* a fascinating new film that plays in many keys—all of them delightful, all of them different.

---

5. This trailer has been usefully appended to the laserdisc version of the film available in the United States from the Criterion Collection. All subsequent quotations from the trailer are taken from this version.

This placement—coupled with the voiceover's delivery, which is remarkably literate and articulate (the text sounds like something read aloud from *The New Yorker* rather than a movie preview) clearly indicates to us that we are meant to regard this supposedly genreless but "classy" (if not classifiable) film as part of another genre, not normally considered as such: the art film.

Shoot the Piano Player's status as art film was also confirmed by its frank sexuality, so different from anything seen on conventional American movie screens at the time. Its sexual content represents, in a sense, another way in which genre conventions and expectations are violated, and it clearly accounts for much of the excitement that the film generated. When Charlie goes to urinate in the beginning of the film while talking to his brother Chico (and comes out zipping up his pants), when one of the dancers at the café tells his partner that his great interest in her chest is justified because he is a doctor, when the prostitute jumps into bed with Charlie (though the most revealing part of this scene was cut in the American version), American audiences were seeing something they were unaccustomed to seeing in Hollywood films.

In any case, the film recuperates its own genre experimentation—its own genre destruction, for that matter, so heavily played up—by reinscribing everything into a larger meta-genre, the "art film," by means of which everything can be understood. In other words, genre is the frame or context that is always necessary for us to begin to understand a film (or anything for that matter); even the destruction of genre must be cast within certain generic terms in order to be read. (In this, the film is similar to, say, a novel that is based as closely as possible on a true story, and that calls the boundaries between fiction and nonfiction into question. The way we deal with this situation is to call it a "nonfiction novel," because we have to call it *something*—even if that something is a contradiction in terms.) The critic James Monaco misunderstands this necessity, I think, when he claims that during this period Truffaut was making genre films and therefore turning his back on "serious art" to make "a commitment to popular art."[6] In fact, the rough playing with generic expectation with which Truffaut is involved here is exactly what removes these films from the level of popular art, where the firmness and unity of genre are always presupposed, allowing them to be understood, really, *only* at the level of the "serious art" film.

This question of the "art film" generic frame that *Shoot the Piano Player* puts around itself, or places itself within, has larger implications as well. The preview (like all advertising of a film, whether in the newspaper, in television spots, or on a poster) puts a frame around the whole film (or the "experience" of the film), or puts it in a context, thus giving us the terms within which to read it. By guiding our interpretation, though, it is also in a sense always *inside* the film as well. Yet the preview is also clearly physically separate from the film, is normally excluded from critical consideration, and is thus outside at the same time.

---

6. James Monaco, *The New Wave: Truffaut, Godard, Chabrol, Rohmer, Rivette* (New York: Oxford University Press, 1976), p. 45.

Not only is a frame of some sort necessary to understand genres and film texts (indeed all texts), but it can also be said that we understand "life" itself *in terms of,* or rather *by means of,* the frames into which we put events that happen to us every day. Life is, after all, also a text, in the sense that *everything* must be read and interpreted, and is not given directly—even, or especially, this text of our lives and of everyday events. Complicating matters is the fact that one of the interpretive frames that we use in life—and the New Wave filmmakers such as Truffaut were very aware of this—is the movies themselves. The Belmondo character in Jean-Luc Godard's *Breathless,* for example (made the year before *Shoot the Piano Player*), very consciously leads his life the way he thinks Humphrey Bogart would and even patterns his physical mannerisms on those of his hero. Truffaut also understood that one of the unconscious ways in which we make sense of experience is to put it into movie terms, in the film frame; in other words, we model behavior according to the narrative and dramatic standards of Hollywood film. Thus, we make movies based on the way we understand life, and we understand life, partially at least, through the movies. What is created is a never-ending loop in which "real life" does not always come first, what postmodernists have described as an "abyssal" structure that has no beginning or end, no firm ground upon which to rest.

Adding to the enhancement of a sense of pastiche in *Shoot the Piano Player* is the fact that, rather than referring to specific scenes from specific films, Truffaut is invoking a certain free-floating visual iconography, a repertory of characters, settings, plots, and themes. Even more importantly, the borrowing is not, despite what many critics have assumed, restricted to gangster films. Truffaut seems rather to be quoting—recycling in an ironic key, really—a myriad of different sorts of motifs and iconographies from previous cinema history. For example, at a crucial moment in the film near the very end—when Léna is killed by Ernest—it is the *Western* that is evoked, rather than the gangster film. Thus in the "shootout" Ernest's hat gets shot off; grabbing it, he calmly replaces it on his head with all the sangfroid of a hardbitten cowboy. Most importantly, the moment immediately before he shoots Léna, he *spins* the gun on his finger (a clear bit of Western iconography). This is also perhaps the zenith of Truffaut's mastery of apparently clashing moods and modes, for we smile at Ernest's gesture and feel sad about Léna's death at virtually the same moment. It is here that Truffaut approaches Shakespeare's legendary ability to mix low comedy and high tragedy.

The particular nature of this mixture bears further comment. Pauline Kael quotes fellow critic Dwight Macdonald as saying that *Shoot the Piano Player*

> deliberately mixed up "three genres which are usually kept apart: crime melodrama, romance, and slapstick comedy." And, he says, "I thought the mixture didn't jell, but it was an exhilarating try."[7]

7. Kael, "Shoot the Piano Player," p. 214.

The point that Kael goes on to make is precisely that the film *is* exhilarating *because* the genres do not mix. One of the other interesting things she mentions, however, is that crime melodrama and romance were in fact routinely mixed throughout the classic era of Hollywood—in *Casablanca, The Maltese Falcon,* and *The Big Sleep,* to name only a few. She does not take this any further, but herein lies a clue, perhaps, to one of the crucial differences between *Shoot the Piano Player* and other films of the time. One of the things that is unique about it, it now seems clear, is its thoroughly unconventional recourse to *slapstick,* which is as much a matter of tone as of genre, and other incongruities. Melodrama and romance, though different genres, are still compatible on the level of tone, are still congruous. Hence the truly innovative aspect of Truffaut's film lies at least as much in its clash of tones as in its mixture of genres, though the terms frequently overlap, as they do in Kael's quotation from Macdonald. (It should be mentioned that Don Allen makes a similar point, using still another term, in *Finally Truffaut,* a portion of which is reprinted in this volume: "it is the unexpected switching of *moods* that gives *Shoot the Piano Player* its particular, elusive quality."[8])

In this country, the debate in 1960 about genre and tone usually took the form of complaints that *Shoot the Piano Player*—really all of Truffaut's films— was disorganized. Pauline Kael's intelligent counterclaim is that

> they are full of unresolved, inexplicable, disharmonious elements, irony and slapstick and defeat all compounded—*not* arbitrarily as the reviewers com- plain—but in terms of the filmmaker's efforts to find some expression for his own anarchic experience, instead of making more of those tiresome well- made movies that no longer mean much to us.[9]

One way we might bring Kael's astute defense up to date is to introduce a term that has become important in contemporary critical theory and is itself a hallmark of postmodernism, the idea of *play.* It is easy to forget this element of the film when one begins to analyze it, as does one critic when he describes this period of Truffaut's career as some kind of laborious "working out [of] problems of film language and logic which had been achingly apparent to him if not to his popular audiences" and when he too severely describes *Shoot the Piano Player* as establishing "a mode of inquiry."[10] It may be useful, and even illuminating, to reconstruct these films in this way, but it also neglects Truffaut's obvious joy and irreverence, the ebullient interjection of his own personality into the making of this and the other films of this period.[11]

---

8. Don Allen, *Finally Truffaut* (New York: Beaufort, 1985), p. 91.
9. Kael, "Shoot the Piano Player," p. 212.
10. Monaco, *The New Wave,* p. 38. He also sees *Shoot the Piano Player* and, even more, Truffaut's next film, *Jules and Jim* (1962), as "introductions to the aesthetic problems Truffaut had committed himself to studying" (p. 39).
11. Allen Thiher, in his essay "The Existential Play in Truffaut's Early Films" (reprinted in this volume), develops a related notion of play and applies it to the characters of these films.

Interestingly, however, the notion of play also moves against the very idea of the art film, as embodied, say, by the immense seriousness of Ingmar Bergman's films and reputation during this same period.[12] Thus, *Shoot the Piano Player,* as both "non-serious" generic romp and "serious" art film, shows how these terms, like the other binary oppositions it puts into play, can never really be rigidly kept apart. Already in Truffaut's first film, *The 400 Blows,* there was a great deal of both lighthearted humor and deadly seriousness, but for the most part they were kept clearly separate and the border between them seemed to hold. *Shoot the Piano Player,* the next logical step, is expressly engineered to break down this border.[13]

In their challenging of borders in the interest of ambiguity and ambivalence, these films also seem to approach "real life" in a way that Hollywood films of the time did not, and most defenses of Truffaut have been cast in terms of a realist aesthetic (remember that the preview discussed earlier compared the film's mixture of tones to "life itself"). As Pauline Kael tells us, for example, "the film is comedy, pathos, tragedy all scrambled up—much I think as most of us really experience them (surely all our lives are filled with comic horrors) but not as we have been led to expect them in films."[14] Similarly, another critic, Annette Insdorf, says that "the film is as unpredictable as experience itself—crazy at some moments, poignant at others."[15] The final test—in other words, the final validation of even the most bizarre work of the imagination, here and elsewhere—is always accomplished in the context or frame of mimesis, that is, the faithfulness of its imitation of "real life." It is this most basic context or frame of reference that seems so "natural" that most critics do not even recognize its existence. In the context or frame of a postmodern aesthetic, however, this assumption clearly demands reconsideration.

An examination of specific details of the film will clarify the dynamics of the processes we have so far been describing rather abstractly. The very opening of the film—a man running wildly here and there, in the dark, on a city street, pursued by a careening automobile—very economically establishes

12. In the preview, the narrator's voice is calm, yet insistent. Notice that his principal promise is that we will regard this as a "great" motion picture, not that we will have a lot of fun or be entertained. Yet he hedges his bets by adding that it will be "delightfully amusing throughout."

13. Annette Insdorf finds the sources for Truffaut's interest in mixed tones as far back as his days as a critic, as for example when he praises Renoir for "the bitterness of the gay moments, the clownishness of the sad"

and calls attention to the qualities in Jacques Becker's *Casque d'or* that would become so apparent in his own films: "*Casque d'or,* sometimes funny and sometimes tragic, proves finally that, through the refined use of change of tone, one can move beyond parody. . . ."

(Annette Insdorf, *François Truffaut* [Boston: Twayne, 1978], p. 28; another excerpt from the book is reprinted in this volume. Quotation from Truffaut is from *Les Films de ma vie* [Paris: Flammarion, 1975], p. 196.)

14. Kael, "Shoot the Piano Player," p. 210.

15. Insdorf, *François Truffaut,* p. 27.

the genre classification of the film, or seems to. He bangs into a lamppost, a passerby helps him to his feet, and, suddenly becoming intimate, they begin to discuss the passerby's marriage, and marriage in general. As several critics have pointed out (perhaps because it opens the film, this scene is the one most frequently discussed), what strikes the viewer first about *Shoot the Piano Player* is this quick shift to apparently "irrelevant" dialogue. Some critics at the time pointed to this shift as evidence of Truffaut's lack of discipline or focus, but most have since seen it as "the way life is," that is, full of things that do not always fit neatly together, as they usually do in the movies. Another more traditional way to think about this scene is that the characters' conversation is in fact *thematically* relevant, for the film is very much about love, finding a mate, and being part of a family. (This subject appears again, with the same kind of multileveled complexity, when the gangsters Ernest and Momo discuss male-female relationships with Charlie and Léna in the car after they have kidnapped them.[16]) On a third level, the very

16. This theme is consistently elaborated in the film, and is perhaps the sole subject that is overtly thematized. As such, it obviously deserves an essay on its own. As the men express their violent attitudes toward women, we laugh perhaps (or we did in 1960), but we also see how stupid they are. Later, Léna tells Charlie that she likes him so much because he "respects women," and he movingly

disjuncture of the scene can itself be seen as thematic in terms of a promotion of the disruptive, the unruly, that which exceeds the usual boundaries. Clearly, it is the interpretive frame that determines which of these three interpretations is "correct."

This interjection of the "inappropriate" quickly becomes a recurring feature in the film, for example in one of Charlie's voiceover debates with himself, when he begins, for no reason at all, to question himself regarding the talent of various American jazz figures like Art Tatum and Erroll Garner. Or at the beginning of the flashback when Charlie/Edouard offers the waitress at the cafeteria a ring; at first we are struck by the inappropriateness of the gesture, then we find out that they are married and are just pretending. Or again, when Ernest tells Momo, who has been criticizing his driving, that if he ever *did* kill a pedestrian while at the wheel, he would actually only be avenging the death of his father, who was run over while ogling women. This constant invocation of the inappropriate serves precisely to call into question, like much post-modernist theory, the very border between the appropriate and the inappropriate, that which belongs or does not belong—which is simply another version of the opposition between the inside and the outside.

Another instance of the inside/outside opposition comes in the frequently discussed scene of Charlie's audition. Here, the diegetic (elements that "belong" to the story being narrated, such as the music from an on-screen phonograph) and the nondiegetic (elements that do not "belong" to the story, for example, music on the soundtrack that does not have a visible source) become completely inter-twined, even if only momentarily. The camera tracks backward, ahead of the young woman with the violin, as she walks away from the impresario's office. Suddenly, the sound of piano music is heard—presumably Charlie beginning his audition—and she stops momentarily. She continues walking away, then out into the huge courtyard of the ugly new building toward the front entrance; what is significant is that during this entire sequence the level of the music stays exactly the same. Since this cannot be explained in logical terms, it can only be read as diegetic music that has become nondiegetic. As the same piece of music con-tinues, we see the poster of Edouard's concert tour and then see him playing on the stage, but it is unclear whether the music is diegetic (that is, what he is actually playing—or better, what he is *represented* as playing, since the actor Aznavour

---

tells her how ashamed he would become when he gave the eye to women who got embarrassed and looked away. When Charlie tries to call their fight a draw, Plyne's macho insistence that there has to be a winner gets him killed, and is a perfect counterpart to his obsessive dichotomization of women into madonna and whore. Truffaut's attitude toward women was complex (as several critics have pointed out, the vast majority of his films, with the exception of the first two, focus on women rather than on men), and cannot be neatly categorized, but there is at least as much evidence for a feminist Truffaut as for a misogynist one. (See Insdorf, "Are Women Magic?" in her *François Truffaut,* the opening portion of which is reprinted in this volume.)

himself is not playing anything) or not.[17] This is only one example among many, but though the distinction between diegetic and nondiegetic is widely relied upon in cinema studies, Truffaut's film provides further evidence of the impossibility of ever rigidly distinguishing between these two terms.

A similar moment comes early in the film when Plyne, the owner of the café, tells Charlie that his problem is that he is afraid. Instead of either agreeing or disagreeing, Charlie in effect self-consciously *tries out* the feeling twice in different tones of voice ("J'ai peur") as though it were a bit of dialogue (which, of course, it is). Finally, the words seem to fit, and the third time he says the phrase it is said "realistically," as though he were finally responding to Plyne within the "normal" terms and boundaries of their diegetic conversation, which his previous two utterances have called into question. (The subtitles unfortunately do not give the sense of the artificiality of the recorded dialogue here.)

This kind of deliberate illusion-breaking is common in modernism, but there it usually has a thematic or other ulterior motive. Truffaut's variety seems to be less clearly motivated, serving as little more than a manifestation of random play, once again, and the effect is different each time. Visually, the insert shot of the gangsters Ernest and Momo in the little mirror in Léna's powder case shows them as though they were only a few feet behind, whereas the medium shot on Léna and Charlie that comes before and after this insert clearly shows that they are far away in the background. Later, when the gangsters are shadowing Charlie's little brother Fido, he buys a carton of milk, enters his friend's apartment building, and then a second later (via what might be called a "whip tilt") is seen bombing Ernest's car from the fourth-floor window. Of course, very few scenes, even in conventional Hollywood films, are ever shot in real time, and temporally elliptical editing is common. Here, however, none of the normal transitions that smooth over these disjunctions and make them invisible are in evidence, and the effect is purposely jarring.

Another self-reflexive visual moment comes with the three medallions of Plyne, as we discover that it was he who betrayed Charlie and Léna to the gangsters. Better known is the series of increasingly closer shots on Edouard's finger as he tries to summon up the courage to ring Lars Schmeel's doorbell; the very radicality of the image's scale self-consciously pulls us out of the illusion of the narrative. The effect of these increasingly extreme close-ups is further enhanced by intercutting them with extreme long shots of Charlie from the other end of the hall. The effect is of violent contrast, another statement of stark difference.

Another visually significant sequence comes during Léna and Charlie's first night together. The sequence of shots seems random, but in fact it is not. It is actually one sequence of a conversation, in which they compare notes about

---

17. This use of music as a bridge from the diegetic over into a kind of montage effect seems clearly borrowed from Orson Welles's *Citizen Kane*, probably Truffaut's favorite movie, in which it is used brilliantly.

their earlier views of each other, that is intercut with random shots, presumably representing other moments during the night. (These intercut, isolated shots can be read as flashbacks, flashforwards, or both, precisely because the frame that would orient them for us is missing.) This sequence is more poetic and visually complicated than almost any other in films of the period, except the one it seems clearly to be borrowing from, Alain Resnais's *Hiroshima, mon amour* (1959).

Most famous of all is the intercut shot of (presumably) Momo's mother keeling over after his oath to Fido that his mother should die if he is not telling the truth. Other more minor visual distancing effects are the *French* subtitles for the song Boby Lapointe sings, "Avanie et Framboise"; the sudden appearance of the ad for *Cahiers du Cinéma* on the back of a truck; and the *very* quick close-up on the wrestling poster in the bar as Plyne and Charlie begin their fight (quite easy to miss on a first viewing), which serves suddenly to distance and stylize their fighting, making it seem like just a wrestling match, not serious yet serious (somebody dies) at the same time. It should also be pointed out that the medallions of Plyne, as well as the picture of Momo's mother and the iris of Lars Schmeel— let alone the ubiquitous mirrors—obviously encapsulate and insist upon the idea of framing, in which the border between the outside and the inside is most obviously posited (and most obviously questioned).

An entire scene can be rich with this kind of playful self-awareness, as when the prostitute Clarisse visits Charlie's apartment. She first sings a little song about the advantages of television over cinema (in 1960, television was just becoming widespread throughout France). The game is further heightened when she shows her bare breasts: Charlie covers them up while saying that this is the way they do it in the movies (a shot that is not in the version released in America). What is amusing here is that this particular example of self-reflexivity that makes us suddenly aware that we *are* watching a movie, also falls back on itself: it *is* what is done in the movies, and in this movie too, but only because he is self-conscious-ly doing it and, moreover, verbalizing that he is doing it.[18] Again, the moment is indulged for its own sense of (expressly) superficial delight.

This film is of course not composed only of visual effects that are ex-clusively antiillusionist or postmodern, and sometimes such effects can work in more than one register at a time. Thus, in a more conventional, organic/formalist analysis, one would want to discuss the way in which

---

18. This sense of the film's being aware of itself as film is carried over to an awareness of itself more generally as spectacle in a curious detail near the end. When Edouard arrives at the house in the country, his brother taps on the ceiling with the handle of an axe to wake Chico up and to let him know that Edouard is there. He taps nine times—six short and three long taps—a gesture that recalls the ceremonial opening of French theater, a custom, according to tradition, borrowed from ancient Roman theater. (I am indebted to Lynne Johnson for this suggestion.)

Truffaut uses the ubiquitous tracking shot (carried over from *The 400 Blows*) for thematic and expressive purposes; the many times that he films through bars (for example, the bars on the window through which we see the trapped Edouard near the end of the film, the bars on the steps inside Charlie's apartment house, and the bars on the sidewalk when Charlie and Léna are being chased); and how he often evacuates one side or other of the frame to indicate an emotional loss on Charlie's part (for example, when Léna suddenly disappears early in the film as he about to ask her if she would like a drink, and in the very last shot, when Charlie is blankly staring forward, as "Fin" finally comes to occupy the emptied right side of the frame). Even more interesting, however, is the moment when Lars Schmeel (who will come between Edouard and Thérésa emotionally), is framed between them in the cafeteria, a matter of conscious but conventional mise-en-scène; a bit later the point is made more artificially—purposely, of course—as the face of Lars is turned into a disappearing iris shot that Truffaut playfully sticks between them as they sit up in bed at the beginning of the next scene.

Emotion itself becomes another element of play. An example is provided by the way in which Charlie tries out the phrase "J'ai peur" to see whether it works, rather than reacting "naturally" in whatever way he "really" feels—though Truffaut cleverly always keeps the emotion illusionistic enough to affect us at the same time. But in many ways, the moments that would ordinarily be the most emotional in a genre film of this sort, or in any film—say, Léna's abrupt departure from Charlie when they arrive at the family house in the country, her sudden death in the snow—are, in fact, massively underplayed and even played with. (Truffaut stylizes what is on one level perhaps the most emotional scene in the film—Léna's death—by employing a quick and highly artificial zoom in on her dead face, one of the very few zooms in the film.) Similarly, we fear the lethal but childish gangsters Ernest and Momo at the same time as we laugh at them. What is called into question here is the coherence of feelings and, by extension, the coherence of the individual self as a fixed unchanging entity—another frequent theme of postmodernist art.

One of the most important elements in the film that expresses the idea of the destabilization of the self is, in fact, the continually doubled characterization of the gangsters Ernest and Momo. These unlikely pipe-smokers in effect act as a kind of vaudeville team who seem to be "playing" gangsters in this or perhaps another movie. On one level—a level that will finally not be denied—they *are* ruthless gangsters, as the death of Léna shows. On another, they diverge from every cliché associated with the type. For one thing, although they are tough at times, they are clearly more juvenile than anything else and seem to be at their happiest when they are showing all their gadgets to Fido after they have kidnapped him. They deliver their lines with incredible speed and with a special kind of uninflected brio that makes them all the funnier, as when they do a little shtick about whether to show Charlie the gun, and then again about whether to show him the money.

This doubleness or contradiction of character is abetted by Léna and Charlie's attitude toward them. When Léna draws the attention of the police by stepping on the gas, instead of accusing the gangsters of kidnapping, she and Charlie treat the whole thing as a joke, as a kind of benign one-upmanship. Their behavior, in other words, and the behavior of most of the other characters, here and elsewhere, is simply not *logical*. As such, it counters the assumed aesthetic of mimesis or realism discussed earlier, and moves closer to the *illogicality* of the postmodern aesthetic that has called the dominance of realism into question. The gangsters goodnaturedly concede to Fido that his trick with the milk was excellent, but insist that they have been winning ever since. And though Fido has ostensibly been kidnapped, and is theoretically in mortal danger, he does not appear frightened at all and in fact has a wonderful time when he gets to steer the car when the gangsters have to push it into a service station. This duality of character serves to highlight the film's duality as well, for its apparent desire to be taken seriously—finally to add up to something—is constantly denied by an anarchic energy that seems to serve no purpose beyond its own expression. The second term of the duality destroys, again and again, the first, every time it appears.

The primary example of the film's interest in doubling, of course, is the way in which the main character is split into two different people, Charlie and Edouard, a division that is abetted by the constant use of mirrors. The doubling is also manifested in Charlie's voiceover, which points to a split between thought and action that is played upon humorously throughout the film. Sometimes Charlie pays attention to the voice (as when it tells him to forget about his brother and just wish him good luck, and Charlie, on camera, quickly says "Good luck!") and at other times he does not (as when he leaves Thérésa alone in the room after her revelations about her liaison with Lars, though he knows he should not). Further complicating things is the fact that the voiceover is actually *not* Aznavour's voice. Another moment that continues the theme of the splitting of Charlie/Edouard is accomplished through an antiillusionistic gesture that is easy to miss on a first viewing of the film. As Edouard's musical career goes into high gear, there is a brief scene (with no specific dialogue) in which Edouard, sitting in a chair, has his picture taken by a crowd of photographers. The next scene begins on a close-up of an oil portrait of Edouard that Lars says he has had painted especially for his office. While the camera is close on the painting, interestingly, several flashbulbs go off, but when the camera pulls back to show the rest of Lars's office, no photographers are present. It is a nice signature bit on Truffaut's part—here he is again, "present" in the film—that further underlines the doubling theme, this time with a hint of *The Portrait of Dorian Gray*. Note also that Léna's voice takes over the film the second after the flashback ends on Thérésa's dead body lying on the street. They too are doubled figures who double the Charlie/Edouard split.

These examples are also manifestations of Truffaut's vaunted concern for *character* above all else. Critics Leo Braudy and Morris Dickstein have remarked, with justice, that for Truffaut, character is always the center of a film's construction.[19] Yet in this film his continuously doubled characters seem to alternate, purposely, in another of Truffaut's self-reflexive gestures, between requiring us to take them illusionistically as real people with whom we identify and at other times as not real people at all, but textual elements, parts of the script, like nouns and verbs or lighting and camera angles. This can be seen in the in-jokes that are connected with their names, as listed by Andrew Sarris,[20] or at other moments, as for example when Léna goes to Charlie's apartment looking for his brother Fido. She moves through the empty apartment calling "Fido," exactly as though she were calling a dog, and the sudden emotional distancing (she is supposed to be worried) provokes laughter in the audience. This sense of name play is verified and doubled a few moments later when Momo remarks to Fido, in the car, that his name sounds like the name of a dog.

Such playing with character also has psychological effects on the audience, since it tends to disrupt the normal process of identification. A psychoanalytic examination of the film would undoubtedly yield interesting results, since the males in the audience, to whom (as feminist film theory has taught us) most mainstream films are principally addressed, really have no one to identify with: all male characters are either "bad" (in the context of the genre story, that is) or completely ineffectual, like Charlie. Nowhere do male spectators find active male heroes onto whom they might project their own self-images. The women are all beautiful, of course, thus fulfilling the normal expec-

19. Leo Braudy and Morris Dickstein, *Great Film Directors* (New York: Oxford University Press, 1978), p. 713 (headnote to Truffaut section). This obsession with character is of course consistent with Truffaut's avoidance of an examination of the larger systems, social and otherwise, within which his characters operate. Like most apolitical directors, he feels that his subject is the "human condition" rather than any specific political conditions that might be alterable. Note, however, that James Monaco, elsewhere in his book on the New Wave, makes a good case for Truffaut as a political filmmaker, one who "was slowly and carefully constructing . . . a politics of intimacy which begins with the smallest political unit—what the French in the late sixties learned to call a 'groupuscule' of two or three—and builds from there" (p. 39).

20. Among the name assignations that Sarris says "have been directly verified by M. Truffaut" are the following. The piano player is given the name of Saroyan as a tribute to William Saroyan, particularly for his volume of stories *The Daring Young Man on the Flying Trapeze,* and also because Charles Aznavour, like Saroyan, is Armenian (according to other critics his first name is a tribute to Charlie Chaplin). One of the hero's brothers in the film is named Chico, a reference to the Marx Brothers. The villainous impresario in the film is called Lars Schmeel, "a take-off on Lars Schmidt, the Swedish theatrical producer and Ingrid Bergman's third husband. Truffaut wished to express his solidarity with Roberto Rossellini, Ingrid Bergman's second husband and a director particularly admired by Truffaut, and his artistic disapproval of Lars Schmidt's activities in the Paris theatre." The stage name of the actress who plays Léna, Marie Dubois, was suggested by Truffaut, who took it from a novel by Jacques Audiberti.

Among the many other references that go beyond names is the theme that Ernest's musical lighter plays, which, according to Sarris, is from Max Ophuls's great film *Lola Montez,* one especially admired by Truffaut. (Andrew Sarris, "Inside the Piano Player," *New York Film Bulletin* 3, 3, no. 44 [Summer 1962], n.p.)

tations for the male gaze—few movies are ever *that* radical—but they are also the center of whatever purposeful action occurs (Thérésa getting Charlie's career going, Léna taking the initiative with Charlie, arguing with Plyne, stealing the car, and so on; even Mammy successfully deals with the police after Charlie accidentally kills Plyne).

There is, however, another contradictory male "character" whose presence in the film is heavily marked: the auteur, Truffaut himself. (This "presence" in turn raises the question of just what it means to be *in* the film, *inside* the film in other words, for if Truffaut is not an actual character, he is nevertheless always clearly "there" and we sense him everywhere.) One of the hallmarks of the New Wave was the direct, personal relationship the auteur tried to establish with his audience. In this it differed greatly from the classic American cinema, whom the New Wave directors claimed to love, but whose ideal was a kind of natural narrative inevitability that, except in such rare cases as the films of John Ford or Alfred Hitchcock, in a sense precluded an actual "author." This assertion of (authorial) self in *Shoot the Piano Player* in effect contradicts that postmodern breakdown of the self that is asserted by other elements of the film. But it cannot overcome it.

Exactly how is this authorial self asserted? According to James Monaco and others, most New Wave critics and directors saw the entire filmmaking process as a dialectical one, chiefly one of innovative auteur pushing against more or less rigid genre conventions. Monaco believes that Truffaut needed genre conventions to oppose to the full expression of his personality in order to avoid a kind of Sartrean nausea of too much freedom.[21] Obviously, however, it is just as possible to see these very "genre conventions"—jumbled and deformed, as in *Shoot the Piano Player*—as the expression of Truffaut's personality, rather than something opposed to them. The personality, after all, if there is such a thing, fixed and consistent, and if it can be manifested at all, can only be manifested through the

---

21. The "existentialism" that some critics have found in this film seems to be part of that large group of themes that Truffaut *mentions* rather than develops, adding to the idea of a pastiche with no true core of motivating ideas. It is indeed possible to see Charlie as existentialist hero (especially when he walks away from the fight between Léna and Plyne), but Charlie's "existentialism" also seems something that is being "tried out," like the phrase "J'ai peur." Charlie could be seen as well as a kind of none-too-serious pastiche of the existential heroes of Jean-Paul Sartre and Albert Camus. (Another "mentioned" theme related to existentialism is the era's concern with the effects of "materialism," as when Ernest tells Fido that he has so many gadgets that he's completely bored.)

What might be called the "romantic" elements of the film are also difficult to place. An example here is Félix Leclerc's song, and, in fact, the whole relationship between Léna and Charlie. How serious is Truffaut about all this? These themes somehow seem posited, taken half-seriously, indulged in and enjoyed, and yet at the same time distanced, made fun of—more bits to be added to the pastiche. Other "serious" themes that are especially emphasized near the end of the film—family loyalty, genealogical determinism, and the like—seem equally to be treated in a mixture of serious and nonserious terms, as for example when Chico is quite pleased to hear that Charlie has "killed a guy," making him finally one of the boys.

film's materiality, that is, what is on the screen—in this case, the genre conventions, however distorted. But the very fact that these conventions *are* confused and inconsistent is an index of the discrepancies, contradictions, and disjunctions that also lie within the authorial self.

In terms of the romantic aesthetic of organic form usually associated with the nineteenth century—the belief that every element of a work must be organically related to every other element, thus contributing to the creation of a vital and coherent whole that makes sense of all its disparate details—an author's "presence" also presumably serves as a guarantee of a work's unity through the concept of authorial intentionality. No matter how self-contradictory the elements of a given work are, in other words, the work's overall meaning can supposedly be ascertained once we discover *what the author meant.*

Intentionality is an immensely rich area that cannot, unfortunately, be discussed in greater depth in the present essay. Let me instead give one small example of the power of an assumption of intention to affect an interpretation. When Charlie justifies his "accidental" murder of Plyne—and everything in the situation, dialogue, and setting seems to back him up on this—he claims that he had intended merely to stab Plyne in the arm, so that he would be forced to loosen his grip on Charlie, but that Plyne *moved* at the last moment and took the knife in the back. In fact, what a close examination of the scene reveals is that Charlie indeed takes a bead, as it were, on Plyne's arm, but when he goes to stab him, he plunges the knife directly into Plyne's back. Plyne does *not* move at the last moment. How do we reconcile this discrepancy? Surely most critics would not claim that Charlie is lying here, so great is the power of the other indicators of his honesty, but if he is not lying, the actual visual evidence indicates that he is mistaken. We reconcile this confusion by positing an artistic intentionality that reads this knife plunge as a "mistake" on the actor's part in the face of Truffaut's "obvious" intentions, despite the contrary evidence before us. Here what is actually a "misreading" of the text is allowed—actually, no one even mentions it—in favor of some presumably higher interpretive goal.

In any case, what is interesting about *Shoot the Piano Player* is that it is precisely the expression of the author's personality, through the mixing of genre and tone, that leads to the destruction of the film's unity, as so many early reviewers insisted. But if it were his *intention* to destroy the film's unity, is this intention, by itself, enough to unify the film at a presumably "higher" level? It seems, once again, to be an abyssal operation, with no origin and no conclusion, a doubling that doubles back on itself and that never comes to rest. The contradiction becomes more understandable, however, if we think of the author himself, in this case Truffaut, not as some coherent, preexisting self with clear-cut desires and intentions, but, as more recent theory does, as himself inherently contradictory. He is, in a sense, a textual *effect,* someone, a self, who attains some sort of imaginary coherence after the fact precisely because he is the author of this (and other) particular films.

For Monaco, this dialectic between the expression of the author's personality and the constraints of genre leads toward a third term that he relates to Roland Barthes's notion of *écriture,* or "writing," a place of juxtaposition between the individual personal style and the larger historical moment. This term, however, has come to have a broader meaning for other poststructuralist writers, to include, among other things, the "excess" that material form always inscribes into any operation of representation. (For example, the material form any representation takes—a photograph, a painting, a poem—will always alter that which is represented; and even merely thinking of something is representing it.) This excess associated with "writing" can also signify the inevitable confusion that is built into any communication (including the communication of the meaning of a film) and that is signaled in *Shoot the Piano Player* in the misspelling ("mis-writing") of Charlie Kohler's name on one or more of the many posters we see as "Koller." (It can be clearly seen on the poster outside the café in the very beginning of the film.[22]) In this way, the film text itself provides a sort of unconscious testimony to the problems and "mistakes" that are inherent in all operations of the transmission of sense and meaning by virtue of the simple fact that they must always be embodied in some material form.

Related to this idea of "excess" meaning is the fact that the title in French, *Tirez sur le pianiste,* can be rendered in English as both *Shoot the Piano Player* and *Shoot the Pianist*—and is, in fact, doubled or split this way between the American version and the British version. But these two titles are quite different, as any native English speaker can tell you (the former pointing to Charlie, say, and the latter to Edouard), and thus the title actually *means more* in English than it does in French. Is this possible? If not, can we say that this extra meaning is somehow illegitimate? The fact that the French title came first and is the "original" means little, for the text that *we* have, for all intents and purposes, is in English. Hence our idea of the relation between original and copy, or between source and translation—more binary oppositions—is disturbed even when we consider such an obviously minor detail as this.

The way in which the film is related to (or doubles) its source, the novel *Down There* by David Goodis, is also relevant to this question of the reversal of binary

---

22. Leo Braudy, in his book *Focus on "Shoot the Piano Player,"* goes into this question at some length in a note:

> In what may be another tribute to his elusiveness, there is no unanimity about the spelling of Charlie's last name. Various books and articles, the English language subtitles, and Suzanne Schiffman of Truffaut's office all say "Kohler." Other books and articles, as well as a hand-lettered poster outside the café advertising Charlie's act, say "Koller." I have not regularized this in the articles that follow, preferring "Kohler" myself because its obviously Germanic origin looks forward to Jules, the German, and Jim, the Frenchman, and because it implies that the murderous obsession of Julie's Kohler in *The Bride Wore Black* may have sisterly affinities with Charlie's detachment.

([Englewood Cliffs, N.J.: Prentice-Hall, 1972], p. 5n.) Braudy might also have added the further detail that *Kohler* in French is pronounced exactly the same as *colère* (anger).

oppositions, and inevitably turns out to be another aspect of Truffaut's abyssal operation. Thus one is not surprised to discover from the interviews that the director felt no special loyalty to his source when adapting a novel for the screen. Unconcerned about capturing its "essence," he regarded the source as a vehicle, more than anything else, for his own ideas.[23] What is interesting for our purposes is that, whereas on one level the film is in fact a fairly straightforward adaptation of Goodis's novel, more importantly, Truffaut felt no compunction whatever about borrowing a great deal of material for his pastiche from *other* Goodis novels that were, in principle, unrelated to the novel that was supposedly being adapted. As Dominique Fanne has pointed out, Truffaut

> draws his inspiration from the entire body of a writer's work, taking here and there a theme, a snatch of dialogue, and so on. Thus the conversation between Plyne and Charlie that opens *Shoot the Piano Player* (a discussion of Charlie's fears and of little Léna-Martha, who has luminous blond hair, so fine and so free) is taken from *Nightfall,* another book by David Goodis. Other dialogues in the film, between the bandits Momo and Ernest, are also taken from this source.[24]

One wonders what the legal aspects of such "borrowing" were. In any case, what is clear is just how shaky such supposedly obvious binary hierarchies—such as, say, original and copy—really are. What *is* the source for Truffaut's film? Clearly, it is and is not David Goodis's novel *Down There.*

Everything doubled and redoubled, over and over again. Opposites stated and dismantled, selves born and questioned, and always in the joyful context of *play.* Though some prescient minds appreciated the purposeful anarchy of *Shoot the Piano Player* even when it first appeared, contemporary critical theory has perhaps given us a means of understanding it better than ever before. Which is not to say that we now know its meaning, its truth. It gives us pleasure, another kind of meaning, and that is enough.

23. In a 1962 letter to a friend and aide, Helen Scott, Truffaut said that "David Goodis wrote me a letter and I realized that he liked the subtitled *Pianiste* less than when he couldn't understand anything and believed the film to be more faithful to his book." (*Correspondence 1945–1984,* ed. Gilles Jacob and Claude de Givray; trans. Gilbert Adair [New York: Farrar, Straus & Giroux, 1990], p. 192.)
24. Dominique Fanne, "The Books of His Life," in Braudy and Dickstein, *Great Film Directors,* p. 719.

François Truffaut: A Biographical Sketch

T he early, emotionally deprived life of François Truffaut has attained almost legendary status in the annals of cinema history. Born in Paris on February 6, 1932, to parents who were too busy with careers and other pursuits to pay much attention to him, he was largely raised by relatives. Although he was a good student during the first few years he attended school, his later years were increasingly troubled.

By the age of ten, he was a frequent truant, making up better and better excuses for each absence. When he went so far as to claim that his father had been arrested by the Nazis, he was so afraid to face the parental wrath that he knew was coming that he slept overnight in a Metro station. As he was to show movingly in his first, highly autobiographical, film, *Les 400 Coups* (*The 400 Blows,* 1959), he spent most of his time watching movies and reading Balzac rather than going to school.

From the first, movies seemed to substitute for the intimacy and emotion that he lacked at home, and Truffaut often saw fifteen films or more per week. Some special favorites like Jean Renoir's *Rules of the Game* or Marcel Carné's *Les Visiteurs du soir* he would see over and over. He preferred crime and love stories with modern settings and showed an appreciation for "art" films that was highly unusual for a teenager.

After definitively leaving school at age fourteen, Truffaut held a series of odd jobs, from which he was fired, one after the other, because of his poor work habits and lack of discipline. He decided to start a ciné-club—a type of society that was quite popular in France at the time—and had just as much trouble making that work. Finally, he went to talk to the director of a rival ciné-club, André Bazin, a man who was to become the most famous film critic and theorist in France and an extremely important influence on Truffaut.

This account depends for many of its details on the excellent and much longer "biographical background" to be found in Eugene P. Walz, *François Truffaut: Guide to References and Resources* (New York: G. K. Hall, 1982), pp. 1–15.

Impressed with Truffaut's passion for movies and his generally intense approach to life, Bazin (who was some fourteen years older than Truffaut) took him under his wing and quickly became the father that the future director felt he had never really had. In the meantime, his real father, angry at the bills Truffaut's insolvent ciné-club had run up, turned the boy over to the police. After spending some five months in a correctional institution for juvenile delinquents, he was released through the efforts of Bazin, who promised to find him a job.

It was through Bazin and his work as a part-time projectionist that Truffaut met many of the other young cinephiles, such as Alain Resnais, Jacques Rivette, and Jean-Luc Godard, who would go on to become the greatest directors of the New Wave. After a few other jobs and an unhappy love affair, Truffaut suddenly enlisted in the French army for three years.

At the time, France was engaged in fighting the revolutionary independence movement in a place called Indochina, which was later to give a great deal of trouble to the United States under the name Vietnam. When he realized how foolish he had been to enlist, Truffaut deserted (several times), was arrested and put in prison in Germany, where he was stationed, and, once again, was rescued by Bazin. Finally, at the age of twenty, he was discharged for "instability of character."

Upon his release, Truffaut went to live with Bazin, who had in the meantime begun a journal, *Cahiers du Cinéma,* which would change the face of film history. After a short period of apprenticeship, Truffaut began writing for Bazin's magazine in March 1953. Even his earliest pieces, interestingly enough, showed many of the themes that were to become the hallmarks of his later work, both as a critic and as a filmmaker. Right from the beginning, Truffaut championed the work of individual auteurs working in Hollywood, often unknown, over the slicker French productions that he felt had corrupted the audience. Instead, he argued for low-budget films filled with energy and enthusiasm that reflected the most personal concerns of their makers.

Truffaut quickly made a reputation for himself as a critic through his take-no-prisoners style, violently attacking the cinema he detested, passionately supporting the cinema he admired. Probably his most significant essay for *Cahiers*—which the editors held for months before finally deciding to risk publishing in January 1954—was "Une Certaine Tendance du cinéma français," a wholesale attack on the French "tradition of quality," which had its roots in literature and which, according to the young critic, failed to exploit the resources of the new medium.

His intemperate, continuing attack on French cinema in *Cahiers* and in another journal called *Arts* finally resulted in his being banned from the Cannes Film Festival in 1958. In the meantime, however, Truffaut had clearly grown tired of being a critic, and, with great trepidation, given the number of enemies he had made, had turned instead to making films. In one of the great turnabouts in film history, his first full-length film, *The 400 Blows*—made for an astonishing

$75,000—would manage to win the first prize at Cannes in 1959, just one year after he had been banned from the festival.

His position as critic had given him access to filmmakers, and he was a frequent visitor to film sets, where he absorbed a great deal of information that would be useful to him later on. During the late 1950s, Truffaut worked with Max Ophuls briefly and, for two years, as an assistant to the Italian filmmaker Roberto Rossellini, though none of their joint projects ever came to fruition. At the same time, he made a silent short, *Une Visite* (*A Visit*), using the apartment of one of the *Cahiers* editors, and, even more importantly, wrote a film treatment called *A bout de souffle* (*Breathless*) that was ultimately to become Jean-Luc Godard's first film in 1959. In 1957, Truffaut shot his first important short, *Les Mistons* (*The Mischief-Makers*) and founded a production company, Les Films du Carrosse, which is still run by the woman he married the same year, Madeleine Morgenstern, the daughter of a well-known producer. His next short, *Une Histoire d'eau* (*A Story about Water*), was completed by Godard.

Truffaut's first feature-length film, *The 400 Blows*, was begun on November 10, 1958, and centered on the amazing presence of the teenager Jean-Pierre Léaud as Truffaut's alter ego Antoine Doinel. Avoiding big-name stars and shooting on location with the smallest possible crew, Truffaut burst onto the international cinema scene with other directors like Godard, Rivette, and Resnais in 1959, that year of wonders that marked the beginning of the French New Wave and forever altered future film practice.

His next film, the subject of this book, was a completely different sort of work, simultaneously a traditional genre film and an avant-garde art film, as though he wanted to move as far away as possible from the autobiographical revelations of *The 400 Blows*. Though European critical response was favorable, the public was baffled and *Shoot the Piano Player* did not do very well at the box office. Truffaut hit his stride in 1961 with his third film, *Jules and Jim*, a thoroughly romantic and delightfully spontaneous work starring Jeanne Moreau that was set during World War I. After taking part in *L'Amour à vingt ans* (*Love at Twenty*, 1962), a compilation film with several other directors (Truffaut's segment again starred Léaud as Antoine Doinel), the director again veered sharply away from public expectation in 1964 by making *La Peau douce* (*The Soft Skin*), a harsh love story set in the present day, diametrically opposed to the romantic spirit of *Jules and Jim*.

Truffaut's next film was *Fahrenheit 451* (1966), an English-language feature that was based on the science fiction novel by Ray Bradbury (the title refers to the temperature at which paper catches fire). The director had a great deal of trouble with the star of the film, the Austrian actor Oskar Werner, during the course of the shooting, and the combination of working in an unfamiliar foreign language and trying to make a film about a subject perhaps too close to his own obsessions as an autodidact—the burning of books—resulted in failure.

In 1968, Truffaut became involved in a struggle with the French government over the firing of the longtime head of the Cinémathèque française, Henri Langlois, which some have seen as a precursor to the more widely known "events of May" that brought the French government to the point of collapse. While making his next film in the Antoine Doinel cycle, *Baisers volés* (*Stolen Kisses*, 1968), which was much more improvisational than his earlier work, Truffaut lobbied to have the Cannes Film Festival canceled that year.

The two films made before and after *Baisers volés*, *La Mariée était en noir* (*The Bride Wore Black*, 1968) and *La Sirène du Mississippi* (*Mississippi Mermaid*, 1969), both drawn from crime novels by the American writer Cornell Woolrich, were made under the strong influence of Alfred Hitchcock, a director whom Truffaut admired greatly. After the expense of these two big-budget color films with international stars, Truffaut returned to low-budget filmmaking with *L'Enfant sauvage* (*The Wild Child*, 1970), a powerful period piece set in the early nineteenth century that is based on a scientific diary concerning a boy raised in the wild, without language, and the doctor who adopted and studied him, played by Truffaut himself. For his next film, Truffaut returned to Antoine Doinel, once again played by Jean-Pierre Léaud, in a domestic comedy called *Domicile conjugal* (*Bed and Board*, 1970).

Truffaut's next project was an adaptation of another novel by Henri-Pierre Roché (the source for *Jules and Jim*), and resulted in a superb, underrated film called *Les Deux Anglaises et le continent* (later shortened to *Les Deux Anglaises* or *Two English Girls*, 1971), which also starred Jean-Pierre Léaud, but for once not as Antoine Doinel. *Une Belle Fille comme moi* (*Such a Gorgeous Kid Like Me*), a somewhat strange and unsuccessful pastiche of earlier Truffauldian themes made in 1972, was followed by one of Truffaut's major films, *La Nuit américaine* (*Day for Night*), a self-reflexive behind-the-scenes look at the process of filmmaking, starring Truffaut as the director. It won the 1973 Academy Award for Best Foreign Film.

After taking a couple of years off to pursue several writing projects, Truffaut returned triumphantly to filmmaking with yet another important film, *L'Histoire d'Adèle H.* (*The Story of Adele H.*, 1975) which starred Isabelle Adjani as the obsessive daughter of Victor Hugo. The year 1976 saw the box office success of a sentimental but pleasant film about children, *L'Argent de poche* (*Small Change*), followed by *L'Homme qui aimait les femmes* (*The Man Who Loved Women*, 1977), a film about a man who, enamored of women's legs, writes an autobiography with the same title, allowing for more self-reflexive gestures in the manner of *La Nuit américaine*.

In 1978, Truffaut directed what is probably his darkest film, *La Chambre verte* (*The Green Room*), a meditation on death and remorse based on some short stories by Henry James, once again starring Truffaut in the lead role. *L'Amour en fuite* (*Love on the Run*, 1979) was a negligible pastiche of previous films in the Antoine Doinel cycle. *Le Dernier Métro* (*The Last Metro*, 1980), a film set in Paris during the Nazi occupation, with Catherine Deneuve and Gérard Depardieu, was the most successful film made during this last stage of Truffaut's career. It treats the theatrical world in much the way the world of cinema was dealt with in *La Nuit américaine,* and won ten Césars (the French Oscar) for the director. *La Femme d'à coté (The Woman Next Door,* 1981), again starring Depardieu, and Fanny Ardant in her first film role, is a story of obsessive love and the past that was not very successful. Truffaut's last film was *Vivement Dimanche! (Confidentially Yours,* 1983), a black-and-white American-style comedy thriller that distantly recalls *Shoot the Piano Player.*

Truffaut died of a malignant brain tumor on October 21, 1984, at the age of fifty-two.

Shoot the Piano Player

Shoot the
Piano Player

The original source of the following continuity script was the script published in French in *L'Avant-Scène Cinéma*, No. 362–363 (July-August 1987). However, when the translation was compared against the 1988 letterbox laserdisc version of the film in the Criterion Collection, which preserves its original widescreen dimensions, serious discrepancies were found in the visual descriptions of many shots. Thus it was necessary to revise the translation from beginning to end.

It is clear in retrospect that the version of the film used by *L'Avant-Scène* for its transcription was a 16mm flat print, in which panning and scanning techniques were used (to allow the film to be shown on television), creating a much different visual impression than the original 35mm wide-screen print, more or less faithfully captured on the laserdisc. The following transcription of the script was also checked against a 16mm copy of the film at the Library of Congress in Washington, D.C., which is also a flat print, and thus it-self often quite disparate from the film's original ratios. (All frame enlargements were made from this print, as the 35mm print was not available, and thus the framing of each enlargement should be visualized as much looser than it appears in the reproduced frames. Nevertheless, none of the frame enlargements chosen for this book has been affected by panning or scanning techniques.) Of course, many of the video versions of the film that are in circulation are also based on flat prints.

Otherwise, there are only two or three short dialogue exchanges that are missing in the American release version, and these have been duly marked. Only one "crucial" shot (and one accompanying line of dialogue) was excised in the American version—a shot of the prostitute Clarisse (Michèle Mercier) nude from the waist up, as she sits up in bed with Charlie (Charles Aznavour). This too has been marked in the text.

The subtitles in both the older 16mm prints of the film and in the recent laserdisc version are usually quite good (though in the laserdisc version, occasionally incorrect, especially those for the songs), but, as with all subtitles, seriously incomplete. Hence, the following translation is completely new, and is based on the dialogue taken directly from the film and from the script published in *L'-Avant-Scène*. Much of the language employed by the characters in this film is filled with 1950s French criminal slang. Since it seemed to me anachronistic as well as awkward to try to find equivalents in 1950s American slang, I have tried instead to make the translation informal and slangy, but more up-to-date.

Standard abbreviations are as follows:

E C U	extreme close-up
C U	close-up
M C U	medium close-up
M S	medium shot
M L S	medium long shot
L S	long shot
E L S	extreme long shot
P O V	point of view

Credits

Director
François Truffaut

Producer
Pierre Braunberger

Production Company
Les Films de la Pléiade

Adaptation
François Truffaut and Marcel Moussy, from the novel *Down There* by David Goodis

Dialogue
François Truffaut

Director of Photography
Raoul Coutard

Assistant Directors
Francis Cognany
Robert Bober
Björn Johansen

Music
Georges Delerue (who also plays the piano for Aznavour)
The song "Avanie et framboise" was written by Boby Lapointe, and is sung by him in the film.
The song "Dialogue d'amoureux" was written by Félix Leclerc and is sung by him and Lucienne Vernay.

Editing
Claudine Bouche and Cécile Decugis

Scriptgirl
Suzanne Schiffman

Not listed in opening credits of film:

Sound
Jacques Gallois and Jean-Philippe

Art Direction
Jacques Mely

Shooting Schedule
Accounts vary. According to Don Allen (*François Truffaut*), filming took place between November 30, 1959, and January 22, 1960, with several scenes being reshot during March 1960. According to Leo Braudy (*Focus on "Shoot the Piano Player"*), the shooting took place between December 1, 1959, and January 15, 1960, at a café, A la Bonne Franquette, rue Mussard, Levallois (near Paris) and at Le Sappey, about fifteen miles from Grenoble, "with an additional two weeks in March 1960 to reshoot several scenes and complete the shooting of others, principally the escape of Charlie and Léna from the attempted kidnapping by Ernest and Momo" (p. ix).

Process
Dyaliscope (black and white)

Release Date
November 22, 1960 (Paris), though Allen and Annette Insdorf (*François Truffaut*) show November 25 in Paris, and Braudy gives August 22, 1960; December 8, 1960, in the United Kingdom (previously at the London Film

Festival on October 21, 1960); July 24, 1962, in the United States

Length

Length varies with version. Usually given as eighty-five minutes, though Allen and Insdorf say eighty; Braudy says eighty in U.S. version, with other versions at eighty-four and eighty-six minutes

Awards

"Prix de la Nouvelle Critique," 1961

Distribution

Les Films du Carrosse (France). Originally distributed in the United Kingdom by Gala and in the United States by Astor. Now distributed by Films, Inc., and on laserdisc by the Criterion Collection.

Cast

Charlie Kohler/Edouard Saroyan
Charles Aznavour

Léna
Marie Dubois

Thérésa
Nicole Berger

Clarisse
Michèle Mercier

Plyne
Serge Davri

Momo
Claude Mansard

Fido
Richard Kanayan

Chico
Albert Rémy

Richard
Jean-Jacques Aslanian

Ernest
Daniel Boulanger

Lars Schmeel
Claude Heymann

Mammy
Catherine Lutz

Passerby
Alex Joffé

The Concierge
Alice Sapritch

The Singer
Boby Lapointe

The Continuity Script

1. CU: *the white letters of the credits are superimposed over the hammers of an upright piano, which are seen at an angle. The hammers rise and fall along with the music playing on the soundtrack.*
   Street, exterior, night
2. LS: *on a darkened street punctuated with the halos of several street-lamps, the lights of a car approach rapidly, its motor accelerating. The camera pans to show a dark figure running wildly down the sidewalk, accompanied by the deafening sound of a motor. The camera tracks left to right. After a moment, the light from a streetlamp allows us to see that it is a man, Chico, who is wearing a tweed overcoat open at the neck, revealing a light shirt and a tie.*
3. MCU: *a low-angle pan from left to right shows the maddened face of the fugitive, which emerges in a sudden flash of light. He tries to look behind him, while the brakes squeal loudly nearby.*
4. MS: *the camera shoots straight ahead as Chico runs toward it. As he runs out of the frame in the foreground, an enormous headlight is revealed, piercing the night.*
5. MCU: *Chico runs from left to right in front of the camera, which pans right to keep up with him. The sound of his footsteps resounds on the asphalt.*
6. MCU: *high-angle, extremely brief shot of car's headlight, with the sound of squealing brakes.*
7. MS: *Chico, running, has the headlights close behind him. The sound of his footsteps resounds on the asphalt. As he runs under the streetlamp, he gets closer to the camera.*
8. LS: *high-angle pan shows the worried fugitive still running, as the camera tracks left to right. For an instant, Chico, barely visible in the darkness, and the headlights that follow him are in the frame together. The camera tracks closer to Chico, who moves into a new area of light, and a short pan to the left frames the streetlamp as he crashes into it. His body is a spot of white in the darkness, seen in high-angle LS.*
9. CU: *from above. Chico, spread out on the sidewalk with his head down, turns over on his back, and briefly feels his head. For the first time since the beginning of the film, there is silence.*
10. MS: *still from above, the camera shows a darkened figure who approaches Chico's body, lowers himself, puts down a package, slaps the inanimate Chico several times, and helps him to get up. While the unknown figure brushes off Chico's coat with the back of his hand, Chico picks up the huge package from the sidewalk and hands it back to its owner.*

CHICO: I don't know how to thank you. I stupidly ran into this street-
    lamp.
PASSERBY: Well, I'm going to take off. She still waits up for me before
    she'll go to bed. (*Making a friendly gesture toward Chico.*) Come on.
*In the same shot, the camera begins to track backward, with the men in a
closer low-angle two-shot. In the darkness one can barely make them out
as they walk side by side while talking. At one point, all that can be seen is
the streetlamp, which is reminiscent of the car's headlight seen earlier.*
CHICO: How long have you been married?
PASSERBY: Eleven years.
CHICO: I wish I was married.
PASSERBY: You say that as if you really meant it.
CHICO: I do mean it.
PASSERBY: It has its advantages. In the beginning it almost didn't work.
    (*The two figures emerge slowly from the night.*) Some days, while I was
    eating breakfast, I looked at her and wondered how I could get rid of
    her. (*The faces of Chico and his companion can now be clearly seen.
    The latter, a heavy man with a jovial air, chews some chewing gum. He
    is wearing a hat and a white scarf, which is tied around his neck, under
    his coat. The package, which he is holding in his hand, is a big bouquet*

of flowers. The camera continues to track backward in front and slightly to the left of them.) And then I said to myself: "Where are you getting such ideas?" And I never managed to find any good reasons.

CHICO (*stopping, as the other man also stops briefly*): Was it a question of your freedom?

PASSERBY: Yep! (*They start walking together again.*) I met her at a dance. I had a helluva time getting to know her. She hadn't really lived very much. You know how it is in Paris; I'll bet there's a lot more virgins there than any other city in the world—at least proportionally speaking—but, listen (*they stop, facing each other in profile*) . . . that's not why I married her.

CHICO: Well, why then?

PASSERBY (*they start walking again; traffic sounds are heard*): I got used to her; we had a good time together. I don't know who you are and I'll probably never see you again . . . but all the more reason to speak frankly. I think it's a good idea to spill your guts to a stranger from time to time.

CHICO (*rubbing his chest*): That's true.

PASSERBY: I ended up having some feelings for her. That had never happened to me before. We went out together for a year and then one fine day I went and bought a wedding ring.

CHICO: That's the way it always happens (*rubbing his face*).

PASSERBY: Not always. I think I really fell in love with her two years after the wedding. She was in the hospital having our first kid. I remember planting myself next to the bed. I looked at her, I looked at the baby, and I think that's when everything began. (*They stop, as does the camera.*)

CHICO: How many children do you have now?

PASSERBY: Three.

CHICO: Three, that's nice.

PASSERBY: Yeah, they're amazing kids. (*They start walking again.*) Well, I'm turning right here. So long, and take care of yourself. (*He walks out of the frame to the right.*)

CHICO: I plan on it. Thanks. (*Waving to him to the right, alone in the frame.*) Good luck! (*Left alone, Chico immediately begins to look hunted again and takes off running left, out of the frame.*)

11. MS: *in the dark, Chico can be made out running at top speed along the sidewalk from right to left. A streetlamp illuminates him for a moment as he passes in front of the camera as it pans to the left to keep him in the frame. Chico starts one way, away from the camera, and then runs back toward it and out of frame, left. The camera briefly moves left and right, as though looking for Chico.*

12. MCU: *high-angle, tracking shot right to left shows Chico stopping at a café and looking inside. To his left,* BYRRH *is seen on the window. The camera swings up and left to reveal, over Chico's shoulder and through the glass, Boby Lapointe, who is singing facing the patrons. Léna, the waitress, moves around the room. The camera follows Chico as he moves toward the door of the café, passing a poster that reads* "CHARLIE KOLLER [sic]. DANCING NIGHTLY" *and that shows a stylized drawing of Charlie at the piano. The singer's voice reaches the street, muted. As Chico reaches the door, the shot ends.*

BOBY LAPOINTE (*singing*): "But it's not monotonous. And even when it's autumn. . . ."

Café, interior, night

13. MCU: *the interior of a café that appears modest and out-of-date. In the foreground, Boby Lapointe, initially in profile, jumps around mechanically while singing. He is wearing a white shirt, a vest, and a dark tie. A beard frames his serious face. To the right, a set of drum cymbals occupies the foreground. Behind him several clients pass from the bar through a swinging glass door into the main room. Chico can be seen entering the bar area, where Plyne, the owner of the café, is serving customers from behind the bar. Chico asks him something, and Plyne points off to the right.*

BOBY LAPOINTE (*singing*): "I cried out when I saw her. Here was springtime. . . ."

14. MS: *Chico emerges through a door on the left into a corridor, down which he walks rapidly, his face moving into* ECU *as it passes the camera, which pans right to follow him. He knocks on a door.*

15. MCU: *Charlie, his back to the camera, as he turns his head when he hears the knock. In the room, various pieces of furniture form a strange combination: a chair is hung on a wall, a blind with a flower motif is spread out across another wall, and another chair is upside down. Three salamis hang in front of the blind.*

CHICO (*off*): Hi, Edouard.

CHARLIE (*drily*): Call me Charlie and wait for me there. (*With a vexed expression, he turns back toward the mirror he had been using to dress, a cigarette at his lips.*)

As Charlie moves out of the frame, Chico moves into it on the left, where he can be seen through an open window that gives onto the corridor.

CHICO: There's something wrong with you. It's been four years since we've seen each other and you greet me like. . . .

As Chico speaks, Charlie moves back into the frame at the lower right, tying his tie.

16. MS: *Chico is in profile at the left, while Charlie, who can also be seen in the mirror, continues tying his tie at the far right. The wall of the corridor separates them.*

CHICO: You'd think I had just gone around the block. (*He points to his swollen forehead.*) Yeah, you see, I hurt myself. It's so dark out there that I ran into a pole.

CHARLIE: Somebody was chasing you.

CHICO: Well, not the cops in any case, otherwise I wouldn't have gotten you mixed up in it.

17. MCU: *as in 15, as Charlie continues to dress.*

CHARLIE (*angrily*): That's exactly why you came, to get me mixed up in it. But I'm not going for it. (*He moves off to the right.*)

18. MS: *as in 16; at first, Charlie can only be seen in the mirror, but then he moves back into the frame as he puts on his coat.*

CHICO (*balancing on one foot then the other*): Fido must have grown a lot since the old days.

CHARLIE: Yeah.

CHICO: And the dough, how's that going?

CHARLIE: I'm getting by. Just don't count on me.

19. MCU: *as in 15; at first Chico cannot be seen through the window, but then he moves into the frame.*

CHARLIE: I don't want to be mixed up in it. You understand? No way.

CHICO: Oh, Charlie, listen. . . .

CHARLIE: How's the family?

CHICO: Everybody's in great shape. The old man. The old lady.

CHARLIE: And Richard?

CHICO: Oh Richard, you know him, he's always up to something. (*Charlie takes a big drag from his cigarette and glances one last time at the mirror as he runs his fingers through his hair.*) But we miss you and Fido.

20. MS: *as in 16, but with both Chico and Charlie now turned in the direction of the camera.*

CHICO: I was telling myself a while ago. . . .

CHARLIE (*leaving the room, moving toward the camera and past the wall, he passes in front of Chico in the corridor and moves left out of the frame; Chico follows him out of the frame*): When they started chasing you.

21. MS: *The camera now tracks backward down the corridor, as Charlie moves toward it, followed by Chico.*

CHICO: Charlie, I'm in big trouble! (*They pass in front of the camera, which pans left to follow them.*) You've gotta help me! I'm in bad shape.

CHARLIE (*lifting the bathroom latch*): So you thought of me. (*He enters the bathroom.*) Who's chasing you? (*He closes the door behind him. A window at the right throws light into the corridor.*)

CHICO (*waiting at the door, on which someone has written* "PLEASE CLOSE THE DOOR" *in chalk. Boby Lapointe can be heard singing in the bar*):

Two guys. We were in on a job together . . . the two guys, me, and
Richard. Well, they wanted to play rough and screw us. So we decided
not to share with them, and me and Richard shook them loose on the
way.

CHARLIE (*who comes out of the bathroom, zips up his pants, and readjusts his jacket*): Great! What do your two guys look like?

CHICO: Well, one had a cap and the other a hat. (*They move off to the
left, followed by a pan from right to left. "*SHIT*" is written with a crayon
in big letters in the passage. The camera then begins to follow them in a
tracking movement.*) They ain't brothers, but they look alike anyway,
and they both smoke a pipe. (*As they move closer to the café, Boby
Lapointe's singing can be heard more loudly.*)

22. MLS, high angle: *the café room, separated from the bar by a half parti-
tion of frosted glass. Léna passes through with a tray. Charlie and Chico
enter by the door at the back.*

BOBY LAPOINTE (*singing off*): Marcelle, I put some salt in the spaghet-
ti. . . .

*The camera pans from left to right, revealing Boby Lapointe at the right of the
frame, as Charlie, followed by Chico, enters the room. He goes toward the
piano and sets himself up there while Boby Lapointe is finishing his song.*

BOBY LAPOINTE: . . . Boom! Boom! (*The singer waves and moves
away.*)

23. MCU: *Closer shot of Charlie, as he sits down behind his piano. He makes
a sign to the musicians and begins playing the piece of music that accompanied the credits at the beginning of the film.*

24. MLS: *slight pan right to left. Couples begin dancing. Clarisse, dressed in
a flower print dress, moves into the foreground and leans her smiling face
toward the piano.*

CLARISSE: Hi, Charlie, how're you? (*She rejoins her dancing partner.*)
The camera pulls back and to the left for a MCU *on Chico as he moves to
the piano, his back three-quarters to the camera, as he looks intently at
Charlie off.*)

CHICO: What the hell are you doing here? (*A backward tracking shot
reveals Charlie from behind, his head lowered over the keyboard.*) Hey,
I'm going to tell it to you straight: you're ruining your life.

CHARLIE (*without moving*): All right, all right.

25. MCU: *Charlie in profile at the far right of the frame, behind his piano,
continues to play. In the foreground on top of the piano lies a package of
cigarettes and a saucer. Several couples are dancing behind Chico, who is
talking animatedly to his brother.*

CHICO (*getting irritated*): Yeah, all right, all right. It's not all right. Well,
you look fine behind that piece of junk (*Léna passes near them*) but you
should be in front of a concert piano, in front of a jampacked hall.

26. C U : *Charlie in three-quarter profile, his eyes lowered, with Chico's head, turned away from the camera, on the left side of the frame.*
    C H I C O : . . . with the audience on their knees. So I'm asking you: what the hell are you doing here?
    C H A R L I E : I can't be in two places at once.
    C H I C O (*turning his face toward the camera with a derisive grunt*): Gimme a break. . . . An international virtuoso who can't even buy himself a used car, that's really screwed up.
    C H A R L I E (*with an irritable expression*): All right, all right. Shut up.
27. M C U : *as in 25.*
    C H I C O (*addressing the whole room, while Charlie, his eyes lowered, seems to get more and more exasperated*): Look at him, a virtuoso who's just banging away. But, my God (*taking off his overcoat*), let's give him a grand piano, a grand piano with candles on it. Well, where are the candles?
    Plyne comes rushing up, a cigarette between his lips, sleeves rolled up, a checkered scarf around his neck.
    P L Y N E : Hey, pal, why don't you pipe down?
    C H I C O (*aggressively*): But I want everyone to hear me.
    P L Y N E : The customers don't want to be bothered.
    C H I C O : That's the trouble nowadays, nobody wants to be bothered.
    Plyne grabs Chico by the overcoat.
28. C U : *Back on Charlie and Chico in* E C U . *Plyne's head is on the right, turned away from the camera.*
    C H A R L I E (*staring at Plyne*): Let him go, Plyne, he's sick.
    Plyne's and Chico's heads move quickly, almost out of the frame, but remain visible at the two edges. Charlie is seen center frame in C U .
    P L Y N E (*off*): So you [tu] know 'im, Charlie.
    C H A R L I E (*in a tone of suppressed anger*): I thought that we understood each other by now. Don't call me by my first name. Call me "Mr. Kohler" when you speak to me.[1]
    P L Y N E (*off*): I asked you [vous] a question: who is he?
    C H I C O (*in* E C U *at extreme left of frame*): Maybe he's ashamed of me, my loving little brother. He's an artist. There's no more Charlie than spinach has butter. His name is Edouard.
29. M C U : *as in 25.*
    C H A R L I E (*off*): Shut up.
    P L Y N E : I didn't even know he had a brother.
    C H I C O : There're four kids in the family, all boys. And Charlie, what do you pay him to do here?
    P L Y N E : To play the piano.
30. C U : *as in 28. Chico in three-quarter profile, with Charlie on the right. Chico makes his speech with a smug expression.*

CHICO: Well, what do you expect? He's paid to play the piano, not to tell the story of his life. If you want to find out more about a guy, you have to shell out, and the more you find out, the more you pay. It's like digging a well—the deeper you go, the more it costs. Sometimes it gets so expensive, ha, ha (*he laughs*). . .

31. MCU: *as in shot 25.*

CHICO: . . . that you have to give up, ha, ha.

Plyne shrugs his shoulders and walks away, running into Mammy, around whom Chico puts his arms.

32. MCU: *high angle, Chico and Mammy dance among the other couples.*

CHICO: You're very desirable, that's why I desire you. Just this evening I decided to get married. You're the first one I'm going to ask.

MAMMY: Aren't you going to ask me if I'm free? (*They both look briefly in Plyne's direction.*)

CHICO: Come on, it's not possible. The abominable snowman is your boyfriend?

MAMMY: Well, he was my boyfriend, but we've never officially broken up. And besides, I don't know who you are.

CHICO: I'm Charlie's brother.

MAMMY (*smiling*): No kidding! I just love Charlie.

CHICO: And how much do you love me?

MAMMY: It's a little early to tell. (*Chico tries to kiss her, but she escapes his grasp.*) You'll have to excuse me now, the customers are waiting.

33. MS: *The camera pans the dance floor, revealing, among the couples, a young man who is contemplating with great fascination his partner's plunging neckline.*

SHE: So my chest interests you that much?

HE: Don't worry about it, I'm a doctor.

SHE (*with a derisive smile*): Yeah.

They dance out of the frame to the right and the camera now frames Clarisse, who's having fun making her partner come closer with little gestures of her hand, then pushing him back onto a bench when he tries to grab her hips. The camera moves backward to put Chico into the foreground of the shot. Along the wall, a row of customers is watching the couples.

34. MCU: *two young men in glasses, one in a jacket, the other in a uniform, discuss the scene from the table at which they're sitting.*

FIRST MAN (*with a grimace*): It's not top quality tonight.

SECOND MAN: Nope. The day before yesterday . . .

35–37. MCU: *hands and hips undulating to the rhythm of the music.*

SECOND MAN (*off*): . . . that was "first-class quality" [in English].

38. MCU: *Back on the two young men.*

SECOND MAN (*in an excited voice, as he jumps up, his finger pointing*): Hey! Look at that, over there!

39. MCU: *from their* POV, *the reverse angle of 35, 36, 37, of Clarisse's hips, in her flower print dress. The camera tilts up toward her bust.*

    FIRST MAN (*off*): Interesting, interesting or just curious.

40. MS: *reverse angle, as at end of 33, with Chico watching on the left, in the foreground, with his back to the camera and the young men at their table in the back. Clarisse continues her little game and pushes her partner back one more time. Exasperated, he slaps her. Chico jumps in, knocks him to the ground with a punch, and gallantly pulls Clarisse away.*

    Café, exterior, night

41. MCU: *Close shot, high angle, tracking right to left: two pipe-smoking individuals, who resemble the description given by Chico, arrive in front of the café, moving quickly. They stop, with their backs to the camera, to look through the same window as Chico looked through earlier.*

    Café, interior, night

42. MCU: *Clarisse, Chico, and Charlie behind the piano, continuing to play. Chico, a satisfied smile on his lips, comes into the shot to get his overcoat.*

    CLARISSE: See you later, Charlie. (*She walks away with Chico.*)

    Café, exterior, night

43. MCU: *Close shot, high angle, tracking right to left: the two gangsters, after looking inside, quickly go to the door, heads down, and enter.*

    Café, interior, night

44. MCU: *as in 42, without Clarisse. Chico, very excited, runs up to Charlie.*

    CHICO: My God! They're here!

    CHARLIE: That's your business. I have nothing to do with it.

    CHICO (*shouting*): I'm really screwed now!

45. ECU: *Charlie, held for only a second.*

    CHARLIE: The door's over there. Get going!

46. MCU: *as in 42, held for less than a second, as Charlie suddenly jumps up to follow Chico.*

47. MLS: *Chico and Charlie run across the dance floor, passing in front of the camera.*

48. MS: *Closer shot: Chico goes through the door while Charlie knocks over some cases of wine to stop the two gangsters. They push everything out of the way while Charlie stands there without moving. One of the gangsters stares hard at Charlie.*

49. MCU: *back on the piano, as in 42. From behind the piano, an unidentified male customer watches the scene.*

50. MS: *as in 48. The two gangsters climb over the cases of wine and run down the hallway. Charlie begins to move toward the piano.*

51. MCU: *the piano, as in 42. Boby Lapointe runs from the background of the frame to the left foreground.*

52. MCU: *Boby Lapointe grabs his coat, but doesn't put it on, and begins to sing, while jumping about in place. He is seen in profile. Behind him is the bass player. As he sings, French subtitles with the words of his song appear at the bottom of the frame.*[2]
    BOBY LAPOINTE: "Her name was Françoise, / But everyone called her . . ."

53. MS: *high-angle pan right to left. Charlie moves among the dancers past Boby Lapointe, toward his piano.*
    BOBY LAPOINTE (*off*): ". . . Raspberry [Clit]. . . (*now back in frame*). . . It was one of the adjutant's ideas, / Even though he didn't have. . ."

54. MCU: *Charlie walks in front of the singer. Boby Lapointe continues to sing "Framboise."*
    BOBY LAPOINTE: ". . . very many [didn't have much balls]. . . ."

55. MS, high angle: *behind the couples moving back toward the dance floor, Boby continues his song. Charlie sits down at the piano.*
    BOBY LAPOINTE: "She gave us a drink / In a little place in the Maine-et-Loire. . ."

56. CU: *Boby Lapointe, behind whom on the left we can see Charlie at the piano. Dancers occasionally pass quickly through the frame.*
    BOBY LAPOINTE: "But it wasn't Maud [she wasn't a prostitute]. / She had another name. / And right off there was no question / Of tickling

her under the chin. / Besides, she was from Antibes. / What an insult! / Insults [vanilla] and raspberries [clits] / are the breasts of fate."

57. MCU: *as in 52.*

  BOBY LAPOINTE: "She was from Antibes, / Which is closer than the Caribbean, / And which is closer than Caracas. / But is it closer than Pézenas? / I don't know! / Even though she was French, / She was nevertheless from Antibes [against fucking]. / And despite being French, / And despite her burning eyes [her eyes looking for cash], / It didn't make me feel any better / To know that she was from Antibes [that she was against fucking], / Since I'm rather in favor of it. / What an insult! / Insults [vanilla] and raspberries [clits] / Are the breasts of fate."

58. CU: *as in 56.*

  BOBY LAPOINTE: "She didn't have many advantages, / But to increase them, / She had herself pumped up / At the beauty institute, ah, ah, ah. / In the Maine-et-Loire you can / Treat yourself to beautiful pear-shaped breasts. / There's an institute in Angers / That operates without danger / On the youngest and the oldest. / You can get just about everything changed, / Except what can't be changed. / What an insult! / Insults [vanilla] and raspberries [clits] / Are the breasts of fate.

  "More advantages, / A great advantage of advantages, / I told her when she returned / With her breasts from Angers. Two times ten!"

59. MCU: *as in 52.*

  BOBY LAPOINTE: "So allow me to play / With this chest from Angers. / But she escaped me, / She took off into a field. / I didn't run after her / Because I didn't want to catch up / With that chest from Angers. / The moral of the story: / Insults [vanilla] and breasts / Are the raspberries [clits] of fate."

The singer makes a little mechanical gesture and disappears while the musicians take up a number with a heavy beat. A pan toward the left passes in front of the bass player and the drummer, stopping on Charlie's profile. The back of the bass player's head can be seen in a mirror in the upper right part of the frame.

  CHARLIE (*voiceover*): He must have run through the courtyard. They didn't really look like they wanted his skin. No, just to talk, to talk about business. You can imagine what kind of business. Every time your dear little brothers get involved in something . . . and the first to get burned is always that big imbecile Chico. Come on, come on, get moving while there's still time and wish him good luck.

  CHARLIE: Good luck.

  Dissolve.

60. MLS: *the customers have left. Plyne is sweeping up when Léna emerges from the back door. He indicates to her to pick up the boxes Charlie knocked*

*over earlier. Léna picks up a box, and as she moves to the left, the camera
pans to follow her. She passes in front of two musicians who are putting
their instruments away and in front of Charlie, who is just walking into the
room, left to right, with his raincoat on. He walks over toward the piano.
The camera tracks in to tighten the shot, as the musicians leave.*

THE MUSICIANS (*to Charlie, while leaving*): Good night.

CHARLIE: So long.

*The camera tracks in even closer as Charlie sits down at the piano and
plays several notes. Plyne, his back to the camera, walks into the frame
toward the piano.*

61. ECU: *Plyne.*

PLYNE: She's really got her eye on you.

62. ECU: *reverse shot of Charlie.*

CHARLIE (*lifting his eyes*): Who are you talking about?

63. ECU: *reverse shot of Plyne.*

PLYNE: Léna. I just thought you'd like to know.

64. ECU: *Charlie.*

CHARLIE (*amused*): Thanks. Thanks all the same.

65. ECU: *Plyne.*

PLYNE: It's a shame you're not interested in her . . .

66. ECU: *Charlie, who gives Plyne a quick look.*

67. ECU: *Plyne.*

PLYNE: . . . I wish she looked at *me* like that.

68. ECU: *Charlie.*

CHARLIE (*ironically*): I can leave if I'm causing problems for you.

69. ECU: *Plyne.*

PLYNE: Oh, don't worry about it. I'm not really her type anyway . . .

70. MLS: *Léna enters from the back door, tying the belt of her raincoat.*

PLYNE (*his back now to the camera*): . . . I'm nobody's type.

LÉNA: See you tomorrow. (*She exits the left side of the frame.*)

71. ECU: *Charlie. After having lightly turned his head in Léna's direction, he
looks back at Plyne.*

CHARLIE (*smiling*): Come on now.

72. ECU: *Plyne.*

PLYNE (*pouting*): I'm just a big lug, and I don't have enough brains to
   make women forget it.

73. ECU: *Charlie.*

CHARLIE (*jokingly*): Maybe it's just your glands.

74. ECU: *Plyne.*

PLYNE: No, it's not my glands. It's just my ugly mug.

75. ECU: *Charlie.*

CHARLIE (*his eyes lowered, still playing some notes on the piano*): You
   shouldn't be afraid of women. They're not poisonous.

76. ECU: *Plyne.*
    PLYNE: It's easy to see you don't believe a word you're saying. You've been through the mill too, pal.
77. ECU: *Charlie, head down, looking at piano keys.*
    CHARLIE: Yeah?
78. ECU: *Plyne.*
    PLYNE: Listen, I bet I know what your problem is. You're shy . . . , you're afraid.
79. ECU: *Charlie.*
    PLYNE (*off*): . . . you're afraid.
    CHARLIE (*looking at him with a surprised expression*): Afraid?
80. ECU: *Plyne.*
    PLYNE: Yeah.
81. ECU: *Charlie.*
    CHARLIE (*pensive, trying out the word*): Afraid. I'm afraid. (*His face tightens.*) Shit, I'm afraid.
    PLYNE (*off*): Come on, pal. Are you okay?
    CHARLIE (*unhappily*): I'm afraid.
82. MLS: *the camera pans left to right. Plyne has his back to the camera. Charlie gets up and goes toward the door, followed by Plyne.*
    PLYNE: The two guys with the boxes, what was that all about?
    CHARLIE: I don't have the slightest idea.
Café, exterior, night
83. MLS: *through the glass door leading to the street, the camera frames Charlie and Plyne, who advance toward it. Charlie opens the door and walks outside.*
    PLYNE (*at the door*): Well, I'm going to bed. After all, you've got to keep doing something.
    CHARLIE: So long. (*He begins moving to the left, followed by a fairly tight tracking shot, when Léna's voice stops him.*)
    LÉNA (*off*): Hey, Mister Charlie.
    Charlie turns around and approaches her as the camera quickly tracks right, in the opposite direction. The shot becomes a two-shot with Léna standing in front of the poster with Charlie's name on it.
    LÉNA: I don't like to talk to you in front of the others. Could you lend me a little bit of dough until tomorrow?
    CHARLIE: Sure. (*He takes out a couple of bills and hands them to Léna.*) Here you are. (*He then quickly exits left.*)
    LÉNA (*smiling*): Thanks. Why don't you walk with me a little ways. I don't like to walk home alone at night, Mister Charlie.
    He comes back toward her, into the frame, and they walk side by side accompanied by a backward tracking shot.
    CHARLIE: Just call me Charlie.

LÉNA: Okay. Call me Léna.
CHARLIE: Why Léna?
They cross in front of the camera in ECU.
LÉNA: Well, first it was Hélène, then Heléna, then Léna.
They walk out of the frame on the right. The camera lingers behind them to reveal Plyne spying on them from behind the window.

84. CU: *Tight two-shot, tracking backward. (Slow music, dominated by a flute, can be heard.) Léna and Charlie walk together without saying anything. He looks at her, his head slightly tilted in her direction, while she looks straight ahead, expressionless.*

85. ECU: *Charlie's hand moves timidly toward Léna's, which she jerks away.*

86. CU: *as in 84. Charlie looks at Léna, who remains expressionless.*

87. ECU: *as in 85. Charlie touches Léna's hand, and she immediately sticks it in her pocket.*

88. MS: *Charlie and Léna are now seen from the back, as the camera tracks forward. They are approaching a tunnel. Charlie's arm begins to move around the young woman's waist.*

89. ECU: *Charlie's hand moves toward Léna's hip, then makes a fist in hesitation and pulls back without touching her.*

90. ECU: *in a disguised cut, Charlie grasps his hands behind his back. His fingers unfold one by one, as if he is counting.*

91. MS: *as in 88, on Charlie and Léna from behind. Charlie, continuing to count, unfolds the fingers of his other fist.*
92. ECU: *tracking backward, similar to 84, but tighter on their faces. Charlie goes into a monologue, his face expressionless.*

    CHARLIE (*voiceover*): Your silence must seem strange to her. . . .
93. CU: *Léna's hand comes out of her pocket, as Charlie's goes into his pocket.*

    CHARLIE (*voiceover*): . . . say something, anything, otherwise she'll think you're trying to scare her. . . .
94. ECU: *as in 92.*

    CHARLIE (*voiceover*): . . . Actually, unless she's an idiot, my silence is probably quite eloquent. It creates an affectionate intimacy. (*Léna turns slightly toward him and he toward her, then they look away from each other.*) She's not a blabbermouth, that's for sure. She's a more serious type, not prissy really, but dignified. Facile jokes won't count much with her. To get her to laugh, it's going to have to be really funny.

    Léna looks over at Charlie, who suddenly wrinkles his face. Léna bursts out laughing. (The music stops.)

    CHARLIE (*feigning seriousness*): What made you laugh?

    LÉNA: The expression on your face. (*Seriously*) Listen. (*Steps are heard.*) Do you know those guys who are after your brother?

    CHARLIE: No, why?

    LÉNA: I think they're following us. (*She takes her compact out.*)
95. ECU: *in the mirror, perfectly framed in a completely improbable way, we see the faces of the two gangsters who are walking forward observing them.*
96. ECU: *as in 94. Léna closes her compact case and begins to run, dragging Charlie along with her. They move quickly out of the frame to the left. Two shadowy figures can be seen in the distant background.*
97. MS: *the camera pans as Léna and Charlie run down a dark sidewalk and up some stairs, an iron fence between them and the camera. Again in the light, they hide behind a wall. The muffled voices of the gangsters just barely reach them.*

    MOMO (*off*): Where'd they go?
98. MCU: *slightly high-angle shot, on Léna and Charlie from behind, pushed up against each other behind the wall, listening.*
99. MS: *similar to the beginning of 97, of the iron bars of the steps. Nobody can be seen.*

    ERNEST (*off*): Ah, they must have taken off that way. Goddamn it! So long! I'm going home.
100. MS: *as in the end of 97.*[3]

    Charlie is looking at Léna and attempts to caress her arm just at the moment she turns and grabs his hand.

LÉNA: Come on, let's go.

101. MCU: *as in 92, tracking backward in a two-shot. The musical theme with the flute begins again. They both remain completely expressionless.*

CHARLIE (*voiceover*): She obviously felt you against her. If she didn't like it, she would have left. So, she agreed. But agreed to what? (*Camera pans over into an* ECU *on Charlie alone.*) That's the mystery. You are going to ask her to have a drink before going home, that will give you more time. Don't mess this up. Take it easy. (*In a peremptory tone.*) "Dear Léna, we can't just separate like this, come and have a drink, that's an order." No. (*More gently.*) "Léna, I'll bet you're thirsty, just like me."

CHARLIE (*turning around*): Let's have a drink. (*He suddenly realizes she's left him, as the camera tracks back faster to reveal her absence.*) What the hell?

CHARLIE (*voiceover*): It's probably better that way. Come on, come on, think about something else, think about Art Tatum, is he talented? And Errol Garner? Yeah, Errol Garner's talented. And Juno Manse? You can't say, you don't even know him.

As he continues to think, the camera slows down and Charlie moves back into an ECU. *The camera holds tight on Charlie for a while until the music ends.*

Charlie's Apartment, interior, night

102. MLS: *at first, only footsteps are heard in the darkness; then Charlie's silhouette is seen in the doorway as he turns a light on. An old-fashioned kitchen can be seen.*

103. MS: *a head covered with brown hair is lying on a pillow in the shadow of a bedroom. A large model airplane hangs on the wall. Charlie comes in and pulls the cover up over the sleeper.*

104. CU: *the sleeping head of a young boy.*

105. MS: *as in 103. Charlie finishes pulling up the cover and looks out between the curtains. A light is blinking on and off on the street.*

106. MS: *as in 102. Charlie turns out the light in the kitchen, then, accompanied by a pan left, moves over toward a window. He closes its curtains and turns on a wall lamp in his bedroom, then turns on another lamp on an end table. The furniture is cheap. On the wall hang several pictures. Charlie begins to take his trenchcoat off.*

107. MS: *we see a door, then Clarisse walks through it onto the landing and listens behind a door to the right, as the camera pans to follow her. She hears Charlie loudly humming a jazz tune and begins to smile. The camera is shooting through the bars of the stairway to frame her. The camera then pans left, moving with her as she goes back into her apartment. At the same time, the camera tilts down to show the lower part of her body as she goes through the door. Finally, only her feet are framed as she kicks off her*

high heels and puts on slippers. The camera tilts back up and pans right as she moves once again over to Charlie's door and knocks.

108. M S : *Charlie, bare-chested, a cigarette between his lips, pages through a magazine in bed. The room is brightly lit.*

    C L A R I S S E : (*off*) Charlie, it's me, Clarisse.

    Charlie gets up and, followed by a pan, disappears for a moment from the frame as he opens the door for Clarisse. He returns to his bed.

    C L A R I S S E (*following Charlie*): Hi, Charlie. You're still sleeping without pajamas.

    C H A R L I E (*getting back into bed*): Yeah, it's healthier.

109. M S : *the camera is now on the right side of the bed. Charlie, in profile in the foreground, smokes in bed. Clarisse sits down on a chair at his side. Charlie hands her the ashtray to put on the table.*

    C L A R I S S E : That reminds me of my skeleton number at the carnival. I started there after I left home. (*She picks up a metronome and starts it going.*) And then . . . I was lying in a coffin, almost completely naked, and with this mirror trick you could see my skeleton. Even the doctors believed it . . . and then I sprained my ankle. (*She extends her leg.*)

110. C U : *reverse angle of Charlie from her direction.*

    C H A R L I E (*with an amused smile*): Being an artist is tough.

111. C U : *reverse angle of Clarisse, much closer than 109.*

    C L A R I S S E : Do you want me to stay?

112. C U : *reverse angle of Charlie.*

    C H A R L I E : I don't know.

113. C U : *reverse angle of Clarisse.*

    C L A R I S S E : I could put it on your tab.

114. C U : *reverse angle of Charlie.*

    C H A R L I E : No, thanks.

115. M S : *as in 109, of Clarisse, with Charlie in profile in the foreground.*

    C L A R I S S E (*in a miffed tone*): Okay, okay, I'm not going to insist. (*She puts the metronome down and gets up.*) I'm leaving.

116. C U : *Charlie.*

    C H A R L I E (*following her with his eyes*): Don't get mad. Take off your dress, even though it's pretty.

117. M S : *reverse angle: Clarisse is already almost out the door.*

    C H A R L I E (*off*): Close the door so Fido won't wake up.

    C L A R I S S E (*doing it*): Don't you think I look pretty?

118. M S : *panning left to right.*

    C L A R I S S E (*walking across the room*): My work goes very nicely with a dress like this. You know, I don't have to bow and scrape to get customers. Nobody can say that. (*She is now in front of a mirror, framed in a* M S . *As she takes her clothes off, black undergarments are revealed.*) "How much? Thirty francs, yes or no, take it or leave it." I'm not trying

Pretty, aren't they?... And a bargain!

to bullshit anybody. It's a free country. (*She walks toward a screen.*) I'm
going behind this.

119. CU: *reverse shot of Charlie watching and listening, with his head on the*
      pillow.
      CHARLIE: You're right. Otherwise, I might get ideas.

120. MS: *an imitation Louis XVI screen.*
      CLARISSE (*hidden by the screen, over which she throws her dress*):   I
      prefer to wear pretty things, rather than those sexy skirts that some of
      the girls wear.

121. CU: *Clarisse's face, which appears over the screen on the right.*
      CLARISSE: Don't you think that everything I wear is always pretty?

122. CU: *reverse shot of Charlie.*
      CHARLIE (*passionless*):   Yes, it's very pretty.

123. CU: *reverse shot, as in 121, of Clarisse, who's pouting.*

124. CU: *Charlie.*
      CHARLIE: No, really, it's very pretty.

125. MS: *as in 120. Clarisse is busy behind the screen.*
      CLARISSE: Anyway, my girlfriends are always asking me where I buy
      my clothes.

126. CU: *Clarisse dangles a pair of black panties at the end of her fingers, this*
      time on the left side of the screen.

CLARISSE: They're very pretty, no? And I only paid four francs for them. That's not very much and they're pretty.

127. CU: *reverse shot of Charlie.*

CHARLIE (*yawning*): I'm not supposed to know anything about your panties.

128. MS: *reverse shot, panning right to left.*

CLARISSE (*walking out from behind the screen in a black slip and crossing the room*). You haven't fallen on your head, I hope.

129. CU: *reverse shot of Charlie.*

CHARLIE: No, but I'm a puritan.

130. MS: *low-angle reverse shot of Clarisse.*

CLARISSE (*taking a pillow out of the armoire*). A puritan! A puritan [*puritain*]! A poor slob [*purotin*]! That's what you are, a poor slob. (*She throws the pillow at him, toward the camera*).

131. CU: *reverse shot of Charlie as he gets hit in the face with the pillow.*

132. MS: *as in 130, on Clarisse, who goes back toward the screen, as the camera follows her, panning right.*

CLARISSE (*bursting out laughing*): That was a good shot!

133. CU: *Clarisse's face, which once again appears above the screen, to the right, and then to the left.*

CLARISSE: Oh, I've upset you, pussycat. Are you mad at me?

134. CU: *reverse shot of Charlie.*

CHARLIE: No, the pussycat isn't mad. He's just tired. Besides, they just said on television that all the pussycats are tired these days. (*He lights a cigarette.*) And I'm sleepy and I only like old-fashioned underwear.

135. CU: *reverse shot, as in 133, of Clarisse, who walks from behind the screen in short steps, one hand behind her ear. The camera is very tight on her face as she moves toward the bed, so that the rest of her body cannot be seen.*)

CLARISSE (*singing*): "Television is like a movie theater you can go to while staying home." (*A pan follows her to the bed.*) Come on, move over.

She gets into bed while a slight panning movement frames Charlie alone. While looking at her excitedly, he grabs the alarm clock and winds it rapidly.

136. MS: *two-shot. Clarisse is sitting up in bed, next to Charlie, her ample breasts plainly visible. She takes off her earrings and lets her hair down.*

CHARLIE (*grabbing the sheet, which he pulls up over Clarisse's breasts*). This is the way it has to be done in the movies.

CLARISSE (*with a knowing air*). Uh, huh.[4] I went to the movies this afternoon and saw "Torpedoes in Alaska."

CHARLIE: Was it good?

CLARISSE: It was a John Wayne film that shows that Americans want peace.

CHARLIE: Well, well. They're just like me.

CLARISSE: Are you making fun of me?

CHARLIE: No, I'm not making fun of you, honeybunch.

He reaches across her and puts the light out. A flash of light coming from outside lightens up the bed at regular intervals.

CLARISSE (*to Charlie, who is smoking next to her*): Gimme a drag.

Charlie passes her the cigarette. After a moment, Clarisse starts to purr, then she starts making little angry cries.

CLARISSE: Hey! I thought you were shy!

CHARLIE (*while Clarisse's cries are becoming sharper and sharper*) Haven't you ever heard of the bravery of shy people?

Clarisse bursts out laughing while their bodies jump around frenetically under the sheets.

Charlie's Apartment, interior, day

137. MS: *in the dim light, we see Clarisse sleeping on Charlie's shoulder, and the alarm clock on a table at the left. Suddenly the alarm goes off.*

CHARLIE (*grabbing the alarm clock*): Clarisse, go back to your room, Fido's going to wake up. Come on, quick!

CLARISSE (*still half-asleep*): Yeah, yeah, I know, I'm only good enough to make him dinner every night.

CHARLIE (*getting up, as the camera pans over to frame him alone*): Don't start, Clarisse. Pass me my pants.

The camera is tight on Charlie's head and back, from slightly above, as he puts on his pants. He gets up and moves over toward the curtains, accompanied by a pan from right to left, as the camera moves slightly backward. He glances down into the street.

CLARISSE (*entering the frame from the left as she speaks, she goes over to him, the back of her dress open*). What are you looking at?

CHARLIE: Nothing, nothing.

CLARISSE (*presenting her back to Charlie*): Hey, how about zipping me up in the back?

The camera pans left to frame them to the right and their reflections in a mirror to the left.

CHARLIE (*zipping up her dress*): Come on, over to your place, I'll see you this evening.

She walks out of the frame, leaving him and his mirror image alone.

138. MS: *low-angle shot from the stairs: on the landing, Clarisse enters her apartment and closes the door.*

139. MS: *a white door, which Charlie opens. The camera pans from left to right as Charlie moves into a dark room (soft, slightly disturbing music begins).*

CHARLIE: Fido!

140. CU: *the head of a sleeping child moves on the pillow.*
CHARLIE (*off*): It's time . . .

141. MS: *Charlie, moving across the room, in which several toys can be seen):* . . . time to get up! (*He goes toward the curtain and looks through it.*)

142. MS: *reverse high-angle shot: in the street, a big two-toned American car, an Oldsmobile, can be seen through the window moving slowly forward. The man at the wheel is looking up toward the window.*

143. MS: *as in 141. Charlie shakes Fido.*
CHARLIE: Come on, let's go, you're going to be late.

144. CU: *Fido, as he turns around in bed in order to look out the window.*

145. MS: *the reverse high-angle shot into the street. Two men get out of the car and station themselves on the sidewalk. They are the two gangsters, and they are rubbing their hands and slapping their arms as if cold.*
Charlie's Apartment, exterior, day

146. MS: *the window, seen from the street. The curtain is pulled back. The two gangsters can be seen in the foreground of the shot, from behind, out of focus to the left and right.*

147. MS: *as in 146, but from slightly closer, and without the two gangsters in the foreground; almost a jump cut. The curtain is still pulled back and Fido can be seen looking through it.*
Charlie's Apartment, interior, day

148. CU: *Fido, as in 144. He leaves the window and grabs his pants.*

149. MS: *Fido as he puts on his clothes.*
Charlie's Apartment, exterior, day

150. LS: *high-angle shot. The two gangsters get back into their car. A mysterious-sounding tune can be heard on the soundtrack.*
Charlie's Apartment, interior, day

151. MS: *low-angle shot from the stairs, as in 138, of Clarisse's door. Fido walks out onto the landing from the right.*
FIDO: Goodbye, Charlie, see you tonight.
He slams the door (the music stops) and goes down the stairs whistling. The camera tilts down to follow him.
Charlie's Apartment, exterior, day

152. LS: *high-angle shot. Fido runs out of the building, crosses the street, and dashes into a store. A second later he comes out again with a package in his hand, then disappears through the door of a neighboring apartment building. A very fast tilt up merges almost imperceptibly with a much closer shot to frame him in an upper-story window along with another boy his own age, even though no time has passed. The camera zooms in more tightly and Fido drops the package. A very fast tilt down follows its fall.*

153. CU: *the camera is inside the car. A muted sound punctuates the explosion of the package as the windshield is flooded with milk. Both gangsters suddenly jump outside. Through the streams of white liquid, their figures can be made out checking the damage.*

154. MS: *panning shot, right to left, of the two kids running across the street, chased by Momo. Seeing that they are going into the school, he stops suddenly and begins walking smartly down the sidewalk to the left.*

155. CU: *Back inside the car, the camera on the back seat. Ernest has just sat down at the steering wheel and slammed the door behind him. The milk still covers the windshield.*

156. *The camera, now on the right side of the front seat, frames Ernest in* ECU *on the right of the frame, and Charlie in* LS *in the doorway of the apartment building as he is leaving. Wearing his raincoat, he turns to the right. The camera pans right to shoot through the windshield as the wipers wipe through the milk, allowing us to see Charlie through the windshield. The car starts and follows him in a tracking shot along the sidewalk, seen through the windshield as the wipers continue. The camera pans to an* ECU *on Ernest. The gangsters pass Charlie, stop, and jump out of the car when he reaches them.*
    ERNEST (*framed through the the open car door*): Hello, Charlie.
    CHARLIE (*calmly*): Whom do I have the honor of addressing?

ERNEST: I'm Ernest (*pointing to his colleague, who enters the frame from the left*) and he's Momo.

MOMO (*off*): Hi.

CHARLIE: Hi.

157. MS: *Charlie on the sidewalk, framed by Ernest and Momo. Ernest grabs Charlie by the arm.*

ERNEST: We're going with you. Get in.

CHARLIE (*trying to get loose*): I'm walking.

ERNEST (*to Momo, who makes a gesture toward the inside pocket of his overcoat*): That's not necessary. (*The wipers are still moving on the windshield.*)

MOMO: I just want to show him.

ERNEST: Well, he knows you have it.

MOMO: Maybe he's not sure.

ERNEST: Okay, show it to him.

Momo takes out a big black gun that he puts under Charlie's nose.

ERNEST: Now do you want to get in?

CHARLIE (*convinced*): Yes I do. (*He gets into the car, followed by Ernest.*)

158. MLS: *Momo runs around the car in order to get in on the other side of Charlie. They start off, followed by a pan down the street.*
Dissolve.

Oldsmobile, interior, day

159. MCU: *a three-shot of Ernest, Charlie, and Momo seen through the windshield. Reflections on the glass keep them from being seen clearly.*

ERNEST: What do you think of our friend, Momo?

MOMO: I think he's tough. What do you think?

ERNEST: Oh, I think he's tough. (*To Charlie.*) We think you're tough.

160. MLS: *reverse-angle shot. The camera is in the car and frames a street lined with bare trees. A backfiring motorscooter passes in front of the automobile from left to right.*

ERNEST (*off*): Fifty thousand, you could handle that. If it's not enough, we can work something out.

161. MCU: *as in 159. All three continue to look straight ahead, through the windshield.*

CHARLIE: I don't need much money.

MOMO: Maybe he thinks we don't have any money.

ERNEST: Right. Show him the package.

Momo shows him a wad of bills.

CHARLIE: It's not very smart to walk around with all that.

Exterior, street, day

162. MLS: *the car comes to a stop alongside a sidewalk that has a lot of people walking on it. A truck passes.*

Oldsmobile, interior, day

163. M C U :   *the camera, on the back seat, frames Charlie from behind. Ernest and Momo are on either side of him.*

ERNEST: This is all just talk. Just where are we now?

MOMO: Well, he doesn't want any money, so let's try something else. (*Turning, in profile, toward Charlie.*) My dear Charlie, we just want to talk to him. We don't want to do him any harm.

CHARLIE: Who?

ERNEST (*irritated*):   I thought we agreed to play fair! You know very well we're talking about your brother.

MOMO: You put us in contact with him, just take us, of your own free will, to his hiding place.

CHARLIE: But I don't know if he's there.

ERNEST: Well, I think he is. Momo, get in the back with him, because here comes our mutual friend.

CHARLIE: Who's that?

Léna appears through the windshield.

ERNEST: The girlfriend who just turned up, the waitress at the bar.

MOMO: Mrs. Charlie.

Oldsmobile, exterior, day

164. M L S :   *Charlie gets out with Momo, who grabs Léna and pushes her into the car. She offers no resistance.*

Oldsmobile, interior, day

165. M C U :   *the camera, on the back seat, frames Léna, who gets into the front, next to Ernest.*

Oldsmobile, exterior, day

166. M L S :   *Momo gets into the back and closes the door.*

Oldsmobile, interior, day

167. M C U :   *the camera, on the front seat, briefly frames Momo and Charlie looking forward. The car begins to move.*

MOMO (*to Charlie*):   No need for introductions.

168. M C U :   *as in 165. The camera, on the back seat, frames Ernest and Léna from behind, against the light.*

LÉNA (*to Ernest*):   Where are we going?

ERNEST: Ask your boyfriend.

LÉNA: He's not my boyfriend.

ERNEST: Anyway, we're going to see his brother Chico.

169. C U :   *the camera, in Charlie's position, frames Léna's face turned toward him.*

LÉNA: The guy last night with the black eye.

170. M C U :   *as in 167, on Momo and Charlie.*

CHARLIE: They must have gotten some information somewhere. First, they knew he was my brother, then they found out my address, and yours too, it looks like.

171. C U : *Léna turned toward Ernest.*
     L É N A : From whom?
172. M C U : *Momo and Charlie.*
     C H A R L I E : I have an idea, but I'm not sure.
173. M C U : *Ernest and Léna, from behind.*
     E R N E S T : I'm going to clue you in.
174. M C U : *in three round frames side by side on the screen, Plyne appears behind the bar in various poses, talking, counting money, and so on.*
     E R N E S T (*off*): The next morning we arranged to have a drink with the owner of your little dance hall.
     M O M O (*off*): If you'd only seen it!
     E R N E S T (*off*): It didn't take long. He spilled everything, the big ape. You know, fifty smackers, that's twenty-five each.
     M O M O (*off*): Twenty-five for Charlie's address, twenty-five for the waitress's.
     E R N E S T (*off*): Greedy, suspicious.
     M O M O (*off*): He was counting his dough.
     In the circles, Plyne grabs the money and peels off the bills one by one.
     E R N E S T (*off*): What a mug—and how he stroked the dough!
175. C U : *Léna turns toward Charlie.*
     L É N A (*with a look of disgust*): Plyne, that pig.
176. M C U : *Momo and Charlie.*
     M O M O : Ernest, watch where you're going.
177. M C U : *Ernest and Léna from behind.*
     E R N E S T : Look, who's driving?
178. M C U : *Charlie and Momo.*
     M O M O : You are, but watch what you're doing anyway. Be careful.
179. M C U : *Ernest and Léna from behind.*
     E R N E S T (*with a syrupy voice, leaning toward Léna*): You're right. We have to be careful with the health of our charming hostages.
180. M C U : *Momo and Charlie.*
     M O M O : You could've passed, you had the time.
181. M L S : *tracking forward along the avenue in front of the car, looking through the windshield. A Renault Dauphine is moving forward slowly.*
     M O M O (*off*): Since he's expecting it, you should move ahead.
182. M C U : *Ernest and Léna, as Ernest turns back toward Momo.*
     E R N E S T : Will you please let me drive?
183. M C U : *Momo and Charlie.*
     M O M O : Oh, if only I had the wheel!
184. M C U : *Ernest and Léna from behind.*
     E R N E S T : Yeah, around your neck!
185. M C U : *Momo and Charlie.*
     M O M O : Don't get upset!

186. M C U : *Ernest and Léna from behind.*
     E R N E S T : I'm not getting upset.
     Oldsmobile, exterior, day
187. L S : *high-angle pan on the Oldsmobile, from left to right, on a large square where cars are hurrying in every direction.*
     Oldsmobile, interior, day
188. M C U : *Ernest and Léna from behind.*
     E R N E S T : If there's one thing I know how to do, it's drive . . .
189. M C U : *Momo and Charlie.*
     E R N E S T (*off*): . . . a car.
190. M C U : *Ernest and Léna from behind, as Ernest turns toward Momo.*
     E R N E S T : In that area, I'm not afraid of anyone. I do what I want with a car.
191. M C U : *Momo and Charlie.*
     M O M O : Except for passing.
192. M C U : *Ernest and Léna from behind.*
     E R N E S T : You just want to get me mad, that's it.
193. M C U : *Momo and Charlie.*
     M O M O : I'm just telling you that instead of ogling the chicks, you should keep your eyes on the road.
194. C U : *the camera is in Léna's position. Ernest, his face turned away from her, is listening to Momo in profile.*
     M O M O (*off*): Some day it's going to end badly.
195. M C U : *Momo and Charlie. Momo's voice is sepulchral.*
     M O M O :   Someday you're going to run someone over!
196. C U : *as in 194, as Ernest leans back toward Momo.*
     E R N E S T : Well, if I do run someone over, I'll only be avenging my father.
197. C U : *Léna, from Charlie's position, listening to Ernest.*
     E R N E S T (*off*): He was a pedestrian, my father.
198. C U : *as in 194.*
     E R N E S T : He got himself run over crossing the street. He wasn't looking at the cars. He was looking at all the women.
199. M C U : *Momo and Charlie.*
     E R N E S T (*off*): One of them must have had a dress that was too short. He looked at her and got himself run over.
200. C U : *Ernest in profile.*
     M O M O (*off, his arm coming into the frame on the back of the front seat*): Well, buddy, your father was quite a dirty old man!
     E R N E S T (*bursting out in laughter*): Well, I must take after him. . . .
201. L S : *lateral tracking shot, right to left along the street, seen from behind the window of the car. In front of the houses is a construction site.*
     E R N E S T (*off*): . . . I'm really sharp-eyed; I know exactly how to find the right moment . . .

202. C U : *Ernest in profile; Charlie is on the left side of the frame.*
     E R N E S T : . . . when the wind is going to blow a dress up, . . .
203. C U : *Léna.*
     E R N E S T (*off*): . . . when a leg is going to be lifted, getting into a bus.
204. C U : *Ernest in profile.*
     E R N E S T (*to Léna*): I'm shocking you.
205. C U : *Léna.*
     L É N A : Not at all . . . .
206. C U : *Ernest in profile.*
     L É N A (*off*): . . . You're not the first bastard I've ever met . . .
207. C U : *Léna.*
     L É N A (*in a provocative tone*): . . . I'm learning something. Go on.
208. C U : *Ernest in profile, Charlie to the left of the screen.*
     E R N E S T : (*leaning menacingly toward her*) I'm going to tell you something.
209. C U : *Léna.*
     E R N E S T (*off*): Whatever women say, they all want it, they all want it.
210. C U : *as in 208.*
     C H A R L I E (*leaning forward*): They all want what?
     M O M O (*leaning into the frame, toward Charlie, then toward Léna*): He's saying that they all want it, and I completely agree with him. And because they want it, they're going to get it.
     E R N E S T : Mind you, I have nothing against women.
211. C U : *Léna.*
     L É N A (*laughing*): Oh, I thought so. (*She directs an amused glance back at Momo.*)
     E R N E S T (*off*): I love them all . . .
212. C U : *Ernest in profile.*
     E R N E S T : . . . and just exactly for what they are . . . .
     Oldsmobile, exterior, day
213. C U : *three small traffic lights.*[5]
     E R N E S T (*off*): . . . The trouble is that they want to talk before and especially after . . .
     Oldsmobile, interior, day
214. C U : *Ernest in profile. Behind him Charlie can be seen.*
     E R N E S T : . . . just when you want to leave . . .
215. C U : *Léna.*
     E R N E S T (*off*): . . . alone.
216. C U : *as in 214.*
     C H A R L I E (*leaning forward a little*): If I may, what my father always said about women was that when you've seen one, you've seen them all.
217. C U : *Léna looking at Charlie.*

218. C U :   *Momo and Charlie and Ernest. Momo breaks out laughing, then Charlie does the same.*
219. C U :   *Léna, who, her eyes on Charlie, also breaks out laughing.*

Oldsmobile, exterior, day

220. L S :   *high-angle pan from left to right. As the car travels around a traffic circle and down a wide avenue, the loud laughter of the four passengers lasts a long time. In the foreground there are several bare branches.*
221. L S :   *high-angle shot of a superhighway. The car, coming toward the camera, passes a truck at high speed. The camera, placed on an overpass, whips quickly to the left to follow the speeding car as it moves further away.*

Oldsmobile, interior, day

222. C U :   *Ernest's profile, in a much tighter shot than previously, stands out against the light coming through the car window.*
     E R N E S T (*staring ahead at the road*): When I see one of them for the first time, it's like being struck by lightning. I love them, my God, I want to marry them, I want to have kids with them . . .
223. C U :   *Charlie, looking straight ahead without expression, listens.*
     E R N E S T (*off*): . . . but as soon as she opens her mouth, there's only one thing that I want, and that's to get rid of her . . .
224. C U :   *Ernest.*
     E R N E S T :   . . . and to see her go.
225. C U :   *Léna, turned toward Ernest.*
     L É N A (*smiling*): That's a nice mentality!
226. C U :   *Ernest.*
     E R N E S T :   Well, I'm sorry, but it's mine.
227. C U :   *Léna, who, smiling, pushes back the curls that the wind has blown into her face.*
     E R N E S T (*off*): Now, look, it's true that . . .
228. C U :   *Ernest.*
     E R N E S T :   . . . you do everything to get men excited . . .
229. C U :   *three-quarter shot of Momo against the light.*
     E R N E S T (*off*): . . . why the lipstick, why the nail polish . . .
230. C U :   *Charlie.*
     E R N E S T (*off*): . . . why the bras, why the skirts . . .
231. C U :   *Léna.*
     E R N E S T (*off*): . . . why the high heels, why the stockings? . . .
     Léna listens, smiling, and shakes her head.
232. C U :   *Ernest.*
     E R N E S T :   . . . why not socks like we wear?
233. C U :   *Momo.*
     M O M O :   Yeah! A girl with knee-high socks, that's horrible.

234. MCU: *Léna and Ernest from behind, as in earlier shots. Léna listens, and turns briefly toward the back. Meanwhile, the road, lined with bare trees, can be seen through the windshield as they pass by.*

    ERNEST (*off*): A real little tease!

235. CU: *Momo.*

    MOMO: One time all my underwear was in the dirty laundry. I found some little silk panties that belonged to my sister. Boy, did that do something to me! . . .

236. MCU: *Ernest and Léna from behind. The car gets ready to pass a truck that is carrying a publicity poster for* Cahiers du Cinéma.

    MOMO (*off*): . . . I understood that day, why they want more, why they all want it . . .

237. CU: *Momo.*

    MOMO: . . . especially since we wear pants, but they, with their dresses, have their thighs touching from morning until night. . . .

238. MCU: *Ernest and Léna from behind. Ernest passes the truck while blowing the horn.*

    MOMO (*off*): . . . Hey, and the priests, that must do something for them, too. . . .

239. CU: *Léna, who is looking out the window at the truck they are passing, the back of her head to the camera. She suddenly turns around and looks into the back of the car.*

    MOMO (*off*): . . . Hey, lovers, isn't that true?

240. CU: *Charlie.*

    CHARLIE: The priests have long underwear on, you jerk!

241. CU: *Léna, looking back toward Charlie.*

242. MCU: *Charlie and Momo.*

    MOMO (*leaning toward Ernest*): Stop, a red light! Shit!

243. ECU: *Ernest's foot on the screeching brake.*

244. CU: *Léna, who shoots a glance backward.*

245. ECU: *Léna's foot, stepping on the accelerator, next to Ernest's on the brake.*

246. CU: *the traffic light turning red.*

    Oldsmobile, exterior, day

247. LS: *extremely brief tilted shot of a car, apparently out of control.*

    Oldsmobile, interior, day

248. ECU: *Ernest's foot trying to push Léna's off the accelerator.*

    Oldsmobile, exterior, day

249. ELS: *the Oldsmobile is traveling very fast down a wide, half-empty road toward the camera.*

    Oldsmobile, interior, day

250. CU: *Momo, followed by a slight pan over to Charlie.*

251. MCU: *Ernest and Léna from behind. A motorcycle cop seen through the windshield blows his whistle furiously, as the brakes screech. Ernest brings the car to a stop while taking off his hat to greet the policeman.*

 ERNEST: Great! Now we're really screwed. (*To Léna, as the camera pans right to include the policeman banging on the car window.*) The two of us will explain everything, okay?

 Léna is in the center foreground, looking back at Charlie, as the policeman continues to knock at the right, and then is seen clearly through the door window.

 POLICEMAN: Well, are you going to open it?

 ERNEST (*off*): The door! Shit, help me!

 The motorcycle cop leans toward the door, a whistle between his lips.

 ERNEST (*off, while the door is being opened*): What's the problem, officer? Have I done anything wrong?

 Oldsmobile, exterior, day

252. MS: *the policeman is leaning over the half-opened door. His motorcycle is parked behind the car.*

 POLICEMAN: Turn off your motor and get out. (*He stands up straight again and takes off his gloves.*)

253. MS: *Ernest gets out of the car quickly, his hat in his hand, and goes around the front of the car to the policeman.*

 ERNEST: I can explain everything.

 POLICEMAN (*to Ernest*): Your papers, please.

 Ernest takes his papers out, as Charlie gets out of the car and stands behind it.

 CHARLIE: He doesn't even know how to drive. He's an awful driver, officer! (*Charlie rushes over to the policeman.*) As soon as there's a little bit of traffic, he goes crazy.

254. MS: *reverse angle. Charlie and the policeman, in profile, are standing on either side of Ernest.*

 CHARLIE (*making a gesture to Léna*): Come on, honey. (*To Ernest.*) That's enough! (*To Léna, who is getting out of the car.*) Come on, we're going to take the bus. (*They move toward the camera and exit the frame on the left, leaving Momo, who is just getting out of the car, Ernest, and the policeman.*)

 ERNEST (*with an impotent gesture*): I can't do anything else.

 MOMO: See you later, Charlie!

255. MLS: *Charlie and Léna move into the foreground while Momo shouts after them. Ernest continues to discuss things with the policeman. A huge truck passes.*

 MOMO: We'll see each other again.

 LÉNA (*turning back toward him*): That's right, come by and see us, we'll be expecting you.

*Charlie and Léna move further away from the car and out of the frame to
the left, as another policeman moves in from the left in the background.*

M O M O (*in the distant background of the shot*): All right! See you later!

Street, exterior, day

256. M L S : *a wide street lined with trees and cars. A bus pulls up in the
foreground and Léna and Charlie get out of it at the back. The bus departs.*

257. M S : *tracking shot, left to right, follows Charlie and Léna in profile (flute
theme is heard again). The camera then makes a turn, and, as they walk
down the sidewalk, settles into a backward tracking, fairly close two-shot,
similar to that of their first walk together the previous night.*

L É N A : They said see you later.

C H A R L I E : Don't worry about it. We'll see what happens.

L É N A : That's right, we shouldn't worry about it. The gun probably just
shoots blanks.

The camera tilts down to show Léna taking Charlie's arm in hers.

258. M S : *as in beginning of 257. The camera tracks backward as the couple
moves toward it. Charlie is looking at Léna. She is looking straight ahead,
expressionless.*

C H A R L I E (*voiceover*): She took your arm all by herself, as if it was nothing. God, it looks like she's taking you to her place.

Camera tilts down once again to show her arm in his.

259. M S : *as in 257, the couple from the front.*

L É N A (*turning to Charlie and smiling*): It's this way.

The camera pans right to follow them.

Léna's Apartment Building, exterior, day

260. M C U : *Charlie in a hallway, with Léna directly behind him.*

L É N A (*going before him*): Wait, let me go in front of you.

She exits the frame to the right. Charlie, in E C U , *follows her as the
camera pans right. The pan continues to the right until it comes upon
Léna's legs, seen through the bars of the stairs.*

C H A R L I E (*voiceover*): Don't look at her legs. It's not very gentlemanly.
But if you don't look at the steps you're going to break your neck. So
just look at the walls (*we see Charlie's face from a low angle going up
the stairs*), they're just all cruddy.

261. M S : *from inside Léna's apartment, we see her door open. Léna enters, followed by Charlie, then moves out of the frame to the right, leaving Charlie
alone in the frame. He looks to the right and then suddenly his face freezes.*

262. C U : *a poster showing Charlie's picture and the following words:*

SALLE PLEYEL

PIANO CONCERT

EDOUARD SAROYAN

BACH—MOZART—CHOPIN—BARTOK

The flute theme stops, replaced by a piece of classical piano music.

LÉNA (*off*): Now it's Charlie who plunks away in Plyne's bar. Before, it was something else . . .

263. MCU: *Charlie, in profile on the right, in front of the poster. Léna stands behind him on the right.*

LÉNA: . . . right, Edouard? (*These last words are repeated, as though in a sound chamber, signifying a movement into the past.*)
A pan from right to left frames the portrait on the poster.
Dissolve, with a lingering superimposition.

264. MS: *Edouard (Charlie) in a tuxedo playing classical music.*

LÉNA (*voiceover, with an echo*): Isn't that right, Edouard? . . . Once . . .

265. ECU: *Charlie's face, staring directly at the camera with a haunted look.*[6]

LÉNA (*voiceover*): . . . once. . . .
Dissolve.

Restaurant, interior, night

266. *A neon sign with the name of a restaurant, "L'Arbois," appears over Charlie's face, then, in a triple superimposition, a* MS *of Lars Schmeel from a high angle. Seated at a table, he is drinking a glass of wine. (Accordion music replaces the classical music.) The superimpositions begin to fade and, in front of Lars Schmeel, Edouard's (Charlie's) profile appears, sitting at another table. He is wearing a sweater over an open shirt.*

EDOUARD (*smiling*): Excuse me, Miss.

THÉRÉSA (*entering the frame from the left*): Yes, sir?

EDOUARD: Do you have crème caramel?

Thérésa is in a black dress and white apron, standing in profile. In the background, and positioned visually between them, Lars Schmeel is looking at her. He is an elegant man in his fifties, wearing a dark suit and a tie.

THÉRÉSA: No, it's crossed off the menu.

EDOUARD: Oh, I see.

LARS SCHMEEL: Could I please look at the menu?

EDOUARD: That's too bad.

THÉRÉSA (*to Lars Schmeel*): Certainly, sir.

She exits the frame to the left, then reappears near Lars Schmeel and gives him the menu.

EDOUARD: Till what time?

LARS SCHMEEL (*to Thérésa, who leaves the frame*): I'm going to look.

EDOUARD: Excuse me, Miss.

Thérésa once again enters the frame from the left next to Edouard's table.

THÉRÉSA: Would you like a cup of coffee, sir?

267. MCU: *Edouard, smiling, from a slightly high angle, her* POV.

EDOUARD (holding out an object to her): Here, take this for your trouble.

268. CU: *low-angle shot of Thérésa, from Edouard's* POV. *The camera tilts down to show her hand taking something from his. She opens a little jewelry case, and takes out a ring.*

THÉRÉSA (*off*): It's too beautiful. (*She puts the ring on her finger.*)
269. MCU: *as in 267.*
   EDOUARD (*voiceover*): She said that it was too beautiful, but what you
   were thinking was that it was too little for two years of happiness.
270. MS: *three-shot, as in end of 266. In the background, Lars Schmeel smil-*
   ingly looks on.
271. CU: *as in 268: Thérésa.*
   THÉRÉSA (*with mock severity, handing back the empty box to Edouard*):
   We never accept presents from customers, sir.
272. MCU: *as in 267: Edouard, who is smiling.*
273. MS: *as in end of 266, three-shot. Then the camera irises in on Lars*
   Schmeel, as we dissolve to Edouard and Thérésa reading in bed. The effect
   is to put Lars's head over Edouard's or to place him between them. As the
   iris gets smaller and smaller, Edouard's head begins to be seen. Finally
   the iris shot of Lars dissolves completely, revealing that Edouard, bare-
   chested, is reading a musical score and Thérésa, in a nightgown, a
   woman's magazine.
   Edouard and Thérésa's Apartment, interior, night
274. MCU: *Edouard and Thérésa in bed.*
   EDOUARD: That guy's been coming around for quite a while now.

THÉRÉSA: A couple of days.

EDOUARD: I think I've seen him somewhere before. (*Putting the score down, and looking over at her.*) You know what I'd like? I'd like you to stop working in the restaurant.

THÉRÉSA (*looking at him and laughing*): Oh, Edouard, you know that your piano lessons aren't. . . .

EDOUARD: Hey, don't make fun of my piano lessons. You liked them a lot once.

THÉRÉSA: Yeah, that's true. Do you remember? (*She puts the magazine down and turns toward him with a mock imploring look.*) Oh, Mr. Edouard, maybe I'll learn something someday. I know that I'm stupid but. . . . (*In a deep voice.*) Oh, Miss, don't say that, you're not stupid at all, but the piano. . . . (*Her own voice.*) Oh, Mr. Edouard, I love these lessons, they take up all my afternoons. (*Deep voice.*) Do you really love the piano, Miss? (*Her own voice.*) Oh, yes, Mr. Edouard.

Thérésa and Edouard break out laughing.

THÉRÉSA (*putting her arm around Edouard's chest, as the camera moves slightly closer*): Tell me, is it true that you'd like to have me with you all the time?

EDOUARD: More than that, much more than that.

THÉRÉSA: I know, and it's the same for me. Every day it's stronger. (*She leans toward him, smiling tenderly.*)

As the accordion music starts again, dissolve.

Restaurant, interior, day

275. MS: *Edouard is sitting at his table. He is wearing a sweater and a jacket. He is on the extreme left and an empty table stands to the right.*

276. MCU: *Lars Schmeel, very well dressed, sits down at the empty table. Thérésa's profile appears in the foreground.*

THÉRÉSA (*to Edouard*): Hello, sir. I recommend the plat du jour.

277. MS: *as in 275. Lars Schmeel is sitting to Edouard's left. Thérésa moves away.*

278. MCU: *Edouard looks in the direction of the young woman.*

LARS SCHMEEL (*off*): Allow me to introduce myself . . .

279. MS: *Lars Schmeel.*

LARS SCHMEEL: . . . I am Lars Schmeel, talent agent.

280. MCU: *reverse shot of Edouard.*

EDOUARD (*slightly getting up*): Edouard Saroyan.

281. MS: *reverse shot of Lars Schmeel.*

LARS SCHMEEL (*in an unctuous and distinguished voice*): I remember perfectly. You're a pianist and you came to my office to see me a year ago.

282. MCU: *reverse shot of Edouard.*

EDOUARD: Yes, that's right.

283. MS: *reverse shot of Lars Schmeel.*

LARS SCHMEEL: I was extremely busy and I wasn't able to talk to you the way I would have liked. Please accept my apologies.

284. MCU: *reverse shot of Edouard.*

EDOUARD: I understand completely.

LARS SCHMEEL (*off*): The lives we lead are crazy.

285. MS: *reverse shot of Lars Schmeel.*

LARS SCHMEEL (*getting up to come closer, he sits next to Edouard*): Do you mind?

286. MCU: *Edouard, as Lars Schmeel appears at the right.*

EDOUARD: Please.

THÉRÉSA (*off*): Would the gentlemen like to have lunch?

EDOUARD (*looking at Thérésa out of the frame*): I have to explain something to you. . . . Well . . . this is my wife.

As Lars stands up, the camera pans left to frame Edouard alone.

287. MCU: *Lars Schmeel and Thérésa, as he kisses her hand.*

LARS SCHMEEL: My compliments, little lady.

288. MCU: *Edouard, as he looks up at them.*

EDOUARD: I have to tell you. . . . We play a little game like this . . . we often pretend to be waitress and customer.

289. MCU: *Lars Schmeel and Thérésa.*

LARS SCHMEEL (*his eyes on the young woman*): That's a great game because there are always two winners.

290. MS: *Edouard. Lars Schmeel comes back into the frame as he sits down once again next to Edouard.*

LARS SCHMEEL: You're very lucky, my friend.

291. MCU: *Thérésa, looking down at them.*

THÉRÉSA: That's very nice of you to say.

292. MCU: *two-shot of Lars and Edouard.*

LARS SCHMEEL (*turning completely toward Edouard*): But I know how to make up for my mistakes. I'd like for you to come and see me tomorrow in my office. Who was your piano teacher?

EDOUARD (*a pan left puts him in the center of the frame*): The old man Zélény.

Lars Schmeel nods his head slightly in respect.

Fade to black.

Lars Schmeel's Building, exterior/interior, day

293. MS: *high-angle shot, panning right to left. We see Edouard, in a tweed overcoat, through the railings of the stairs as he climbs up. Violin music is heard far away. He walks down a hallway, preceded by the camera, which is now tracking backward, and looks at the numbers on the doors. The violin music gets louder and louder.*

294. CU: *Edouard, turned three-quarters away, looks at a plaque on a door that reads* "LARS SCHMEEL, IMPRESARIO."

Charles Aznavour and Claude Heymann

295. E C U : *a three-quarter shot of Edouard's face, which is on the right.*
296. M S : *Edouard, whose hand is hesitating on the door handle.*
297. C U : *Edouard's hand. He removes it from the door handle, flicks the plastic tag hanging from the key in the lock, and moves his hand back up.*
298. E C U : *Edouard's index finger pointing toward the doorbell.*
299. E C U : *even closer, the button of the doorbell and the finger moving toward it.*
300. E C U : *even closer, the tip of the index finger a half inch from the bell. The bell and the finger completely fill the frame. The finger pulls back, just before contact. The violin is still playing very loudly.*
301. E L S : *slightly high-angle shot of Edouard's tiny figure at the end of an immense, empty hallway. (The music stops.)*
302. M S : *Edouard is looking at the door as it opens suddenly. A young woman with a violin case and a serious look on her face comes out and moves into the foreground. The camera, panning left and then tracking backward, precedes her along the corridor in C U for several seconds. Halfway down, piano music can be heard. She stops, but the tracking shot keeps moving backward and then stops, framing her in M L S . Dressed in a coat that is knotted at the waist, she is carrying a violin case in her hand and a purse over her shoulder. Continuing toward the*

camera, which is now stationary, she moves into c u *and then suddenly turns left, exiting the frame.*

Courtyard, exterior, day

303. m s : *extreme low-angle shot of the young woman moving forward, preceded by the camera tracking backward, in the courtyard of a large modern complex, which can be seen behind her. The camera stops and, panning to the right, follows her from behind as she goes toward the big door that gives on to the street. (Piano music, very loud, accompanies her the whole way.)*

304. c u : *a poster, which reads:*

Salle Gaveau   Monday, November 23
Piano Recital
Edouard
Saroyan [in gigantic letters]
Chopin—Liszt—Debussy—Ravel

The piano music continues.

Concert Hall, interior, night

305. m s : *slightly high-angle shot of Edouard's face, which appears behind the raised cover of a piano that fills three-quarters of the frame. He is playing, dressed in a tuxedo.*

306. M S :   *Edouard, behind the piano, from a different angle.*
307. M L S :   *Edouard, in profile at a piano on a stage. In the foreground are the base of an enormous Greek column and many floor lights. He finishes the piece to loud applause.*
308. M S :   *low-angle shot of Edouard and Thérésa, in evening clothes, coming down the staircase in the middle of an elegant crowd. Both of them have serious expressions on their faces. The camera pans left to keep them in the frame as they move into* C U.

Street, exterior, night

309. M S :   *high-angle shot of Edouard and Thérésa, seen through the windshield of a white sports car. The car starts off, followed by a pan to the right, and then moves away.*

Hotel, interior, night

310. M L S :   *high-angle shot of Edouard and Thérésa climbing the stairs of a sumptuous hotel. They get to the landing and, followed by a pan, walk along the corridor, then into a room. They are both silent and expressionless.*
311. M S :   *from inside the room, as the couple enters through the door. A pan left frames Thérésa alone while she takes off her coat.*

T H É R É S A :   Why are you making such a face?

E D O U A R D (*off*): Oh, it's nothing.

T H É R É S A :   Yes, it is! You were a barrel of laughs in the car.
Edouard walks into the frame, followed by the camera, and over to the fireplace. His face is reflected in the mirror.

T H É R É S A (*off*): You suddenly stopped talking as though I had said something you didn't like.

E D O U A R D (*while emptying his pockets in front of the mirror, in which Thérésa can now be seen*): No, you didn't say anything. I just stopped talking when I realized you weren't listening. You pretend but you don't really care. (*Turning around and moving forward in the room.*) You tell yourself "he's talking, so he's happy," but meanwhile (*putting his jacket on a chair, alone in the frame*) you're thinking about your tablecloths, your furniture, your dressmaker. (*He comes back toward the mirror, followed by a pan left, which includes Thérésa in the frame. She is standing in front of the mirror lighting a cigarette.*) I'm trying to explain to you what I liked in the concert and I look over at you and your expression is saying, "keep talking, buddy." *He approaches Thérésa, who moves away, and follows her as the camera pans right*) Well, I'm sick of it! Do you hear me, I'm sick of it! This is no life for an artist. (*She walks into another room.*) I'm probably not a real artist anyway, but I need for people to believe it so that I can try to become one. (*The camera pans left as he moves back toward the mirror.*)

312. C U :   *Edouard in the mirror. He is taking his bow tie off.*

EDOUARD (*in a exasperated tone*): I don't think that's asking too much, for God's sake!

THÉRÉSA (*who, reflected in the mirror, walks around the room*): You don't know how much patience, how much incredible patience, it takes to live with you. Your conversation's been just great over the last year. (*Edouard remains in the foreground of the mirror shot, Thérésa in the background.*) "I wonder what you think of Hemingway. Apparently he collects all my recordings. And So-and-so who didn't come to my concert, and Thingamajig who told Thingamabob that he thought I was the greatest living pianist. (*She moves closer to the mirror, next to Edouard, while he covers his eyes with his right hand, overwhelmed. The camera pans right to show Edouard to the right, with Thérésa reflected in the mirror on the left. A small part of his face can also be seen reflected on the left. The visual effect is that she appears to be looking in the opposite direction, away from him.*) And am I right to accept this and refuse that? What does Smith think of me? Did the concierge see me on television?" (*Lowering her voice, which has become tired.*) My God, you repeat everything ten times, but I have to pretend as though I'm hearing it for the first time. (*Edouard still has his hand over his eyes.*) You think this is a life? Don't you think it's getting a little gross, finally? . . . (*She moves away, and her mirror reflection disappears to the left. Edouard takes his hand away from his face and moves to the right, the camera panning to follow him in* ECU.)

313. MCU: *Edouard. He moves toward Thérésa, whose image is reflected for a moment in the mirror front of a large armoire.*

THÉRÉSA (*putting clothes into the armoire*): . . . I'd prefer it if you were pretentious and more sure of your talent. At least that way I'd have some peace. The least little criticism makes you ill.

314. MCU: *the couple from a different angle. She seizes him by the shoulders. He looks very depressed. They occupy the left of the frame, while Thérésa is also reflected in the armoire mirror on the right.*

THÉRÉSA (*in a sweet voice*): I'm sorry. I'm saying stupid things because I'm jealous.

EDOUARD: No, I know that everything you say is true. (*As he speaks, the camera pans slightly to the right so that he too can be seen in reflection in the mirror.*) I think about it myself sometimes. What is there to do? I'm just not the guy for you.

THÉRÉSA: No, don't say that. It hurts too much.

The camera pans left as she pulls him toward the bed, where they lie down. Edouard's back is toward the camera.

Fade to black.

Lars Schmeel's Office, interior, day

315. ECU: *the poster of 304.*

LARS SCHMEEL (*off*): What a lucky guy, what success! You must be
really happy, and your wife too (*a pan moves left around a luxurious
room; Edouard is seated near a window, seen against the light. The camera
keeps panning until it reaches Lars, seated at his desk on the left.*) Now
there's something else I've got to talk to you about. Your press conference
was a complete failure. You put the journalists to a lot of trouble, they get
everything set up to see the rare bird. And then they can't get a single anec-
dote, a single word, nothing, out of you! Shyness is also a disease, you
know, it can be cured. Luckily, I'm doing your work for you. (*He gets up, a
newspaper in his hand, to show it to Edouard. The camera follows him over
to the right, where Edouard is seated.*) Look, I'm quoted in "The Day's
Gossip": "Lars Schmeel, Edouard Saroyan's agent, told us today. . ."

316. CU: *the newspaper. A column is circled in pencil.*

LARS SCHMEEL (*off*): ". . . I love everything and everyone that is beautiful, without regard to sex."

The camera moves down the page and stops on an ad with big print: HOW
TO CONQUER SHYNESS. (*A piece of slow music begins to get louder.*)

Street, exterior, day

317. MLS: *Edouard, in an overcoat, walks toward a wall to which a series of
photographs has been attached.*

318. MCU: *Edouard, in a three-quarter shot of his back, looks at the photos. A
distinguished man with graying hair illustrates, with the appropriate*

*poses, the following captions: "Sad thoughts"—"The Unshy"—"Energy"—
"Will Power"—"Indecision." Edouard puts his glasses on.*

319. C U : *closer shot of the photograph entitled "The Unshy." The man, exuding confidence, is seated on a chair, his chest swelling, his hands in the pockets of his vest, his legs crossed.*
The music gets louder.

320. M S : *very brief shot of Edouard, as in 318. He takes one more look a the photographs and begins to move away. Behind him can be seen two extra poses: "Courage"—"Butterflies in the Stomach."*

321. L S : *panning shot from left to right of Edouard walking along the sidewalk.*

322. E C U : *Edouard's hand checking the books lined up in a bin in front of a bookstore. He picks out some books with titles like* The Practical Treatment of Shyness, Shyness, *and* I Got Over My Fear.

323. M S : *Edouard walks into the store, the books in his hand.*
The music stops.
Dissolve.

Press Conference Room, interior, day

324. M S : *slightly high-angle shot of a figure, in a dark outfit, sitting in an armchair. We cannot see his head at first. In the foreground a flashbulb goes off.*
M A N ' S   V O I C E : Hey, Mr. Saroyan!
A tilt up reveals Edouard's relaxed face.

325. M S : *slightly high-angle shot of Edouard, behind a row of reporters, with a self-confident air. Flashbulbs pop and the indistinct hubbub of voices is heard shouting at the virtuoso.*

326. M C U : *Edouard casting a conquering glance all around him.*

327. M S : *slightly high-angle shot, from a different angle than 325, of journalists on their knees shooting Edouard with their cameras.*

328. M C U : *Edouard, who is smiling slightly.*

329. M L S : *Edouard smiles broadly at the group that surrounds him.*
General hubbub. Since the image moves slightly, the camera seems to be hand-held.

Lars Schmeel's Office, interior, day

330. C U : *Edouard's portrait, lying flat on the floor. Lars Schmeel's hands pick it up to put in on the wall. Flashbulbs, as in the previous scene, illuminate the canvas, but when Lars picks it up, no photographers are to be seen.*
L A R S   S C H M E E L : There you are, Edouard. Now, in spite of your many escapades, you'll never be able to escape from me again. (*A pan reveals the impresario, in a three-quarter back shot, putting the painting against the wall. He moves back to admire it.*) Thanks to this masterpiece that I can contemplate every day. (*Turning toward Edouard, and*

moving into the foreground of the frame, as the camera pans right to fol-low him.) How's Thérésa?

He moves over into a dark place between two windows, where Edouard is.

EDOUARD *(off-screen at first; then he can barely be seen in the dark)*: She's tired all the time.

LARS SCHMEEL *(moving over next to him)*: These trips, this nomad life. . . .

EDOUARD: No! It's because of me.

LARS SCHMEEL: You've been arguing a lot?

EDOUARD: At first we argued, now it's much worse.

LARS SCHMEEL: You can tell me everything.

He takes Edouard over to a window, then opens it.

331. MS: *Edouard and the impresario walk out onto the little balcony, and lean against the iron railing, over the street. Behind them, cars can be seen on a wide avenue.*

EDOUARD *(eyes lowered)*: She doesn't want me anymore.

LARS SCHMEEL: Come on.

EDOUARD: You don't believe me. I didn't believe it at first either. It's as though she was fighting against something. It's become very obvious. *(Lars Schmeel takes out a cigarette.)* For example: we'll be talking and suddenly she turns her back on me and walks out of the room. Now it's gotten to the point that if I try to stop her, she locks herself in her room and doesn't answer. That's where things are. *(Looking at the im-presario.)* It's over!

LARS SCHMEEL: Did she tell you that?

EDOUARD *(eyes lowered again)*: No, but it's just the same. I think she's hated me since, well, since I began having some success.

LARS SCHMEEL: Listen, I honestly think this is all just a misunderstand-ing. You have a cocktail party to go to at 4 P.M. at the hotel, well, take her with you and I'll talk to her.

EDOUARD: I'll try. *(Looking at Lars Schmeel with gratitude.)* Thanks.

Dissolve.

Hotel, interior, day

332. MS: *panning shot left to right of Edouard, in a dark overcoat, who rushes through the crowd in a hotel lobby and runs up the stairs.*

333. MCU: *high-angle tracking shot left to right of Edouard in profile walking quickly along the corridor. Behind him can be seen the rich ceiling of the hotel lobby.*

334. MS: *slightly high-angle shot of Edouard climbing the stairs. As he reaches the landing, the camera tilts up slightly to keep him in the frame. A pan follows him as he crosses in front of the camera on the landing and runs toward a door, behind which he disappears.*

335. MS: *from inside the room, of Edouard as he enters the room, toward the camera.*

E D O U A R D : Thérésa. . . . (*He moves toward the bed, on which his wife, in a bathrobe, is half stretched out; the camera follows him, panning to the left. The camera tracks in closer.*) Listen, Thérésa, I've come to get you. I'd like you to come with me to the cocktail party.

T H É R É S A (*sitting up, supported by one arm*): Leave me alone, please, just get out of here.

E D O U A R D (*raising his voice*): Oh, I've had enough!

T H É R É S A : Why are you shouting? You never shouted at me before. Why are you shouting at me now?

E D O U A R D : I'm sorry, I didn't mean to.

336. E C U : *Thérésa, from Edouard's* P O V , *in a three-quarter face shot.*

T H É R É S A (*in a low voice*): That's all right, after all, you have a reason to shout. I'm making you unhappy. I know it's bad, but I can't help it. (*She seems to be lost in a dream.*) When it's the middle of the night, you can't stop the night. It's dark, and it's getting darker and darker. There's no way out of it, no way to know what to do. (*Looking at Edouard.*) I think there's only one thing left for me to do, one thing, and that's to say goodbye and to leave.

337. M S : *as in 335. He makes a gesture toward her, but she gets up suddenly and flattens herself against the wall, as the camera pulls back. Discouraged, he moves away.*

338. M C U : *Thérésa against the white, bare wall.*

T H É R É S A : Yes, I'm going to tell you everything.

339. C U : *Edouard, who, in a very brief shot, turns suddenly and stares intensely at her.*

340. M S : *Thérésa, her back against the wall on the extreme left, and Edouard, his back to the camera on the extreme right.*

T H É R É S A : I must tell you. It's always necessary to explain . . . to confess.

341. M C U : *Edouard.*

E D O U A R D : Confess? (*He looks at her uncomprehendingly.*)

342. M S : *reverse shot of Thérésa.*

T H É R É S A : I made a mistake. . . . I did a very bad thing and now you're a famous musician. I'm very happy about that.

343. M S : *reverse shot of Edouard.*

T H É R É S A (*off*): Thanks to me, you got your chance.

Edouard's face tightens.

344. E C U : *very tight on Thérésa, looking into Edouard's eyes.*

T H É R É S A : Lars Schmeel.

A pan moves rapidly over the wall, stopping at Edouard in an E C U . *He closes his eyes with an expression of intense pain.*

345. M S : *Wider shot, as in 335. Thérésa and Edouard are on either side of a small table on which rests a bouquet of flowers. There are several suitcases on the floor.*

THÉRÉSA (*moving closer to him, and then forward, toward the camera*): It was the week you signed your contract . . . a couple of days before that. (*A slight pan follows Thérésa, who keeps moving toward the camera.*) He came to the restaurant. (*She turns back to Edouard, who is in the background; she is in the foreground of the frame, the back of her head to the camera.*) But not for coffee.

Slow music begins to be heard.

346. MCU: *reverse shot of Thérésa, from the front, Edouard's POV.*

THÉRÉSA: Not for lunch either, but to make me an offer. At first I didn't understand. (*She begins to walk back and forth, as the camera pans to follow her from behind.*) It was like a riddle. I was wondering what he was talking about, and he was looking at me as if to say, "Think about it, you'll figure it out." I thought about it all night; I couldn't sleep. The next day he came back (*stopping to look at Edouard*). You know how a spider works. It was as if he had cut me in two (*making the gesture*), as if my heart was one thing and my body something else. (*Walking again, now to the left, as she moves again into an ECU.*) It wasn't Thérésa who went with him, just Thérésa's body. As if I wasn't there, I was with you, I was getting you on the stage. (*Here there is a disguised cut, but the shot remains the same.*)[7] That afternoon he got a room near the restaurant. (*She stops.*) Then that evening, you told me the news (*she is walking again*), that the contract had been signed. Afterward when he came to the restaurant, he was just a customer like all the others (*she passes in front of a photograph of her and Edouard in evening dress*), he ordered his meal, and I told myself that now it was finished . . . you could be Thérésa again. But, you know, it's strange, what you did yesterday . . . stays in you today. . . . I,look into the mirror and what do I see? Thérésa? Your Thérésa? (*Shaking her head.*) No, not Thérésa. Nowhere. . . . Just a dirty old rag (*looking away, then at Edouard*). That's why I don't want you to touch me . . . to touch this dirt.

She falls down on the bed, her face buried in the pillow.

347. MCU: *straight ahead, of Edouard, looking at her.*

EDOUARD (*voiceover*): Yes, look at her, go to her, lower your head. Get on your knees, quick, while there's still time. Think, try to think. If you walk out the door, she'll be all alone. You can't leave her alone. (*He suddenly turns and runs out of the room, slamming the door.*)

348. MS: *panning shot from right to left on Edouard walking slowly in the darkened corridor. (Muffled drumbeats punctuate the music.) A faraway noise is heard. He turns around suddenly and runs desperately toward the door.*

349. CU: *Edouard, who runs into the room (the drumbeats are getting louder and louder). The camera pans left to follow him across the room, then races ahead of him, panning rapidly over to the open window. At first we see only the sky and some bare trees, then the camera suddenly*

points straight down revealing Thérésa's curled-up body lying on the as-phalt in E L S *(the image is punctuated by loud music).*
Dissolve.

350. C U : *Thérésa's photograph in the newspaper, under the following headline:* THE WIFE OF THE GREAT PIANIST EDOUARD SAROYAN JUMPS FROM A FIFTH-FLOOR WINDOW. *On the next line:* THE VIRTUOSO HAS DISAPPEARED. RECITAL TOUR CANCELED.
The music dissolves into the piano theme at the beginning of the film.
Slow dissolve.

Street, exterior, day

351. L S : *high-angle pan on a landscape in the poor outskirts of the city, full of refuse and old cars.*
    L É N A (*off*): You disappeared, you started your life over. Edouard Saroyan became Charlie Kohler. You went back to see your brothers in the snow and you asked them to let you have Fido. (*The pan passes over a poor, empty street to end on Plyne's café:* A LA BONNE FRANQUETTE. *The music stops.*) Then one day you ended up at Plyne's. . . .

Café, interior, day

352. M L S : *lightly high-angle shot of Charlie, from behind, sweeping the floor near the piano.*
    L É N A (*off*): They really needed you to sweep up that old dive. There was an old piano in the corner, a real piece of junk. (*Charlie tidies up the piano with a rag.*) You spent your time looking at it, looking away, then looking at it again. (*Charlie opens the keyboard. Plyne can be seen on the right fixing a chair.*)
    L É N A (*off*): One day you asked Plyne:
    C H A R L I E : Can I play a little bit?
    P L Y N E (*getting up*): Yeah, sure.
    C H A R L I E : I think I know how.
    P L Y N E : Go ahead. Just get it to make some music.
    Charlie takes a chair and sits down at the piano. Léna enters the frame from the left and picks up a bucket, dustpan, and pushbroom. She moves toward the camera and out of the frame while Charlie, behind her, looks at the piano keys.

353. E C U : *Charlie's profile, his eyes concentrating on the keyboard. He begins to play a piece of classical music. A slight tracking movement to the right and a pan left and tilt down frames his hands, then tilts up and left to frame the hammers that we saw under the opening credits of the film.*
    As the music continues, dissolve, both aurally and visually.

Café, interior, night

354. M S : *Charlie's face and hands reflected in a mirror. A cigarette between his lips, he is playing the musical catch phrase we have heard earlier.*

LÉNA (*off*): Who is Charlie Kohler? Little is known about him (*pan left on Charlie, at whom the camera looks directly from the front*). He's a piano player, he's raising his little brother, and, above all, he doesn't want any trouble.

355. MS: *Charlie is behind his piano next to the drummer, who is smiling broadly. To the right is the bass player, and behind them a large mirror hangs on the wall.*

LÉNA (*off*): Thanks to you the local folks are coming to dance every evening and the dump is becoming something big. Plyne has hired more waiters and more musicians.

356. CU: *the smiling drummer.*

LÉNA (*off*): Victor the drummer, who laughs all the time without knowing why.

357. CU: *the bass player, who is also smiling broadly.*

LÉNA (*off*): . . . and his brother, François, the bass player . . .

358. CU: *hands covered with black hair playing the bass.*

LÉNA (*off*): . . . with his long, hairy hands.

359. MS: *Léna leaning on the bar, seen behind the café window.*

LÉNA (*off*): And then . . . there was me, who was looking at you all the time and you didn't even know.

A fairly quick tracking shot right passes over the poster on which Charlie's name is written, then over another window behind which couples are dancing, and finally a third window. (The piano theme is heard throughout.)

Dissolve.

Léna's Apartment, interior, night

360. CU: *the poster of Edouard in Léna's bedroom. A pan left moves lightly over the walls and the furniture (a softer, slower version of the main musical theme begins to be heard), while in superimposition Léna and Charlie, in ECU, their eyes closed, cover each other with kisses. We see a window adorned with a curtain, a glass jar in which goldfish are swimming, an unidentifiable statuette, Léna's clothes on one chair, and Charlie's on another. The superimposition of the lovers in ECU ends as the pan continues left, finally stopping on Charlie and Léna in bed in MCU. The young woman's head is resting on Charlie's shoulder.*

361. CU: *Léna, facing the camera, caressing Charlie's cheek, which is seen in profile.*

LÉNA: On my birthday, when I said, "Now a big kiss for everyone," it was for you, you know. I saw that you were looking at me, so I started looking at you too.

Charlie smiles.

Dissolve.

362. M S : *from above on Charlie and Léna asleep. She squeezes closer to him in her sleep.*
     Dissolve.
363. C U : *as in 361, Léna caressing Charlie's cheek, as though a continuation of 361.*
     L É N A : What were you thinking when we were walking together down the street last night?
     Dissolve.
364. M S : *Charlie and Léna asleep, from a different, lower angle. He is holding her in his arms.*
     Dissolve.
365. C U : *as in 361, Léna caressing Charlie's cheek.*
     L É N A : Did you like me right away? Remember that night you told me. . . .
     Dissolve.
366. M S : *as in 364, Charlie and Léna asleep. Charlie moves his arm.*
     Dissolve.
367. C U : *Léna caressing Charlie's cheek.*
     L É N A : When I took your arm, I was afraid that you'd think I was being too forward, you know.
     Dissolve.

368. MCU: *a closer, high-angle shot, very brief, of Charlie and Léna asleep.*
Dissolve.
369. CU: *as in 361, Léna caressing Charlie's cheek.*
LÉNA: I wanted so badly for you to take my hand.
Dissolve.
370. MS: *Charlie and Léna asleep, slightly further away, and from a higher*
angle. She opens her eyes and moves closer to him.
Dissolve.
371. ECU: *Léna looking at Charlie, out of the frame, with a happy expression*
on her face.
Fade to black.
Fade up.
Léna's Apartment, interior, day
372. MS: *Charlie, in the bedroom, is putting on his shirt and tie in front of a*
mirror. He is humming a classical tune very vigorously.
373. CU: *Léna, seen from behind in the kitchen, is putting lipstick on. She is*
wearing a bathrobe and her face can be seen in a mirror. Charlie's happy
humming can be clearly heard.
374. MS: *Charlie, as in 372, who is now putting his pants on. He is still hum-*
ming loudly.
CHARLIE (*taking a cigarette and looking for a match*): You know, I think
that Plyne is madly in love with you.
375. CU: *Léna, as in 373.*
LÉNA: You're crazy. That's all I need.
376. MS: *Charlie, who is buttoning his sleeve.*
CHARLIE: No, really. Besides, he told me himself. After all, Plyne is just
a man like all the others.
He goes toward the kitchen, followed by a pan, and opens the door.
377. ECU: *Léna, who turns toward Charlie.*
LÉNA: But I love you because you're not like all the others. You don't
act like a big ladies' man, you don't act like a tough guy. You're shy and
you respect women.
CHARLIE (*off*): Don't believe it.
A tilt down finds Charlie lighting his cigarette from the flame of the gas
heater.
378. MS: *Charlie from behind with Léna in front of him.*
CHARLIE: I'm really just like the others. (*He readjusts his tie in front of*
the mirror while she brushes her hair.) When I had some money and
was famous, a lot of women recognized me in the street. I stared at them
shamelessly, as if I wanted to undress them (*Léna is brushing Charlie's*
hair), and since most of them just stared back at me and seemed to
enjoy it, I got bolder and bolder. (*He turns toward the stove and pours*
some milk into a bowl.) When I ran into a nice girl who lowered her

eyes (*he comes toward the camera*), I was ashamed. (*He walks out of the frame at the right.*)

379. MCU: *Charlie, as he goes and sits at the table.*
CHARLIE: I couldn't stand it if someone looked at my mother, my wife, or my daughter like that.

380. MS: *Léna in the kitchen as she moves toward the camera and out of the frame, closer to Charlie.*

381. MCU: *Charlie at the table. Léna comes up behind him, takes him by the shoulders, kisses him on the cheek, and moves away.*
LÉNA (*off*): You just have to want it. We're going over to Plyne's to quit, and get back our freedom and become a team.
Charlie bites into his piece of bread.

382. MS: *Léna as she moves around enthusiastically in front of Edouard's poster.*
LÉNA: *I'm* going to wake you up. You're going to become Edouard Saroyan again.

383. MCU: *Charlie, as in 381.*
CHARLIE: For what?

384. CU: *Léna, looking straight ahead at him.*
LÉNA: Not for what, for whom. For me and for you too . . . for the two of us.

385. MCU: *Charlie eating his bread.*
LÉNA (*off*): I've been on welfare. I'm used to fighting.

386. CU: *Léna.*
LÉNA: You're going to work, go to auditions, and give concerts. Charlie is dead . . .

387. MCU: *Charlie. Léna enters the frame and squeezes her face tightly against his.*
LÉNA: . . . long live Edouard! (*She kisses him on the cheek.*)

388. MS: *Charlie is drinking his coffee, his bowl in his hands. Behind him is a door and a big, old-fashioned radio with a porcelain vase on it. To the right is his poster. Léna goes into the side room.*
LÉNA (*off*): Would you do me a favor? Go buy me a pair of stockings. Then we'll go get rid of that pig Plyne. (*She comes back into the room.*)

389. MCU: *Charlie.*
LÉNA (*off*): "Scandal" stockings, number two.

390. MS: *Charlie, as in 388. He is wiping his lips.*
LÉNA (*passing next to him*): Tangerine . . . that's the color.
CHARLIE (*getting up and putting on his jacket*): Fine!
He walks through the door, and Léna follows him.

391. MCU: *the front door, seen from the landing. Charlie leaves.*
LÉNA (*sticking her head out the door*): Charlie! (*She hands him his raincoat. Charlie turns around and taps her cheek lightly.*) The only thing

I've ever asked from a man is to tell me it's over, when it's over. And not one has ever done it. When you don't love me any more, tell me. *Charlie nods, and immediately exits from the frame on the left, leaving the frame half empty. His footsteps can be heard going down the stairs as Léna looks after him.*

Street, exterior, day

392.   MLS: *high-angle shot of Momo and Ernest waiting in the street. They are wearing overcoats and are leaning against a wall.*

393.   MS: *a sign on the front of a building, which reads:* BOYS' SCHOOL. *A tilt up frames the French flag above. The shouts of schoolchildren can be heard.*

394.   MS: *Children coming out of the school preceded by the camera tracking backward. Fido and a young friend walk forward; Fido is singing. Fido gives his bookbag to his friend and does a little song and dance number while snapping his fingers. The camera keeps tracking back while Fido, in a two-shot, continues his demonstration for his friend. The camera pans slightly to the right to reveal a car, the Oldsmobile, following them along the curb.*

395.   MS: *(A disguised cut, almost exactly identical with the previous shot.) Seeing the Oldsmobile, Fido grabs his friend's arm and takes off at full speed, as the car door opens. The camera pans left, away from the car, to follow the two children as they race out of the frame.*

Charlie's Apartment, interior, day

396.   MS: *Fido and Clarisse are seated at the table. A wine bottle is at the right, and Fido is eating a soft-boiled egg.*

CLARISSE: Wait a minute, I'm going to make you some mouillettes.[8]

FIDO (*playing with his egg with a spoon*): I don't like the white part very much. I like the yellow part better.

A knock is heard at the door.

CLARISSE (*handing a mouillette to Fido*): Come in.

A middle-aged woman, dressed in a black shawl, comes into the room from the right.

WOMAN: Miss Clarisse, you have a customer. (*She goes over and ruffles Fido's hair.*)

CLARISSE (*irritated*): A customer? Why doesn't he come during working hours? Tell him to go find somebody else. As if there weren't enough of them walking the pavement. . . . It's unbelievable!

WOMAN (*standing between Clarisse and Fido, with an insistent tone*): He wants Miss Clarisse and no one else. He was very definite about it. And besides he looks like a nice man, very clean, and pretty good-looking too.

CLARISSE: Okay, okay, I'm going. (*She gets up. To Fido.*) There's sugar here, a yogurt, and some fruit, and by the time you're finished, I'll be back. (*She goes out.*)

397. M S : *high-angle shot, through the stair railings, of Clarisse coming out onto the landing behind the woman.*
W O M A N (*to Clarisse*): Here's the gentleman. I'll leave you now.
C L A R I S S E (*turned back toward the kitchen*): I'll be right back, Fido. (*To Momo, who is revealed by the camera tracking slightly backward and panning left.*) Hello.
M O M O (*taking off his cap and kissing Clarisse's hand*): Hello, Miss. How are you? Where do we go?
C L A R I S S E (*moving toward her bedroom*): It's over here, honey. (*She looks at Momo.*) Hey, I recognize you, you've been up here with me before.
The camera tracks forward slightly.
M O M O : Me? No, not really.
C L A R I S S E (*opening the door*): Do you have any money?
M O M O (*following her in*): A little.
The door closes on them. After a moment, the door opens slightly, and Clarisse's hand reaches out and takes the keys out of the door.
398. M S : *The same shot, but pulled back a little. The door opens and Momo runs out, locking the door behind him.*
C L A R I S S E (*off*): Hey, honey, where are you going? What the hell is going on! Shit!
M O M O (*turning his head toward the steps*): Ernest!
E R N E S T (*running up to the landing*): I'm coming.
They run toward Fido's door and enter.
399. M S : *Fido at the table. He jumps up when he sees Ernest and Momo come running in. They grab him and start to drag him away, putting his coat on him, backwards, at the same time. We hear some indistinct shouts from Fido.*
400. M S : *low-angle shot of the two gangsters, each holding one of Fido's arms, as they go out onto the landing and down the stairs followed by a pan.*
Charlie's Apartment, exterior, day
401. L S : *low-angle shot of the front of the building. Clarisse, beside herself, is at the upper window.*
C L A R I S S E : Kidnappers!
A tilt down reveals Ernest and Momo dragging Fido toward their car across the street. He is fighting wildly.
402. L S : *Clarisse at the window.*
C L A R I S S E : Kidnappers!
403. M C U : *slightly high-angle shot of the car's windshield. The car starts loudly and disappears. Two other cars pass in the opposite direction.*
Café, exterior, day
404. L S : *Léna and Charlie walking along arm in arm. Both of them are wearing their raincoats.*

CHARLIE (*nodding toward a very old car next to the sidewalk*): My carriage! (*They laugh and walk toward the camera, which follows them with a pan left.*)

405. CU: *the couple, close on their faces, from the side.*

CHARLIE (*looking at Léna*): So, it's decided, we're going to quit.

LÉNA: I hope you don't hesitate. Just let me handle things and you just watch.

Café, interior, day

406. MLS: *Plyne is inside, perched on a stepladder washing the café windows.*

PLYNE (*turning toward the bar*): Here they are!

Léna and Charlie walk along behind the glass façade and go into the café. A pan right, and a fast track backward, reveal Mammy, who is drying glasses at the bar. All four can be seen in the shot at once.

MAMMY: Well, do you think you're on vacation?

CHARLIE: I got up late.

LÉNA (*leaning against the bar*): Yeah, he got up late. Then we took a drive and then we took a walk.

MAMMY: Both of you together?

407. MS: *Léna, from the front, leaning on the bar. She and Plyne are also reflected in the mirror behind her.*

LÉNA: Yeah, the two of us together. Do you want me to draw you a picture?

MAMMY (*off*): Yeah, I'd like that. I'm curious. Usually he likes to hang out by himself.

LÉNA (*her eyes lowered*): Even when he's with someone, he's alone.

408. MLS: *a full shot of the whole café, as at the end of 406.*

LÉNA: In any case, we've come to get our pay. (*Plyne turns around.*) And since we're here, we might as well tell you we're quitting too.

409. MS: *Mammy. The wall behind the bar is covered with bottles and with posters advertising wrestling and judo matches. Charlie's back is to the camera in the right half of the frame.*

MAMMY (*in an irritated tone*): That's all I need. It's not bad enough to get screwed by the customers, but I have to get it from the help as well. Did you hear that, Plyne?

410. MLS: *the full shot.*

PLYNE (*getting down off the stepladder*): Hi, Charlie. Where did you take off to? I looked everywhere for you because I was worried about the two guys who were here last night.

LÉNA: Where did you expect him to take off to since the two guys from last night had his address? Mine too, by the way.

MAMMY: I don't get it. I had nothing to do with that.

411. MS: *Léna, as in 407.*

LÉNA: Ask your boyfriend, since after all, he's the guy you live with.

412. M S : *Mammy.*

    M A M M Y (*grimacing*): Saying that I'm "living," is saying a lot.

    Charlie moves left, to occupy more than half the screen in the foreground.

    P L Y N E (*off*): Shut up! What are you two doing here?

    L É N A (*off*): You're the one who's going to shut up!

413. M S : *Léna faces Plyne, whose back is toward us in the foreground. Léna is also reflected in the mirror on the right.*

    L É N A (*acidly*): So the two guys from last night came back here this morning. In exchange for some dough, they got Charlie's address and mine at the same time.

414. M S : *Mammy. Charlie is expressionless, looking toward Léna.*

    M A M M Y (*surprised, to Plyne*): It was you who gave it to them?

    L É N A (*off*): And how! I want you to meet Plyne the big informer!

415. M S : *behind Charlie, who is walking toward the camera in the foreground, Léna, Plyne, and Mammy are arguing.*

    P L Y N E : That's not how it happened.

    C H A R L I E (*in voiceover, while the argument continues behind him*): Plyne acted like a bastard, sure, but she gives him a hard time. He sees her every evening, he wants her, but no way, what a pain! Even now while she's dragging him through the mud, he can't take his eyes off her. She's going overboard, but what can I say to her? That Plyne is not as big a jerk as he seems, that he's just a poor slob who wanted to be someone and who didn't make it? It's true, and you can tell her that, but it really has nothing to do with you, nothing does. You're going to go sit down at your place in front of the piano. (*Camera pans right, following Charlie as he moves toward the piano and starts taking his coat off.*) You can't do anything for Plyne or for anybody else. You're not in it anymore. For you, nothing matters any more.

    He finishes taking off his coat, sits down, and starts to play. Léna and Plyne can still be heard arguing loudly. Charlie stares straight ahead, expressionless, then looks to his right, back at Plyne and Léna.

416. M S : *Léna and Plyne face to face in profile in front of the bar. Mammy is behind it.*

    P L Y N E : Take back what you said!

    L É N A (*articulating very carefully*): Fuck you!

    P L Y N E (*lifting up his right arm and making a muscle*): Look at my biceps, Léna. I'm not just anybody. Feel it.

    M A M M Y : This is bullshit.

    Plyne pushes past Léna and slaps Mammy, who ducks down behind the bar.

    L É N A (*directly in his face*): She's right, this is bullshit!

    P L Y N E (*the camera moves in tighter, as Mammy passes by in the background rubbing her cheek*): "Fuck you." "This is bullshit." What dirty words in such a pretty mouth.

LÉNA (*defying him*): Speaking of mouths, why don't you shut yours? (*Her face is very close to Plyne's.*) Big pig!

PLYNE: As sure as you see me, Léna, I'm going to kill you!

LÉNA: I can't see you because you're too short!

PLYNE: So much the worse for you. (*Raising his hand over his head to hit her.*) You bitch!

Charlie suddenly moves into the frame from the right, as the camera pans slightly to the right, and grabs Plyne's arm. Plyne turns around, and the two men are framed in MCU.

PLYNE: Well, Charlie, you're daydreaming!

CHARLIE: Just leave her alone.

PLYNE: Right now I'm not interested in her (his index finger jabs Charlie in the chest), but in you! You bastard! You touched her, didn't you? Confess! You dirtied her, didn't you? (*Shaking Charlie by the lapels of his jacket, Charlie's whole head along with it.*) I'm going to break your head!

417. CU: *very briefly, on a poster announcing a wrestling match. (Fast music starts playing.)*

418. MS: *Plyne and Charlie start fighting. Mammy runs toward them from behind the bar, and hugs Léna at the far end. Charlie throws Plyne off and reaches over the bar.*

419. ECU: *very brief shot of a hand grabbing a long kitchen knife in the sink.*

420. ECU: *a hand grabbing a telephone.*

421. ECU: *the hand with the knife.*

422. ECU: *the other hand as it tears the receiver from the phone.*

423. MS: *Charlie is holding the knife and Plyne, the receiver in his hand, is facing him.*

424. ECU: *the telephone receiver hitting Charlie's knife in a sort of mock fencing match.*

425. MS: *Charlie throws himself after Plyne. A very fast pan follows the two men across the room. The two combatants end up around the soccer game. Plyne has lost the telephone receiver and tries to escape from Charlie. He disappears through a door, the same one that Chico had escaped through the previous night, and Charlie follows him.*

Courtyard, exterior, day

426. MS: *shot from the end of an alley of Plyne, who is running away from Charlie, toward the camera. He throws a ladder in front of Charlie.*

427. MS: *Plyne is trapped in a cul-de-sac and tries to jump out of it. Charlie knocks him down, stops next to him, and throws the knife down. We follow its movement on the ground.*

The music stops.

Serge Davri and Charles Aznavour

428. M C U : *Charlie and Plyne, both exhausted, are sitting on the ground at op-*
     posite ends of the frame with the knife between them.
     C H A R L I E : Come on, who cares?
429. M S : *as in 428, only pulled back about ten feet. A tilt up shows a woman*
     looking out of her window onto the courtyard.
     P L Y N E (*off*): You're not mad at me any more?
     C H A R L I E (*off*): Let's forget the whole thing.
     P L Y N E (*off*): That's not possible, . . .
430. M C U : *the two men, as in 428. Plyne is now against Charlie.*
     P L Y N E : . . . there has to be a winner.
     C H A R L I E : Let's just say that I chickened out.
     P L Y N E : No, the women saw me take off. I have to get revenge. They
     have to know, they can't believe what she said.
     Motioning Charlie closer to him, Plyne suddenly grabs Charlie's neck in a
     hammerlock and begins to squeeze.
431. M C U : *Plyne tightens his vicelike grip while Charlie's face grimaces in*
     pain.
     P L Y N E (*in a calm voice*): I don't love Héléna any more because she used
     certain words that aren't worthy of her. If she had a soul, she wouldn't

have acted so vulgar. (*Charlie is suffocating.*) She's a bitch, she's not
a young girl, she's not a woman. Because a woman is pure . . . delicate . . . fragile (*Charlie is gagging*), woman is supreme, woman is
magic (*Plyne seems to become illuminated as Charlie is in agony*). For
me, woman is supreme. Allow me to call you by your first name [de te
tutoyer]. My old buddy Charlie, you're going to die [tu vas mourir]. (*He
rolls over on top of Charlie, and begins to strangle him with his right
hand.*)

432. ECU: *Insert shot of the knife on the ground. Charlie's hand gropes for it
and finally gets it. His gasps can be heard.*

433. CU: *Charlie's face, with Plyne's back in the foreground. Charlie plunges
the knife into Plyne's back; he drops down, leaving Charlie, his eyes
closed in exhaustion, alone in the frame.*

Café, exterior, day

434. LS: *Léna and Mammy run out of the café and stop near the car of the two
other musicians, which has just pulled up alongside the curb. They hur-
riedly pull the two men into the café.*

Courtyard, exterior, day

435. MLS: *the camera tilts down from the wall to show the two women run
into the alley and lean over the inanimate bodies of Charlie and Plyne.*

436. MCU: *Léna grabs Charlie under his arms. The pianist's face, eyes closed, crosses the frame. The camera pans left to find Plyne, who is also being carried, the knife sticking out of his back.*

437. MLS: *behind Léna, who is pulling Charlie, we see Mammy and the bass player moving Plyne's body. The camera is tracking backward in front of the group moving back down the alley.*
    Slow music can be heard.
    MAMMY (*raising her head toward the neighbors*): Come on, get back inside. It was just an accident. (*The camera pans right to follow them into the café.*)

Café, interior, day

438. MLS: *the group comes into the café by the back door, moves toward the camera (which is very low and close to the floor) into the room, then turns, followed by the camera tracking laterally, to cross the room and lay Plyne's body down. The two women carry Charlie behind the bar.*

439. MS: *from the basement, we see the two women lower him down the steps, which are illuminated by the light from above. Loud knocks can be heard.*
    LÉNA: Listen, someone's there.
    MAMMY: Shit! I forgot the light. Ah, that must be the police. I'll go. Look, his eyes are open.

440. CU: *Charlie's and Léna's faces as they bump into the lightbulb that weakly illuminates the basement.*
    LÉNA (*out of breath*): Get going!
    CHARLIE: Why are you pushing me? I've got legs. (*His head passes in front of the camera in ECU.*)
    LÉNA: Move them, then. Oh, you're worse than a drunk. Come on, get going! (*He sits down as she passes out of the frame to the right.*)
    CHARLIE: The knife, the knife. I threw it down on purpose to prove that the whole thing wasn't serious. (*Léna comes back into the frame, picks Charlie up again, and drags him further, followed by a pan.*) I was starting to suffocate . . . I found the knife. I tried to stab him in the arm so that he would let me go. (*She puts Charlie on a mattress.*) But he moved at the same moment, he moved so fast that he got it in the back.
    LÉNA (*off*): You want to bet?
    CHARLIE: Bet what?
    LÉNA (*off*): They'll believe that.
    CHARLIE: No they won't. The police need proof. I'm the one who did it, so they won't have to look any further.
    The music ends.

441. MS: *a looser shot of Charlie on the mattress. Léna is sitting on the end of the bed at the left.*
    LÉNA: You have to explain it to them.

Marie Dubois and Michèle Mercier

CHARLIE: Yeah, sure, but I think I'd rather do it by letter. Anyway, go
   get Fido, in case the cops go to the apartment.
442.   MS: *tighter shot of Charlie on the bed. The shot is slightly bumpy, as
   though the camera were hand-held. The light goes out and Charlie is seen
   in the dark for a few more moments.*
   Charlie's Apartment, interior, day
443.   MS: *the camera is on the darkened stairway, shooting down. A tilt upward reveals Léna in the shadows climbing the stairs. She rushes in
   through Charlie's open door and can be seen at intervals through the door.*

LÉNA (*calling*): Fido! Fido! Fido!
She goes back out onto the landing and cries out.

444. MCU: *suddenly the light goes on and Léna finds herself face to face with Clarisse, who is sitting on the steps.*
     CLARISSE (*aggressively*): What do you want?
     LÉNA: I got scared. Excuse me, Miss, but I'm looking for little Fido Saroyan.
     CLARISSE (*drunkenly*): There's no more Fido, Fido's disappeared, kidnapped by two bastards.
     LÉNA: You're completely drunk!

Oldsmobile, exterior, night

445. MCU: *Ernest and Momo, with Fido between them in the front seat, seen through the windshield. Ernest is driving, a cigarette in his mouth. A dog can be heard barking.*

446. MLS: *reverse shot, camera tracking forward: on the road in front of them we can see patches of snow and ice illuminated by the headlights. They are passing through a village.*

447. CU: *Ernest at the wheel and Fido next to him, seen through the windshield.*

448. MLS: *reverse shot: in the headlights, a cat can be seen running across the road as the car plunges through the night.*[9]

449. CU: *Momo and Fido, seen through the windshield.*
     MOMO (*to Fido*): Hey, Fido! That sounds like the name of a dog.
     FIDO: Fido means "faithful."

450. CU: *Ernest and Fido, as in 447.*
     ERNEST (*to Fido*): The milk trick was pretty good, but you have to admit we won the second round.

451. CU: *Momo and Fido, as in 449.*
     MOMO: If I were you, I would have never left the door open. Besides, my father always used to say: "When you hear somebody at the door, assume it's a murderer." That way, if it's only a robber, you'll be happy.

452. CU: *Ernest and Fido, as in 447.*
     ERNEST: How're you doing in school?
     FIDO: So-so.

453. CU: *Momo and Fido, as in 449.*
     MOMO: What's your best subject?
     FIDO: Science.

454. CU: *Ernest and Fido.*
     ERNEST: I wasn't good in any subject. Any kind of work gives me a migraine. I'm making up for all the fathers and grandfathers who worked before me. All those generations of workers! (*Offering a cigarette to Momo.*) Here.

455. CU: *Momo and Fido.*
     MOMO: No thanks. I prefer snuff. (*He puts a pinch of tobacco up his nostrils.*)

FIDO: You're putting tobacco in your nose. That's disgusting.

MOMO: No it's not. It's great, especially in the morning. (*Sniffing loud-ly.*) Besides, the first one is always the best. (*Fido looks toward Ernest.*)

456. CU: *Ernest and Momo. Ernest is lighting a cigarette with his lighter. Music, as from a music box, can be heard.*

FIDO: What's that?

ERNEST: It's a . . .

457. CU: *Momo and Fido.*

ERNEST (*off*):   . . . musical lighter.

FIDO: That's super!

MOMO (*to Ernest*):   Show him your watch.

458. MCU: *a wider shot of Ernest, Fido, and Momo. Through the rear window, behind them, can be seen the lights lining the road.*

ERNEST (*holding out his wrist toward Fido*):   Here. And that's not all. I also have a great gadget for parking meters.

FIDO: Is that all?

ERNEST (*with a conceited air*):   No. I've also got a pen, a new Snorkel from America, with a retractable nib and automatic filler, a belt made of fiber from Oceania, an air-conditioned hat, my suit comes from London and it's made from Australian wool, and I have air-conditioned shoes made of Egyptian leather. So, really, there's nothing else that I want. . . .

459. CU: *Ernest and Fido, as in 447.*

ERNEST (*in a mournful tone*):   I'm bored as shit.

460. CU: *Momo and Fido.*

MOMO (*feeling his scarf*):   It's like my scarf, huh, you'd think it was made of silk. Well, it's metal! But it's a special metal, really flexible. It's Japanese metal (*holding it out toward Fido*). Go ahead, touch it.

FIDO (*feeling it*):   It's not metal, it's made out of cloth.

MOMO: I'm telling you, it's Japanese metal.

FIDO: No, it isn't. It isn't even Japanese.

MOMO: I swear I'm telling you the truth.

FIDO: Come on, give me a break.

MOMO (*putting his scarf back on*):   If I'm lying, may my mother keel over dead this instant.

Apartment, interior, day

461. MS: *an oval shot, framed, as in old family portraits. In a room with old-fashioned furniture an old woman with a bun suddenly grabs her chest, opens her mouth, and keels over dead, her feet kicking up at the end.*

Oldsmobile, interior, night

462. CU: *Momo and Fido.*

FIDO: Now I believe you.

MOMO: I told you it was true.

Café, interior, night

463. CU: *Mammy leaning over in profile in the basement.*
464. MS: *Charlie is laid out on a mattress, a cloth on his forehead. Mammy, seated on the edge of the bed, wipes Charlie's face with a wet towel. She picks up a basin from a stool and walks out of the frame. Slow music begins to be heard. As the camera tracks in closer to Charlie, the light goes off and the trapdoor is heard closing again. Fade to black.*
465. MCU: *Charlie, his eyes closed, the cloth on his forehead. Groaning, he puts his hand to his head and tries to get up.*
    LÉNA (*coming to him*): It's me, Léna. (*She picks him up by the arms.*) Come on, but don't make any noise.
    CHARLIE: Yeah, yeah, yeah. Oh, my head! Oh, shit. (*Léna is pushing him from behind, followed closely by a pan.*) Christ, do I feel groggy.
    LÉNA (*goes to the trapdoor alone*): Wait a minute, I'm going to take a look.
    POLICEMAN (*off*): Yes, yes, and what were you doing?
    LÉNA (*rushing back to Charlie*): They're still there!
    CHARLIE: And Fido?
    They are now moving toward the camera.
    LÉNA: I'll explain later.
    She leans him against a wall, and moves out of the frame, up a different set of stairs.
    CHARLIE (*wiping his face*): Ouch, ouch.
    LÉNA (*after listening above*): The way out is clear now. I borrowed a car.
    CHARLIE: From whom?
    LÉNA: From my landlady.
    CHARLIE: You must be in really good with her!
    LÉNA: No, but I know where she keeps the key. Can you climb up?
    CHARLIE: Yeah.
    LÉNA: Hang on to my waist.
466. MS: *Léna, pulling Charlie along with her, emerges from a door. They go down a corridor, followed by a pan from behind.*
467. MS: *Léna walks through another door, toward the camera, still helping Charlie. She leans him up against the wall, and moves quickly to the right, accompanied by a pan.*
    MAMMY (*off*): Yes, officer, everything I told you is true. Just ask the tenants.
468. MS: *Léna, who moves toward a glass door, behind which Mammy can be seen talking to two policemen.*
    MAMMY: You know how it goes. One thing leads to another.
    Léna comes back toward Charlie, followed by a pan, and, putting his arm over her shoulder, leads him toward the left, out of the frame.

Café, exterior, night

469. MLS: *Léna comes out into the dark street holding Charlie. They are illuminated, for a moment, by a single bright light.*

470. MS: *Léna and Charlie as they emerge from the darkness, and struggle down the street. Léna pushes Charlie into the passenger side of the front seat of a car and slams the door shut. She runs around to the other side as the camera tracks closer to shoot them in profile in the front seat. The camera moves in closer on Léna, while Charlie's head can be seen on the left, leaning against the back seat. Mammy comes up to Léna's window, and shoves Charlie's raincoat through it to Léna.*

    LÉNA (*to Mammy*): The cops?

    MAMMY: They asked me a bunch of questions and now they're questioning the tenants. (*She hands her a bottle of cognac.*) Here, this might come in handy.

    LÉNA: I'll call you when we're on the road.

    CHARLIE (*weakly*): Fido?

    LÉNA (*starting the car*): I'll explain later.

    The camera pans right to follow the departing car, as Mammy comes into the frame at the left. She walks forward a few steps.

Car, interior, night

471. CU: *the camera, placed in the back seat, shoots Léna and Charlie from behind. The car moves down the road.*

    CHARLIE: You've got the bottle?

    Léna hands him the cognac.

    LÉNA: Here.

    CHARLIE (*who, after taking a big gulp, gives the bottle back to Léna*): Here.

472. CU: *Léna and Charlie are now seen through the windshield, brightly lit by the passing lights. She also takes a big gulp.*

    CHARLIE: I'm still thirsty. (*She hands the bottle back to him.*)

473. LS: *reverse shot, tracking ahead; the camera is in the car as it moves down into a long, lighted underground passage. The car's motor is very loud.*

    CHARLIE (*off*): I'd have to be the king of assholes not to have expected that. They got to me through Chico and to Fido through me. There we go again, all of us in trouble, the horrible Saroyan brothers.

Oldsmobile, interior, night

474. CU: *Ernest, Fido, and Momo through the windshield. The motor is making funny noises.*

Oldsmobile, exterior, night

475. LS: *the car's motor continues to make noises and hiccups a few times; the car slows down on the freeway.*

Oldsmobile, interior, night

476. C U : *Ernest, Fido, and Momo, from behind, in the dark. (The camera is on the back seat.)*

   E R N E S T (*trying to start the motor again*): Here we go, that starts again! Goddamn car! This is the third time. Whatta string! I'd rather have one of those chairs people carry you on.

   The car stops and Ernest and Momo get out, leaving Fido alone in the middle.

   M O M O (*off*): What's wrong with it?

   E R N E S T : How should I know? Some lucky break!

   Fido remains on the seat while Momo and Ernest, barely visible, can be seen through the windshield as they open the hood.

   E R N E S T : Well, we'll just have to push it.

   M O M O : Come on, let's go.

Road, then Service Station, exterior, night

477. E L S : *the freeway plunges into the night and far away a big neon sign glows. The sign says* DUNLOP.

   M O M O (*off*): Well, look in front of you. Over on the right, straight ahead.

478. M S : *slightly high-angle shot from the front on Momo and Ernest pushing the car. A pan reveals, through the windshield, the joyful face of Fido at the wheel.*

   F I D O : Come on! Push!

   M O M O (*off*): If you screw up, you're going to be in trouble.

479. E L S : *a service station on the freeway. The two gangsters and a mechanic are standing around the raised hood of the car.*

   Fido walks over and begins playing with the gas pumps.

480. M L S : *tighter on Momo, Ernest, and the mechanic, who are arguing while they look at the car's motor. A pan right frames Fido in a* M S . *He stops playing with the pumps to watch a car hurtling down the freeway. In a pan, the camera follows Léna and Charlie's car as it passes the service station, its motor roaring.*

Car, interior, night

481. L S : *tracking shot backward. The camera is in the car and frames, through the back window, Fido and the service station as they quickly get smaller and smaller. A whip pan left, in the dark, which merges with:*

482. C U : *Léna's profile as she drives. A pan right frames the road ahead of her as they pass through a small village.*

   C H A R L I E (*off*): Does the radio work?

   L É N A (*off*): I don't know. Try it.

   The voice of the singer Félix Leclerc can be heard.

   F É L I X   L E C L E R C (*off*): Very far away, violins . . .

483. L S : *a disguised cut to the same shot of the road ahead through the windshield.*

FÉLIX LECLERC (*off*): . . . and shepherds . . .

484. LS: *same framing, with an almost imperceptible cut. Now, however, the backs of Léna's and Charlie's heads can be seen. We come to a crossroads and the car turns left.*

FÉLIX LECLERC (*off*): . . . dressed as knights. Forty jesters of the King . . .

485. LS: *Same framing, again in a scarcely perceptible cut. The road is lined with streetlamps.*

FÉLIX LECLERC (*off*): . . . all painted, the angels watching over us on the horizon.

486. LS: *Similar framing, though tighter, as their heads cannot be seen. We are going through a town.*
Dissolve.

487. LS: *same framing. A freeway.*
Dissolve.

488. LS: *same framing. A curve on the freeway.*
Dissolve.

489. LS: *same framing. A freeway.*

FÉLIX LECLERC (*off-screen, beginning another song*): When I start to hate you, so that you'll know, when I start to hate you, I'll start wearing my cap. . . .

Dissolve.
Car, interior, day

490. LS: *Same framing. The sun is coming up on a snow-covered road that winds up through mountain cottages.*

WOMAN'S VOICE (*off, the voice of Lucienne Vernoy continues the song*): When you don't love me any more, so that you'll know, when you don't love me any more, I'll start wearing my hair down.

FÉLIX LECLERC (*off*): Since then, my girlfriend's been wearing a chignon.

LUCIENNE VERNOY (*off*): And in all kinds of weather . . .

491. MCU: *Charlie and Léna through the windshield. Charlie finishes the bottle with a gulp as Léna grabs it and throws it out the window.*

LUCIENNE VERNOY (*off*): . . . he walks around . . .

492. MLS: *reverse shot, tracking ahead: through the windshield we can see a small road in the middle of the pine trees. The landscape is covered with snow.*

LUCIENNE VERNOY (*off*): . . . with nothing on his head. (*The song ends.*)

CHARLIE (*off*): Stop.

LÉNA (*off*): We're not there yet.

CHARLIE (*off*): Didn't you hear me? I told you to stop.

493. MCU: *Léna and Charlie from the front. She stops the car. A dog can be heard barking.*

494. MS: *Charlie and Léna through the car door, as Charlie opens it.*

LÉNA: What are you doing?

CHARLIE (*his face tight*): We're separating. You go back to town and put your landlady's car back where it belongs.

495. ECU: *Léna, looking squarely at Charlie. Her head is framed by the white of the snow behind her.*

LÉNA: Look at me.

496. ECU: *Charlie, staring straight ahead, with an uneasy and unhappy look.*

CHARLIE (*voiceover*): If she had let you drink the whole bottle, the separation would have been easier.

497. MS: *Léna and Charlie, as in 494.*

CHARLIE: When you get to the crossroads, turn left. (*He does not look at her.*)

498. ECU: *Léna, her eyes lowered as she looks away.*

LÉNA: You don't have to explain. I know the way. (*She looks at him.*) What are you waiting for?

499. ECU: *Charlie.*

CHARLIE (*voiceover*): You want her to stay with you and she knows it. But, too bad, it's not possible.

500. MS: *the two-shot, as he gets out of the car.*

CHARLIE: And thanks for all the fun.

501. ECU: *Léna as she lowers her eyes and turns her head.*
Snowy Landscape, exterior, day

502. MS: *low-angle shot of Charlie getting out of the car, closing the door, and disappearing to the left. The car moves away to the right, followed by a pan, between two snow embankments. We watch as it disappears.*

503. ELS: *far away, in a very-high-angle shot, Charlie can be seen, against the light, going over a small bridge that crosses a stream. He is climbing through a field of snow toward the camera. As he moves into a MS, a figure appears suddenly on the right.*

CHARLIE (*without much feeling*): Hi, Richard.

RICHARD: Hey! You're all alone. I thought I heard a car.

The two men move forward toward the camera, which begins to track backward in front of them.

CHARLIE: It was just a friend who brought me up here.

RICHARD: Ah, okay. You understand, we're a little defensive here because there are some guys looking for Chico to give him a little welcoming party. Chico must have told you. He went to see you.

CHARLIE: He's here? When did he arrive?

RICHARD: He got here this afternoon, half dead. You know, hitchhiking, running, etc. Now he's doing better. He's taking a little snooze. When he got here he ate enough for four.

CHARLIE: Are Mom and Dad here?

RICHARD: We got them set up down in the village.

CHARLIE (*stopping*): You guys are completely crazy.

RICHARD: Do you think it was fun? Hey, I like them too. We've got some nice old folks, not pains in the ass at all. But, what are you going to do, they're not bulletproof.

CHARLIE: Yeah. Have you had any visitors?

RICHARD: No.

CHARLIE: So we're the first ones.

RICHARD: Anyway, good old Chico.

CHARLIE: Well. . . .

RICHARD: Don't try to cover up for him. He's always screwed things up. If assholes could fly, he'd be the squadron commander.

CHARLIE: He was in a bad situation.

RICHARD: He's always in a bad situation. And you know why? Because he doesn't know what the hell he's doing.

CHARLIE: But still, it's not his fault I killed some guy.

RICHARD (*flabbergasted*): What!

CHARLIE: Yeah . . .

504. MS: *Charlie and Richard walk out of the frame to the right.*

CHARLIE (*off*): . . . yesterday evening.

House in the Country, interior, night

505. MS: *Charlie, still in his raincoat, and his brother Richard are seated at a table in a brightly lit room. Richard is wearing a black turtleneck sweater; his hair is dark and curly. Behind them a cuckoo is bobbing up and down, marking the passing seconds.*

RICHARD: We're in a nice fix. The two guys who grabbed Fido. On the other side, the cops are looking for you, of all people. Hey, so what, I'm happy to see you.

CHARLIE (*looking at him, completely expressionless, his hands in his coat pockets*): I'm happy to see you too.

RICHARD: "Me too," as the Brits say.

CHARLIE (*turning his head*): Hey, is that your coffee that's boiling?

The camera tracks backward quickly.

RICHARD (*getting up*): Shit! Boiled coffee is spoiled coffee!

On the table is a storm lamp and a plate of apples.

RICHARD (*bustling around behind Charlie*): I'm going to tell you something. (*Ironically.*) It's really exciting . . .

506. CU: *Charlie, his eyes fixed straight ahead.*

RICHARD (*off*): . . . to stay like this, without being able to budge. In the morning you don't feel like getting up. You're a prisoner of the shack. At first we had a lot of fun with Chico.

507. MS: *Charlie and Richard, who is still near the stove.*

RICHARD: That was great fun. I'm going to wake him up to tell him you're here.

He grabs a hatchet and pounds on the ceiling with the handle, in a series of six quick raps followed by three long ones.[10]

CHICO (*off*): Yeah!

The door at the right opens. Coming down the last few steps, Chico appears, dressed in a wool checkered jacket. The camera pans right slightly, in order to reframe. Chico is holding a pistol in one hand and, under the other arm, a black attaché case.

CHICO (*surprised, he stops to look at Charlie*): You're here!

CHARLIE: Yeah. How's your black eye?

CHICO (*smiling*): Oh, it's all right. It doesn't hurt any more. (*He puts the attaché case down.*)

CHARLIE (*off*): What's that?

CHICO: The dough. That's what I went up to Paris for. (*He sits down next to Charlie, as the camera tracks forward into a two-shot of Chico and Charlie at the table.*) 'Cause all of that is in new bills, with all the numbers registered. Now in order to pass them you have to come up with a scheme, you know. (*Richard comes closer and puts some bowls on the table.*) Richard and I (*laughing*) had found some honest job at a place where they exchange money. One day we were making an exchange and these two guys pulled guns on us. It was fun. Not a good idea, because we know a little bit about pulling guns ourselves. Then they said: "Okay, if you know something about it, let's split it four ways." Richard and I looked at each other. We didn't have much choice, so we went along with it, and left with these two guys. (*Richard is pouring coffee.*) And then, we thought right away about coming up here. I don't know what happened then. In the car the two guys started bitching, it was too far, what's with this house in the snow, and all that. Hey! (*With a gesture.*) So we dumped them and decided to forget about sharing the dough. The only problem is that these two guys now want our hides.

508. MCU: *Chico and Richard, from slightly above Charlie's* POV, *as Richard sits down.*

  CHICO: We should have blown them away.

  RICHARD (*to Chico*): By the way, Charlie killed some guy.

  CHICO (*dumbfounded*): No shit! (*Grabbing him.*) No way! (*With a smile.*) Shit! Well, hey, what if I told you I was glad? (*The melancholy musical theme begins.*) Now . . .

509. MS: *Charlie walking away from the table, his back toward them.*

  CHICO (*off*): . . . you're just like us.

  Charlie walks over to a cracked mirror that is hanging in the window. His face is reflected in it. He smiles.

  CHICO (*off*): Do you remember the slingshots?

510. MCU: *Richard and Chico seated at the table.*

  RICHARD: What slingshots?

  CHICO: And the limousine. The people who came to get you in the limousine, the young prodigy, the fourteen-year-old virtuoso, to take you to the Academy of Music, to the old man.

511. MS: *reverse shot of Charlie, as in 509.*

  CHARLIE (*turning back toward his brothers*): Yes, to Zélény's. (*He moves to the left as the camera pans to follow him around the room.*) While we were going through the woods, you and Richard bombarded the car with slingshots. The two guys didn't know who you were, of course. The lady in the car, who had blue hair and glasses with little shells on them, asked me who you were. I said, "Do you mean those young boys, Ma'am?" And she said, "They aren't boys, they're wild animals."

512. MCU: *slightly high-angle reverse shot of Chico and Richard from Charlie's* POV. *They occupy the right-hand side of the frame.*

  CHICO: What did you say?

513. MS: *Charlie as he sits down in a rocking chair near the window.*

  CHARLIE: "Those are my brothers, Ma'am." Naturally, she changed the subject. She told me about the Academy of Music, the great teacher I was going to have, a bunch of stuff like that. The whole time, stones continued to rain down on the car. (*He is rocking back and forth.*) It was as if you and Richard were talking to me. As if you were telling me that I couldn't leave for good and that some day I'd come back forever.

514. M C U : *Chico and Richard.*

R I C H A R D (*getting up*): . . . come back to the wild animals!

C H I C O : Well, you had to come back, Charlie, because we're all the same, you, me, Richard (*he gets up*), and even Fido.

R I C H A R D : Well?

C H I C O : What?

R I C H A R D : Let's go hit the sack, Charlie. Chico, you take the first watch. *The camera pans right to frame Chico alone. He has the revolver in his hand.*

515. M S : *Charlie.*

C H A R L I E : Go to bed, Chico, I'm not sleepy. I feel like having a smoke.

516. M C U : *Chico, who is waving his gun.*

C H I C O : Okay, well, I'll leave this for you. (*Throwing the gun on the table; the camera pans to frame it.*) Man's best friend. *A pan right and tilt up follows Chico as he picks up the attaché case. He is smiling at Charlie.*

517. M S : *reverse shot of Charlie, who half-smiles at Chico. The music ends.*

518. M C U : *Chico and Richard as they go up the stairs and close the door behind them.*

519. M S : *Charlie, who is rocking in his chair as he lights his cigarette. The music starts again. The camera lingers on Charlie as he pulls his coat more tightly around him, and then fade to black.*

House in the Country, exterior, day

520. E L S : *High-angle shot that tilts down to show the little house in the snow. Smoke is streaming from the chimney. Dissolve.*

House in the Country, interior, day

521. M S : *Charlie, in three-quarter face forward, rocking on his chair. Through the window next to him, snow can be seen falling. He is wrapped up in a checkered blanket, and is still smoking. The music continues.*

522. M C U : *Charlie, seen from the outside, from the other side of the window, in a closer shot. Through the bars of the window, his head can be seen rocking back and forth as the music continues and the snow continues to fall. Dissolve.*

523. M S : *Charlie seen from the inside.*

524. M C U : *Charlie seen from the outside. He gets up, picks up the gun from the table, and moves out of the frame.*

525. ECU: *Charlie's face. He moves around the room, glancing briefly at a picture of a bicycle racer on the wall, followed by a very tight panning shot.*
    CHARLIE (*voiceover*): There you are! You're a murderer in a family of
    thieves. No problem! Yes, there is a problem, this kind of craziness. (*He
    suddenly turns to look back at the cuckoo, bobbing up and down, and
    for a few moments follows its bobbing path with his head and the gun.*)
    From whom did you and your brothers get it? (*He starts moving around
    again.*) Not from Mom and Dad. It must have jumped a couple of
    generations. These things happen. It disappears for a hundred years, two
    hundred years, and then it comes back. (*He passes in front of the crack-
    ed mirror and feels his whiskers while munching a piece of sugar.*)
    Going back to our ancestors, you'd probably find Saroyans who were
    frenetic, passionate, doing crazy things, then holing up in a corner, just
    like us, now. You could write a poem about it . . . a comic one, of
    course. And this useless gun: "I'm leaving this for you, it's man's best
    friend." Saying that to you. (*He rubs some of the ice off the window.*)
    You, who hate guns of any kind.

526. MLS: *reverse angle: through the window and the bars we see Léna,
dressed in her raincoat, walking toward the house, through the snow.
The music stops, but the sound of the ticking cuckoo clock can be heard
louder than ever.*
    House in the Country, exterior, day

527. LS: *Charlie, the blanket on his back, runs out of the house and rapidly crosses the surrounding field of snow toward the camera. A quick pan to the right
reveals Léna coming into the frame in* MCU. *She is smiling at him.*

528. MS: *Charlie coming closer.*

529. MCU: *Léna. Left side of frame is empty.*
    LÉNA: And Fido?
    CHARLIE (*coming into the frame, making it a two-shot*): Nothing, still
        nothing. I think we screwed up in our calculations.
    LÉNA: We're leaving. I'm going to take you back.
    CHARLIE: What about the police?
    LÉNA: There's nothing to worry about. You're in the clear. Self-defense!
        The neighbors were very good. They told the truth. That you threw the
        knife away, that Plyne was trying to strangle you. And you wanted to
        stab him in the arm, just an accident!
    CHARLIE: If only it's true! And the car?
    LÉNA: The car is over there. Come on, let's go!
    CHARLIE: I can't just leave without telling them. I'm going to go ex-
        plain. Wait for me.
    Charlie leaves the frame, leaving Léna alone.
    LÉNA: Are you coming back, for sure?
    A quick pan to the left frames Charlie alone.

CHARLIE (*looking at her and smiling slightly*): You know I told you that when I started hating you, I'd start wearing my cap. (*He goes back toward the house followed by a pan left. A church bell can be heard in the distance.*)

530. MS: *Léna moves right through some bare trees in the foreground. Behind her, snow and more trees.*

531. LS: *Charlie, who is near the house.*

532. ELS: *high-angle pan on the Oldsmobile moving forward along a small snowy road bordered by pine trees.*

Oldsmobile, interior, day

533. MCU: *tracking forward on Ernest, Fido, and Momo in the car, seen from behind. A pan toward the windows on the left side of the car allows us to see the house first over Ernest's shoulder, then, as the pan continues left, framed through the back window.*

House in the Country, exterior, day

534. MS: *Léna is waiting in the snow, looking up toward the house. A quick pan left frames the car, which can be seen through the trees stopping on the road.*

535. ELS: *on the little bridge over the creek. In the foreground, a tree branch blows in the wind.*

536. ELS: *through the bare branches Momo, Ernest, and Fido can be seen running forward down the road in single file.*

537. MLS: *high-angle shot. They run across a snowy field and start walking across the bridge in MS. Fido pushes Momo, who falls down on the bridge.*
MOMO: Goddamn it!
Fido dashes away and runs along the creek followed by a very rapid left-to-right pan. We can hear his heavy breathing, and his steps, and nothing else. He moves through some trees in MS.

538. MCU: *Léna, who is following him with her eyes, as though they are panning, in a brief, very fast, and exaggerated gesture.*

539. LS: *Fido running quickly through the trees to the right.*

540. MCU: *Momo's lower body gingerly stepping on some rocks in the creek. A tilt up reveals the rest of his body and Ernest at his side. They both have guns.*
ERNEST: Shit! It's snowing!

541. MS: *low-angle shot of Chico, from outside the house, as he appears behind a window, which, after pulling down a curtain, he then opens from the top.*

542. MS: *the two gangsters coming closer, moving left.*

543. MS: *Chico, who fires two shots through the window. A pan left reveals a second window whose glass is broken from inside. Richard sticks his arm out and also begins shooting.*

544. MS: *the gangsters. Ernest's hat is shot off, but he manages to catch it and puts it back on his head. They begin to shoot back.*

Richard Kanayan

545. M S : *Richard, who is still shooting.*
546. M C U : *Ernest and Momo in profile as they aim carefully before firing and then move forward.*
547. M S : *Chico, who fires twice more through his open window.*
548. E C U : *Léna's face, as she turns to scream out.*
     LÉNA (*wildly*): Charlie!
549. C U : *a disguised cut to another* C U *on Léna. She runs right in profile, followed by a pan. More exciting, "chase" music begins, as she continues to run. Suddenly, she falls.*
550. M C U : *reverse angle of 544. Ernest, in profile, spins his gun three times around his finger, and aims.*

Daniel Boulanger and Claude Mansard

551. ECU: *Léna gets up again and runs, followed by a pan. Her face is not in clear focus, and the camera has difficulty keeping her in the frame.*

552. MS: *Léna is running through the trees, as the camera pans right to follow her.*

553. MS: *Ernest, who fires at something to the left. A blurred pan, as though following the bullet, moves quickly toward Léna, who is at the top of a small hill. She collapses.*
The music ends. Another blurred pan moves right, toward the house, to frame Charlie behind a window. He hears, looks quickly to his right in an exaggerated gesture, and runs outside. The camera pans quickly right and picks him up again at the corner of the house.

554. LS: *Léna's body slides smoothly and quickly down a hill of snow, followed by a pan.*
Slow, sad music is heard.

555. LS: *Charlie runs through the trees to the left. In the background, Momo and Ernest are running in the other direction.*

556. ELS: *pan from left to right as Léna's body, at first merely a speck against the snow, continues to slide down the hill.*

557. MS: *pan from left to right as Léna's body turns over on the snow and the gun that Léna was holding in her hand drops. Her body becomes immobile. End of the music.*

558. ELS: *high-angle shot: in the foreground, the tops of some pine trees. The two gangsters run past, behind the house to the left. After a moment, Chico and Richard go out the front. Momo and Ernest, after having circled the house, reappear at the right. As the fast music theme begins again, the four men exchange shots and Richard falls. He gets up again and takes off with Chico, followed by the two gangsters.*
     Fast music continues.
559. MLS: *Richard and Chico run down the road and jump into the car that Léna and Charlie have brought. Richard, in the back seat, points his gun behind him out the window.*
560. MLS: *pan from right to left on the Oldsmobile as it starts up and briefly spins its tires in the snow.*
561. LS: *high-angle pan from right to left on Léna and Charlie's car as it quickly moves further away, followed by the Oldsmobile.*
562. ELS: *high-angle shot. Under the falling snow, the two silhouettes of Fido and Charlie, tiny dots that are barely visible, can be seen coming, one from the right and the other from the left, converging on the half-buried body of Léna, which is in the center of the frame. Charlie reaches her first and falls down at her side.*
563. CU: *Charlie turns Léna over on her back and puts his hand under her neck. Her face is covered with snow. Fido comes into the frame from the left. Fido and Charlie, kneeling, surround Léna's face, which is upside*

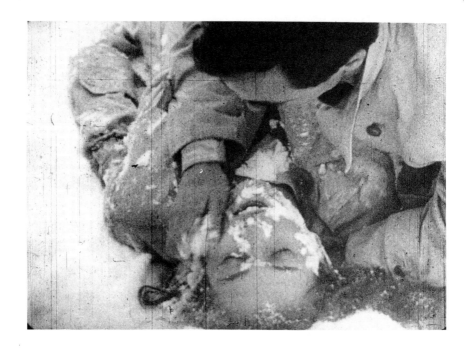

down at the bottom of the frame. Charlie closes her eyes. (Slow music replaces the earlier music.) The camera reframes so that only Charlie and Léna are in the frame as he wipes away the blood forming on her lips with a piece of snow. Momentarily, the camera pans too far to the right, leaving Charlie half out of the frame.

564.	CU: *Léna's upside-down face, as Charlie brushes snow from her hair and, uselessly, the snow next to her body. A zoom-in frames her face in an* ECU, *as the musical theme comes to a climax and ends.*
	Dissolve.
	Café, interior, day

565.	MS: *a matched dissolve from Léna's face to Mammy behind the bar, which is filled with customers. The camera follows her to the left and stops on a two-shot of Mammy and a young girl behind the bar, who is putting glasses on her tray. Her hair is braided.*
	MAMMY: No, honey, that's not the way to do it. You'll break the glasses that way. Here's how to do it. (*She arranges the glasses herself.*) You have to put them down gently.
	CHARLIE (*coming into the bar from the door behind them*): Hi.
	MAMMY: Charlie, this is the new waitress. (*To the waitress.*) This is Charlie, the piano player.
	WAITRESS: Hi. (*Shaking his hand.*)

Charles Aznavour

Charlie moves away and the waitress leaves the frame with her tray, and then walks in front of the camera in E C U .

566. C U : *Charlie's hands, in profile, on the piano keyboard. He starts the theme originally heard at the beginning of the film as a tilt up and pan right frames his serious face from in front. The music gets louder, hammering the notes. The space at the right of the frame is empty, and Charlie is at the extreme left. He occasionally blinks or looks down at his hands playing, but mostly he just stares straight ahead.*
Suddenly, in the blank space to the right, appear the words:
   THE END.
   Production:
   FILMS DE LA PLEIADE
Fade to black. Music comes to a climax and ends.

Notes on the Continuity Script

1. In French, Plyne uses the overly familiar pronoun "tu" (you) with Charlie, who insists on being called by the more polite "vous" form. The traditional translation of this sociolinguistic distinction into English is first name vs. last name, but this is clearly inadequate.
2. What follows in the script is a more literal translation of Boby Lapointe's notorious song "Avanie et framboise" than that which appears in either version of the subtitles (16mm print or new laserdisc). The wonderful rhymes are lost, of course, but the benefit of literalness is that it enables one to capture more of the song's sometimes gross double meanings, which are indicated in brackets. Here is the complete text of the song in French:

Elle s'appelait Françoise . . .
Mais on l'appelait
Framboise.
Une idée de l'adjutant
Qu'en avait très peu pourtant,
Des idées.

Elle nous servait à boire
Dans un bled du Maine-et-Loire
Mais ce n'était pas Madelon
Elle avait un autre nom
Et puis d'abord pas question
De lui prendre le menton.

D'ailleurs elle était d'Antibes
Quelle avanie!
Avanie et Framboise
Sont les mamelles du destin.

Pour sûr qu'elle était d'Antibes
C'est plus près que les Caraïbes
C'est plus près que Caracas
Est-ce plus près que Pézenas?
Je n'sais pas.

Et tout en étant française
Elle était tout de même Antibaise
Et bien qu'elle soit française
Et malgré ses yeux de braise
Ça ne me mettait pas à l'aise
De la savoir Antibaise
Moi qui serais plutôt pour

Quelle avanie!
Avanie et Framboise
Sont les mamelles du destin.

Elle avait peu d'avantages
Pour en avoir davantage
Elle s'en fit rajouter
A l'institut de beauté ah, ah, ah.

On peut dans le Maine-et-Loire
S'offrir de beaux seins en poire.
Il y a un institut d'Angers
Qui opère sans danger.
Des plus jeunes aux plus âgés
On peut presque tout changer
Excepté ce qu'on ne peut pas.

Quelle avanie!
Avanie et Framboise
Sont les mamelles du destin.

Davantage d'avantages
Avantage d'avantages
Lui dis-je quand elle revint
Avec ses seins angevins.

Deux fois dix
Permets donc que je lutine
Cette poitrine angevine

Mais elle m'a échappé
A pris du champ dans le pré
Mais je n'ai pas couru après
Je ne voulais pas attraper
Une angevine de poitrine.

Moralité:
Avanie et mamelles
Sont les framboises du destin.
(This is reproduced from the mimeographed dialogue script for the film,
sent to me by Madeleine Morgenstern of Les Films du Carrosse.)

3. At this point, the *Avant-Scène* script of the film shows the following
   dialogue exchange between Ernest and Momo. It is missing from all
   American versions of the film, including the laserdisc version:

   MOMO (*off-screen*): Hey, wait a minute. Lend me fifty francs.
   ERNEST (*off-screen*): I can't. Here's ten.
   MOMO (*off-screen*): Ten francs? You must be joking. Well, I'll take it, but
   I'm not paying you back.
   ERNEST (*off-screen*): Okay. It's a present.
   MOMO (*off-screen*): Well, lend me twenty, I'll pay you back, and that way
   you'll do better.
   ERNEST (*off-screen*): No way. I'd rather lose ten and have peace.

4. Shot 136 and its accompanying dialogue to this point are missing from all
   earlier American versions of the film, but have been restored in the laserdisc
   version.
5. These are the small lights the French put at the base of a traffic light so that
   they might be more easily seen by motorists waiting at the light.
6. There is an unidentified woman in the background of this shot. It is impossible to determine its location; it seems to be connected with the past, but
   seems to be neither in the apartment nor on the concert stage.
7. There is no artistic, narrative, or psychological reason for this cut, which is
   virtually invisible to the normal viewer. It is probably there because the
   camera ran out of film before this long take was over or because Truffaut
   wanted to combine the best parts of two different takes. (See the article by
   Reisz and Millar, reprinted in this volume.)
8. Long, thin pieces of toast that are dipped in soft-boiled eggs.
9. The following line of dialogue occurs at this point in the *Avant-Scène* version of the script, but is not in any American version of the film:

   ERNEST (*swearing*): Shit! These goddam cats!

10. Similar to the traditional ceremonial opening of French theater.

Interviews, Reviews, and Commentaries

Interviews

Truffaut liked to talk about his films nearly as much as he enjoyed making them. From the hundreds of interviews he gave during his lifetime, I have chosen several that specifically concern *Shoot the Piano Player* and that illuminate different aspects of that film. The interview with Hélène Laroche Davis appears here in print for the first time. Also included are two pieces in which Truffaut—whose initial training was as a critic, of course—spoke of the film more or less directly, without the benefit or hindrance of an interlocutor.

Interview with François Truffaut

Hélène Laroche Davis

A t the end of a little street, filled with the voices of children playing in the schoolyard, are the offices of Les Films du Carrosse, François Truffaut's production company in Paris. This is where we first met in 1978 to discuss a project for a book on *Shoot the Piano Player*. Images of *The 400 Blows* and *Small Change* came to my mind as I entered the building. The walls of Truffaut's office were lined with books. He had a genuine love for books, especially old and rare books. After a warm and friendly welcome the conversation focused on *Shoot the Piano Player* and he responded with characteristic enthusiasm to the project. He immediately began searching for material about the making of the film— newspaper clippings, documents, and photographs, as well as his own recollections. He spent time telling me anecdotes about the actors, anecdotes always tinged with affection. He even began to design a cover for the book. This stimulated a renewed interest in the film on his part and resulted in a revival of it in 1982 with beautiful new prints made possible by the financial success of *The Last Metro*.

After several meetings in Paris and California, and an extensive correspondence, we decided to tape a formal interview in his office at Les Films du Carrosse in January 1980. What follows is a translated and edited version of the interview. It deals with the making of *Shoot the Piano Player,* the casting of actors, the reaction of the press, and the affinity of Truffaut for the novels of David Goodis.

Davis: What place would you give *Shoot the Piano Player* in relation to your other films?
Truffaut: No place. Simply, the second film I made. I have said before that this film was made in reaction to *The 400 Blows,* which was so French, I needed to show that I had also been influenced by American cinema. It is so true that, at the time when I used to see Rossellini a lot—I had worked with him for years, and he had loved *The 400 Blows*—he told me he was going to see *Shoot the Piano Player.* I said "Do me a favor, do not see *Shoot the Piano Player,*" because I knew deep down that I had made this film almost against him, maybe.
Davis: Was *Shoot the Piano Player* a victim of criticism against the New Wave rather than against the film itself?
Truffaut: Yes. There was a polemic. I did receive the Young Critics Prize, a prize that existed only for two or three years. A few critics used to get together; Françoise Sagan was among them. They gave the prize to *Shoot the Piano Player* so they must have liked it. Other critics attacked it, as they did all the second films

Taped at Les Films du Carrosse in Paris, January 1980. Technical assistant: Robert Ernest Tompkins.

of New Wave directors. The idea was that these young men were capable of making a first film because they told the story of their childhood. But they could not make a second film. Thus we were refused entry into the profession.

Davis: Your first three films—*The 400 Blows, Shoot the Piano Player,* and *Jules and Jim*—were shot in CinemaScope. Why did you start with the large screen? Are you satisfied with the results?

Truffaut: When we were critics at the *Cahiers du Cinéma,* we defended Cinema-Scope against older critics and some French directors. In *The 400 Blows,* as in the first New Wave films, we were shocked by the simplicity of our technical means for shooting. We had only a noisy camera. We did not record the sound directly, only a vague test sound. We were shooting on real locations, with a reduced crew. Our means were so limited that we thought the result would not be a real movie. I was very surprised when *The 400 Blows* was selected for the Cannes Film Festival, because I told myself that at Cannes they should not show a film that had not been shot with direct sound. (However, if we go back to 1946, at the first Cannes Film Festival, they showed René Clément's *La Bataille du rail,* which must have been shot under these same conditions.) Yet it is strange to think that in 1959 in Cannes the three French films presented—*Orfeu Negro* (*Black Orpheus*), *The 400 Blows,* and *Hiroshima, mon amour*—had been shot without direct sound and outside a studio. In spite of the fact that he liked our films, Jean Renoir reproached us for not defending direct sound and was not satisfied with post-synchronization. In *The 400 Blows* it worked rather well because children are easily dubbed and Jean-Pierre Léaud is so well dubbed that you can't tell. With the parents it is not so good. Besides, there are parts shot with direct sound. For instance, the interview with the psychologist, which could not have been dubbed. I used this silent film system with postsynchronization up through *Jules and Jim.* Afterwards we switched to direct sound.

To answer your question on CinemaScope: by shooting *The 400 Blows* in scope, I had the rather naive feeling that the film would look more professional, more stylized; it would not be completely naturalistic. CinemaScope has this strange peculiarity of being an oblong window that hides many details. When someone moves in a room, if you have a square frame (1:1.33) you have all the details, what is on the table, on the wall, you judge the decor at the same time. Whereas in a CinemaScope room, the character moves abstractly, almost like in an aquarium. It is very clear in *Shoot the Piano Player,* during Thérésa's confession, for instance. You are left with a face moving against a gray background. It becomes more abstract. And I liked that. I thought that in movies, we give actors absurd motivations to justify their movements, for instance "Go over there to put out your cigarette in the ashtray." And I did not like these motivations. I believed that we could ask actors to move without a reason. That is why I liked CinemaScope. But afterwards, I abandoned CinemaScope when I learned that for *The 400 Blows* and *Jules and Jim,* 16mm reproductions were made, reducing the film to a flat screen. So CinemaScope, which had been invented to fight against television, was completely assimilated into the system; it was even harmed.[1] We ended up seeing our favorite films massacred in movie theaters, with the top and bottom of the frame cropped. At first I thought that shooting a film in scope meant preserving it. Now that my films are shown on television cropped right and left, we know that there is no other solution than the 1:1.75 screen, which is the format used for most American films.

Davis: What made you decide to adapt Goodis's novel?

Truffaut: I read the book when it came out. It must have been at the time I was shooting [*Les Mistons*]. I had just written the scenario of *Breathless,* which I did not think I would make myself, but I didn't really know what I would do with it. It was a true story that happened in the Pigalle district, where I was born. At that time I discovered *Shoot the Piano Player* and I was enthused by the dialogue, the poetic tone of the book, the love story, the evocation of the past. I gave the novel to Pierre Braunberger, who was the only producer to take an interest in the young directors, and he liked it a lot and bought the rights to it. Then, while working on the adaptation, I felt that it was not right to start with this film. So I offered the script of *The 400 Blows* to him and he turned it down. He preferred *Shoot the Piano Player.* So I made *The 400 Blows* with my father-in-law who was a retired producer. My experience with *Les Mistons* had taught me that I worked well with children, that I was not quite ready for adults, and that I would work better on a subject close to me. After I discovered *Shoot the Piano Player* I started reading all of Goodis's books, looking for what they had in common. When we talk about the attraction that hard-boiled detective novels have for French people we have to remember that it is not only the American material in which we find a certain poetry, but, because this material has been transformed by the translation, we get an almost perverse pleasure out of it. For instance, I believe that the version of *Johnny Guitar* dubbed in French is more poetic than the original film, because there is a certain style, a theatrical style that touched us in France, a sentimental style. I think that Americans like *Johnny Guitar* now in retrospect, after the French reaction. For instance it is the only Western in which the characters say "vous" to each other. "Jouez-nous un air, Monsieur Guitare." The French text of *Johnny Guitar* leads the film in the direction of classical tragedy.

There is also a rhythm of synchronization. When we like a book like *Shoot the Piano Player* it is difficult to explain why to an American audience. We even like the distortion. When I wrote an article for *Cahiers du Cinéma* on Humphrey Bogart, I not only described what I liked in Bogart, but also paid homage to the two actors who used to postsynchronize his voice. Dubbing, like subtitling, is a technique that distorts and sometimes enhances the meaning. The printed word reinforces and makes things funnier. This is what happened to some of my films

1. Everything Truffaut says here about *The 400 Blows* and *Jules and Jim* is also true, of course, of *Shoot the Piano Player.*

when they were shown at the New York Film Festival. It is the only time I ever saw my films in the States. I noticed more laughter than in France at certain points, just because of the printed words.

Davis: Is that what happened with "Avanie et framboise," the Boby Lapointe song?

Truffaut: It's quite different. Boby Lapointe's song was an accident. Pierre Braunberger didn't like this singer. He said that he did not understand a word he was saying and wanted to cut the scene. So, I said that I would subtitle the song so he could understand. I remembered the Canadian films of Norman MacLaren that I loved. In these films, people in the audience were supposed to sing along. The words appeared syllable by syllable with a little ball bouncing on the syllable at the time it was to be sung. I had the syllables appear at the time Boby Lapointe pronounced them.

Davis: Did you plan the changes of tone in *Shoot the Piano Player* because they appear in the novel, or did this style come spontaneously during the shooting?

Truffaut: They were planned but they were reinforced in the shooting because I realized that I was faced with a film without a theme I clearly understood. In a movie like *Adele H.*, I know that I have the same idea repeated, that the heroine must be excessive in her character, which becomes obsessive. Whereas with a film with an unclear subject, such as *Stolen Kisses* or *Love on the Run,* some days I stress the comical side, other days the dramatic side. It is only when the film is finished that I know what it is about. The first time I showed *Shoot the Piano Player* to Jacques Rivette, he told me something that upset me. He said: "Do you realize that the main character of your film is a bastard?" I suppose that he said it because the character is a complete introvert who never expresses his thoughts, who is withdrawn, who refuses to intervene when he sees that women are victimized. Later on Rivette liked the film. But it is unusual to have so little control over what one is doing. The scenario was really a compromise between what I liked best in Goodis and other things I wanted to say. I found Goodis's book too chaste. The film is not as chaste as the book. I was advancing instinctively, according to the actresses, too. I saw what was appropriate for these three very different women. I consciously wanted to show three portraits of women who can pass through a man's life. That part was planned.

Two years before making *Shoot the Piano Player,* I was a critic at *Cahiers du Cinéma* and *Arts.* There had been such an exaggerated reception and publicity for *The 400 Blows* at the Cannes Film Festival. We were in the news and were interviewed over and over. It did not go to my head, but it created a certain agitation in my mind after this disproportionate success of *The 400 Blows.* Afterwards in *Shoot the Piano Player,* there was an echo of the notion of celebrity and obscurity. It is reversed in *Shoot the Piano Player* since it is a famous person who becomes unknown. There are touches here and there of this feeling that troubled me. For instance, a small detail, when Aznavour is sitting and there are photographers who call him in a more and more familiar way: "Monsieur Saroyan, Charles, Charlie. . . ." It is something that had struck me at the Cannes Festival, where Cocteau insisted that I go up the stairs with him before the showing of *The 400 Blows*. And Cocteau, who was very popular with the photographers, was hailed in that manner: "Cocteau, Maitre, Jean. . . ." It made me laugh. And the scene with Aznavour is an echo of this.

Davis: Why did you choose to stress the poetic atmosphere of Goodis's novel?

Truffaut: In spite of my admiration for Ernst Lubitsch, I have to disagree with him when he says "In a film one must never speak of the past." He thinks it is wasted time and we lose the audience. As for me I have always been moved by scenes that are told but not seen, or when there is a reference to the past. So there is that style of interior monologue in *Shoot the Piano Player* that excited me, and I wanted to reproduce it in the film. I was very meticulous. In a first version, I used Aznavour's voice. Later I realized that his voice was good for dialogue but not for voiceover, because his voice was not soft enough. Maybe we can see here something that is in several other films I made, that is, an attempt to include literary forms in the soundtrack of my films because I like commentary, flashbacks, and evocations of the past. Even the imperfect tense of a verb: when Marie Dubois says "You were here, you started playing piano again," it is very literary. It is funny because this film is an homage to American cinema, and at the same time this verb tense is not used in American cinema.

Davis: What about the superimposed images in their first intimate scene, where this very literary dialogue takes place?

Truffaut: The superimposed image expresses the passage of time. I liked the idea of intimacy being born. Also, because Aznavour's voice was not soft enough, I used only her words and no words from him. It emphasized the feelings and was rather well done.

Davis: Did you ever meet David Goodis?

Truffaut: Yes, he gave me a view finder. It was a very different one from what we have in France. He got it when he worked on a film as a second unit director. I remember one night in New York, he told us he wanted to go on walking. The next day Helen Scott, my agent in the United States, told me that he had been in a fight and was in the hospital. I could not speak any English and could not understand him. Helen translated very well, simultaneously, so it was as if I were talking with him. I remember more what he said about his publishers. In France we think that these authors are better known than they are. In France we are familiar with all the names of the Série Noire [detective fiction], and in the United States no one knows them because they disappear in the crowd of that enormous production. I must have been impressed by the fact that he was unknown, humble, modest, and that he had so much difficulty with his publishers, who always wanted to change his books.

Davis: What was the role of Marcel Moussy in the writing of the screenplay of *Shoot the Piano Player*?

Truffaut: His role was not as important as for *The 400 Blows* because *The 400 Blows* corresponded to the work he had done on television for a program called *If*

Truffaut and Aznavour in the restaurant

It Were You (*Si c'etait vous*), which presented problematic social situations. For *Shoot the Piano Player*, I had not been able to explain to him why I liked the book, and he wondered why I wanted to make this film. In our first discussion, he wanted to establish social roots for the characters, to situate them socially. I realized that I could not answer his questions, because I felt like making an abstract film. In the script, there were precise references to places in Paris or in France and during the shooting I changed that, I decided to remain abstract; I wanted to say "the town," "the snow," to stress more the Série Noire aspect. There was an attempt on my part to oppose certain French films that adapted novels by James Hadley Chase taking place in America and transposed them to the French Riviera. That transposition was always done in bad taste. I did not want to give French equivalents for the locations. I wanted to remain abstract.

Davis: So Marcel Moussy did not continue.

Truffaut: After a few weeks, we gave up, and we said that we would work together on another script, some other time. Then I went to the Colombe d'Or at Saint Paul de Vence, and I wrote the script alone, up until the part when the characters have to leave Paris, because it was urgent to start shooting.

Davis: How did you develop the character of Fido?

Truffaut: There is a link with the previous film. The little boy had a part in *The 400 Blows*. He was in the classroom, tearing his notebook page by page because he had blotted the pages. Finally he had only three pages left. He made us laugh a lot. Also when he tried out for *The 400 Blows,* he imitated Aznavour. And he has a scene in *Shoot the Piano Player* where he imitates a singer as he walks away from the school.

Davis: How did you choose the other actors?

Truffaut: I had been moved by Aznavour [Charlie] when I saw him in Franju's film *La Tête contre les murs* (*The Keepers*). I liked his face, the way he moved. Nicole Berger [Thérésa] I had known for a long time. She was Braunberger's stepdaughter. She had acted in several films, even, when she was very young, in *Le Blé en herbe* (*The Game of Love*) by Autant-Lara. She was a very sensitive girl, sad and interesting. Michèle Mercier [Clarisse] was not well known. She was a dancer in a few films.

Marie Dubois [Léna] was the result of a search. I was looking for someone to convey the idea of purity. I looked at many actresses and photos. Then Marie Dubois's picture came to my attention, but she never came to our appointments because she was very busy. Her agent told me that she was going to appear on TV and, when I saw her, I was sure she was the right one. She finally came at the last minute. We hardly had time to buy her a raincoat for her part and she started right away. Actually I named her Marie Dubois, because her name was not good for an actress. Her name was Claudine Huzé. [In French *Huzé* is pronounced like *usé,* and means "worn out."] Since I liked that novel by Jacques Audiberti entitled *Marie Dubois,* which is a great portrait of a woman, I proposed that name to her, and she agreed to be named Marie Dubois. And Audiberti was very happy.

Albert Rémy [Chico] was the father in *The 400 Blows,* and I felt like giving him a nice role, because he was my friend and I was embarrassed to have given him this harsh role in *The 400 Blows.* There also was a clown side to him, very innocent, pure comic, which I wanted to show.

The gangsters are Daniel Boulanger [Ernest], who had played a small part in *Breathless* by Godard and was Philippe de Broca's scriptwriter, as well as being a novelist. Claude Mansard [Momo] was from the theater. He had acted in many plays by Ionesco, a very emotional actor. The two gangsters looked like two big cats. I was ill at ease with these gangsters, and it was while shooting the film that I realized that I did not like gangsters. I had grown up in Pigalle and I only had bad memories of them. One night when I was very young, I was alone at home because my parents had gone out. There were guys making noise under my window, so I threw a pan of water on them. They took it badly and came up and kicked the door. I was dying of fear, and I pushed a heavy armoire against the door. When my parents came home I got in trouble because the door had been damaged. Those guys were gangsters. Often there were shots in the middle of the night in Pigalle. It is snobbism on the part of artists to like gangsters. There is no reason to like them, they are bad guys. During the war, they often worked with the Gestapo. That is why I made them comical. I never included gangsters in my later films, even those taken from the Série Noire, like *The Bride Wore Black* and *Mississippi Mermaid.*

"SHOOT THE PIANO PLAYER"
BUDGET REPORT of 12/31/1960

Screenplay—author	Fr	30,000.00
Screenplay—adapters		50,575.00
Screenplay—copies and miscellaneous		7,303.83
Music		5,748.36
Technical direction		5,500.00
Director		24,795.38
Technicians		125,397.66
Principal actors		92,626.65
Secondary actors		15,569.10
Lighting—electricity and equipment		13,191.42
Studio shooting—labor		23,425.86
Dubbing—PA system, auditorium		38,319.51
Sets, furniture		9,788.41
Miscellaneous—expenses for shooting		3,976.89
Editing projection		15,652.36
Cameras—scope		20,589.75
Film—stock for image and sound		20,740.88
Magnetic-strip film stock		18,533.28
Laboratory—work and print		61,956.08
Miscellaneous work		23,367.72
Wardrobe		7,506.82
Miscellaneous exteriors		8,757.78
Transportation and reimbursements		24,412.32
Insurance		37,807.54
Publicity, including photos		45,491.25
Miscellaneous direction costs		12,355.69
Benefits		47,536.21
Miscellaneous—release taxes		10,158.00
Financial expenses		11,402.97
Preparations—screentests— synchronization		15,229.81
Publicity trailers		4,318.00
		831,834.53
7% General expenses		58,228.42
Total cost of the film		890,062.95

This budget report has been translated from a copy of the
original budget given by Truffaut to Hélène Laroche Davis in
1980.

The scene in the street with the passerby is taken from another book by Goodis. The title escapes me. Catherine Lutz [Mammy] had never acted before; I liked her a lot. She worked in a movie theater, I found her beautiful, with a Marlene Dietrich look. Her facial structure was beautiful. She acted again in *Stolen Kisses,* where she was a detective. Serge Davri, who played Plyne, was crazy. I first noticed him in the music hall, where he is still doing the same act after thirty years. He breaks plates on his head as he recites poems. Sometimes he is funny, and sometimes it is a fiasco. He made me laugh, that's why I chose him. But it was difficult to work with him, because some days he refused to work.

Davis: We noticed a difference in the timing of the various copies of *Shoot the Piano Player.* How do you explain that?

Truffaut: People are not accurate in the timing, they print anything. But I did make mistakes and changed a few scenes. I was ashamed of the dialogue in the car [when the gangsters discuss women], which I found too raw. So I put so much traffic noise in the scene that one could not hear the dialogue. People blamed me for it, and I made a second cut where you could hear better. There may be other short scenes cut or moved. There was a scene in which you saw Aznavour in a Monoprix buying a pair of stockings for Marie Dubois. That scene was to be accompanied by a song in the Monoprix, a very famous song by Tino Rossi called "Petit Papa Noel." But it took very long to obtain the rights for this song and, when we finally got them, I was in the middle of editing and I had decided to cut the scene. Probably those timing differences are due to small things like this. It is also very difficult to make films with Pierre Braunberger at the Films de la Pléiade because it is quite disorganized. It often happens that there are several versions of a film. One time *Shoot the Piano Player* was on French television, and for four minutes a scene was shown with the soundtrack from another scene. Nobody noticed, because they thought it was another pretentious experiment of the New Wave. I was furious. But this illustrates the chaos of the Films de la Pléiade and Pierre Braunberger—in spite of his love of cinema, which is real.

Davis: How much did the film cost?

Truffaut: I think the film cost $150,000 at the time.

Davis: So a budget was imposed on you.

Truffaut: Yes, but although I was not working in luxury, it was all right. In black and white we do not pay so much attention. Of course some sets were ugly. Everything was done sparingly. At one point, we needed a cocktail party in the film; we needed a crowd. It was decided to use a cocktail party that had been organized to publicize the film. People had to be filmed secretly.

Davis: In general did those restrictions hinder you?

Truffaut: No. I was rather carefree and happy then. I had made *The 400 Blows* with a lot of anxiety because I was afraid that the film would never come out, that people would say that after having insulted everybody as a critic, I should have stayed home. Whereas *Shoot the Piano Player* was made in euphoria thanks to the success of *The 400 Blows.* It was the discovery of some unusual material that I did not master, that I did not understand. But there was a great pleasure in filming, much greater than in *The 400 Blows,* where I was concerned about Jean-Pierre Léaud. I was wondering if he would show up each day, or if he had had a fight and would have marks on his nose. With children we worry more because they do not have the same self-interest as adults.

I Wanted to Treat *Shoot the Piano Player* like a Tale by Perrault: An Interview with François Truffaut

Yvonne Baby

My critical tendency leads me to work always "in reaction against." Thus, *Shoot the Piano Player* is in reaction against the primitive detective film in which the overemphasis on violence attempts to make up for the lack of talent. I also react against the humanized film noir in which the gangsters look at each other with watery eyes and the honest people act like scum. That's why I showed gangsters who were simultaneously grotesque and sympathetic, but stripped of sentimentality. Instead, there are no privileged persons in the entire *Shoot the Piano Player;* you must love them all equally.

Because spectators see the same scenarios in so many films, they have become good scenarists and can always foretell what's coming and how it's going to end. With *Shoot the Piano Player* I would like them to go from surprise to surprise.

I also wanted to react against the brutality of the idea of the invulnerable "tough guy." Charles Aznavour—whom I wanted to hire since I saw Georges Franju's *La Tête contre les murs*—is vulnerable, and, in spite of his timidity, women are attracted to him.

Baby: What's the real theme of the film?

Truffaut: The love and relations between men and women. Around this story of a piano player who once had been a success, but who chose anonymity after a personal tragedy and now plays an old honky-tonk piano, there is a unity in the theme of love.

The visual action of the film is strictly detective story. So the dialogue never concerns itself with the action but with the relations between men and women in all their modes: sentimental, conjugal, carnal. . . .

Baby: How have you treated the subject?

Truffaut: I systematically practiced a mélange of genres and sometimes I didn't hesitate to parody. For example, the scene in which Nicole Berger throws herself out of the window is a melodramatic and respectful parody of certain American films. In this way I pay homage to the works of Nicholas Ray and Samuel Fuller, to name only two, and more generally to American B movies.

I wanted—it's a structural idea—to delimit the subject in the manner of a tale by Perrault. I had already been struck by the tone of Goodis's novel, which, at a certain point, passes beyond the usual gangster novel to become a fairy tale. *Shoot the Piano Player* isn't made to be believed, but to divert, to amuse.

Translated by Leo Braudy from "J'ai voulu traiter *Tirez sur le pianiste* à la manière d'un conte de Perrault," *Le Monde,* November 24, 1960.

Baby: Do you pay attention to public reaction?

Truffaut: For me the cinema is a show, and I compare a film to an act in the circus, or in a music hall, where for once death spoils the entertainment. There are two kinds of writers: those who think about the public and those who don't. For the first kind, of whom I'm one, a commercial failure is a failure of the whole film. I agree with Hitchcock on this point: when one of his films flops, he says, 'I made a mistake.' That means that *Shoot the Piano Player* is a work for people who love movies; that means it isn't meant for those who go to the movies only once a year.

Baby: Why did you hire an unknown for the principal female role?

Truffaut: The French cinema has at its command a parcel of young actresses less than thirty years old who seem to me to have a dismaying lack of authenticity. These Mylenes, Pascales, Danys, Pierrettes, and Danicks are neither "real" young girls nor "real" women, but "sex kittens," "dames," or "pinups." You have the feeling they were created by the movies and for the movies, and they wouldn't exist if the movies didn't. They appear for a year, sometimes two, and then vanish the way they came. For three seasons the distributors and the producers make you use them in films as if they were stars, when in fact they haven't made one viewer come to the film, and nine times out of ten their personal sophistication threatens the verisimilitude of the role they've been given. That's why I wanted to use an unknown for the principal role in my film. Marie Dubois (her pseudonym is the title of a novel by Jacques Audiberti) is neither a "dame" nor a "sex kitten"; she is neither "lively" nor "saucy." But she's a perfectly worthy young girl with whom it's conceivable you could fall in love and be loved in return. You wouldn't turn around to look at her on the street, but she's fresh and gracious, a little bit of a tomboy, and very childlike. She is violent and passionate, modest and tender.

Baby: Does *Shoot the Piano Player* have anything in common with *The 400 Blows?*

Truffaut: Yes, in the sense that both films follow a character from one end to the other of a story and draw his portrait. In *The 400 Blows* it was Jean-Pierre Léaud; here it's Aznavour. Talking about childhood carries a terrible responsibility and makes you more conscientious. That's no doubt why it was much easier to direct *Shoot the Piano Player* after *The 400 Blows.* I had no qualms about the subject. I wasn't afraid of bad taste or excess. I felt more detached, more gay, more relaxed. There isn't any scene in the film that wasn't made for pleasure.

Baby: Is the film more comic than tragic?

Truffaut: It's both. With *Shoot the Piano Player* I wanted to make women cry and men laugh.

Adapting *Shoot the Piano Player*

François Truffaut

I don't like my films, except the sketch in *Love at Twenty*. I know their problems, their development, the intentions, and the result. Sometimes I'm unhappy with the intentions or the result, but I'm always convinced that I would like them much more if they had been made by someone else, because then I would see only the intentions and the annoyances that occurred in the course of filming. Abel Gance says that when you make a film, you get onto the screen 10 percent of what you wanted to do, although I wouldn't make it the same proportion. Perhaps my dreams are less frenzied than Gance's, but I do believe that I achieve on the screen only part of what I wanted to do, and in the case of *Shoot the Piano Player,* it's very hazy. Yet, as a spectator seeing the film, I'd love it because I like what's gone into it. I prefer American films that are dubbed and that's the feeling I get from this film. Everything that people do and say, all their intentions, the little cabin—I just adore it. In fact, I know it's not normal for them to go out in the snow in the middle of the day and then suddenly talk about going and hiding (we had so many problems with this film), but in fact, speaking as a critic, I like that better than "successful" films that don't agree with my state of mind.

I couldn't adapt a film from a book I hated. Even if I didn't like the style of a book, I could try to tell myself: "The style doesn't matter; it's the facts that count." But you can't do that. Because the irritation that style brings out in me sprouts so well that each time a producer gives me a book to read, even if there is a synopsis, I have to say no, because the resumé that somebody else makes never seems to me to have any flesh and I think that a book can be adapted only for its stylistic qualities. It's a little dangerous to talk about how an image is equivalent, but still . . . I like a lot of things in Goodis: characters, actions, and the style he writes in. For example, Thérésa's confession before she commits suicide is something I would be incapable of writing or even imagining. If some scriptwriter friend brought it to me, I'd refuse it . . . and still she's what she is. She is exactly as she is in the book. But sometimes there is more than one influence . . . I remember that I wanted to do the book because I admired it. At the time of *The 400 Blows* and all the euphoria at Cannes, I told Braunberger that there was a book I really wanted to do, which I really enjoyed when I read it several years before; I also liked Aznavour very much and thought, well, if we can put two good things together, let's do it! Braunberger bought the rights and made a contract with Aznavour. Subsequently, as I was rereading the book, I realized that I had made a reckless

Excerpted and translated by Leo Braudy from "Ce qu'a dit François Truffaut," *Cinéma 67* 112 (January 1967): 41–44.

decision. The book really required a very strong character, a character with physical presence like Sterling Hayden. And the famous scene when he kills Plyne in the bar is a scene that had been based on the principle of the strong man toying with his prey without taking advantage of it; but the other man (Plyne) has a knife and the main character has to kill him in spite of himself.

This whole idea dissolved because of the choice of Aznavour. I was tormented for several days. Then I changed direction. That's why I contacted Marie Dubois for the role of Léna. I said to myself: "You have to go to the exact opposite and take a girl who will be stronger than he and who will carry him on her shoulders, this guy who's as light as a feather. That opposition would clear everything up." And we were able to work it out. Sometimes there were still other influences. When I saw the film again, I remembered that there's a whole part of Aznavour's relationship with Nicole Berger that's influenced by Moravia's *Contempt*. It's the story of a woman who has facilitated her husband's success; he thinks she's contemptuous of him. This appears in the first scenes with Nicole Berger. That's why you can say that this genre of film is an amalgam, filled with references to the American films I've loved. The strongest influence was Nicholas Ray's *Johnny Guitar*.

The adaptation was made very casually. The end in the snow was worked out among ourselves. Albert Rémy, Daniel Boulanger, and I were sitting around a table and wondering who's going to shoot whom. Down there the cold weather had taken its toll of the cast, and we decided to shoot with those who weren't sick. Finally we quickly killed off the ones who had to go back to Paris. The whole end was made that way, with the one exception that, despite the friendly insistence of Braunberger, I had planned to have Marie Dubois die; so beforehand I had filmed the small section of the final scene where there's a new waitress.

Another influence was Audiberti. I was rather sad that he hadn't liked *The 400 Blows,* and that he hadn't dared tell me. In general, he liked everything and never rejected anything. One day he told me: there's a Simenon aspect there that bothers me. It also lacks something else, the idea that it's only a story." I thought about Audiberti during the filming of *Shoot the Piano Player,* and a part of Plyne's character is clearly influenced by him. I said to myself: "This one has to be a character like Audiberti, who has a completely magical idea of young people." At that moment there's a reversal in the film. You realize that the sympathetic and timid little guy isn't so shy after all and copes pretty well, and that the true victim of Society is someone who puts women on a pedestal, like Audiberti and the bar owner had. There the film is more influenced by Audiberti's own character than by his books.

It's not necessary to look for reality in *Shoot the Piano Player*—neither in the Armenian family in the snow near Grenoble, nor in the bar in Levallois-Perret (there's really no dancing in that kind of bar). All I wanted was the pleasure of mixing things together to see whether or not they were miscible. I strongly believe in this idea of mixing. I think it controls everything.

I don't want to compare the two films at all—mine is a *divertissement*—but I think that in *Hiroshima, mon amour* Resnais's pleasure was to see if you could mix the story of the atomic bomb with the story of a girl in Nevers who had her hair sheared at the Liberation because she slept with a German. Resnais wanted to see if the two things were miscible, his work then being to make them mix. But it couldn't be accepted in that film. The idea of acceptance is also important. Otherwise you could do anything, leave the screen white, or leave it black. Your interest, when you make that kind of bet, is to win.

Should Films Be Politically Committed?
François Truffaut

Why did you make this film? What relation does it have to you? How are you attached to it?

It's a film that singularly lacks any *raison d'être* . . . in the exact sense that one couldn't make the same charge about my first film, *The 400 Blows*.

When I made *The 400 Blows* I economized on the film stock, the lighting, and the studio time because I had no reason to think it would be a commercial success. I was very conscious about that: I was making a little French film on the same scale as Leenhardt's *Les Dernières Vacances*, Lucot's *Les Dieux du Dimanche*, Riera's *La Grande Vie*, or Wheeler's *Les Premières Armes*. It was, therefore, a little French film that was neither erotic nor a detective story, likeable and gently encouraged by the press, but a film that people wouldn't go see. The success of *The 400 Blows* was a total surprise for me and I attribute it to a series of extraordinary coincidences: its selection for the Cannes Film Festival (what would have happened to the film if it had been finished in November of the preceding year?), the birth of the New Wave (I benefited from *The Lovers, Hiroshima, mon amour, The Cousins*), that year's crisis in French production, etc. I therefore saw this modest family enterprise suddenly become a great international film that was picked up by all sorts of associations, groups, organizers of galas—how could I know?

The film escaped from my hands and became something academic that I didn't recognize anymore.

It belonged to a public that doesn't like movies, to the spectator who goes to the movies twice a year, the public of René Clair and *The Bridge on the River Kwai*, which I dread most in the world. With my second film I felt myself being watched, waited for, by this public, and I really wanted to send them all packing. I had a number of projects for films with children; I put them all aside since I didn't want to seem to be exploiting a trick that worked well before. This time I wanted to please the real film nuts and them alone, while leading astray a large part of those who liked *The 400 Blows*. Maybe everybody was led astray by the piano player, but so much the worse.

I refused to be a prisoner of my first success. I discarded the temptation to renew that success by choosing a "great subject." I turned my back on what everyone waited for and I took *my pleasure* as my only rule of conduct. You won't

Translated by Leo Braudy from "Questions à l'auteur," *Cinéma 61* 52 (January 1961): 7–11. This selection is an extract from a discussion that followed the showing of *Shoot the Piano Player* to members of the French Federation of Ciné-Clubs.

find any exposition scene in *Shoot the Piano Player* (nothing useful: everything is there for my pleasure as a filmmaker and I hope for your pleasure as a spectator).

I was free as a breeze. Therefore I chose some limit so that I wouldn't go crazy. I put myself in the position of a filmmaker who had orders imposed on him: a detective novel, American, that was to be transposed to France. Nevertheless, I chose *Shoot the Piano Player* because I admired the author, David Goodis; perhaps you movie lovers know his novel *Dark Passage,* which was made into a film by Delmer Daves and starred Humphrey Bogart and Lauren Bacall, or Paul Wendkos's film of *The Burglar* with Jayne Mansfield and Dan Duryea. Ever since I saw *La Tête contre les murs,* I wanted to make a film with Aznavour; now I would reconcile two dreams by uniting Goodis and Aznavour.

I know that the result seems ill-assorted and the film seems to contain four or five films, but that's what I wanted. Above all I was looking for the explosion of a genre (the detective film) by mixing genres (comedy, drama, melodrama, the psychological film, the thriller, the love film, etc.). I know that the public detests nothing more than changes in tone, but I've always had a passion for changing tone. The shot I like best in *Zazie dans le métro* is Albertine's tears. But I do think that there's a coherence in *Shoot the Piano Player:* love. In the film men talk only about women and women talk only about men; in the most strenuous brawls, settlings of accounts, kidnapping, pursuits, everyone talks only about love: sexual, sentimental, physical, moral, social, marital, extramarital, etc.

In spite of the burlesque side to certain scenes, it's never a parody (because I detest parody except when it begins to rival the beauty of what it's parodying). For me it's something very precise that I would call a *respectful pastiche* of the Hollywood B films from which I learned so much.

Infancy isn't the only subject. Why avoid the great problems of our time? You could always stay a film critic!

You can say my film's useless, a failure, nothing, anything you want, but I don't recognize your right to tell me that I ought to make another film in its place, or treat this or that subject. You have to judge the film I show you, that's all. I hate the kind of articles that are appearing more and more in the newspapers, which totally condemn various films of the New Wave because of the themes they've treated. The great problems of our time? I don't know the answers to them; many more intelligent, cultivated, and able people than I have broken their heads on these things you want me to mix into. I'm talking only about the things I know or I think I know. In point of fact I could undertake a film about the Algerian war if I wanted to. But I don't want to, because the reality of it is too complex for me and I could only make a negative film, a purely negative film that would add to the confusion. Apart from Algeria I'm also interested in Hitler, in the concentration camps, and in racism; I read all the books that come out on those subjects. When a journalist asks why don't the young filmmakers make a film about Algeria, I'd like to answer: "Why don't you write a book about Algeria?

Because you wouldn't know what to write? O.K., imagine that I wouldn't know what to film!"

Deportation fascinates me. How you get deported isn't complicated; what's strange is how you become a "deporter," how and why *everyone* can find it normal to deport or to see other people deported. I've read so many books about the camps that it seems to me that I could make a film about them. But I think for a minute: what's a deportee? A sixty-six-pound man. Look, sixty-six-pound characters can't act; to select skinny walk-ons as in *Le Bal des maudits* is pure infamy. The margin of cheating between a skinny walk-on and a deportee is blasphemous and unacceptable. A documentary film is the only solution, and there Resnais has made *the* film that it was necessary to make, the only one possible, the greatest film I have ever seen [*Night and Fog*]. Some imbecile wrote that *The 400 Blows* was a film against public schools because the teacher was overridden by the events. If I had been raised by the Jesuits, I would have been given the "Lay Office Prize," if it existed.

Let me tell you of my contempt for certain "great subjects." For me, Stanley Kramer is an outrageous schemer and his films, *The Defiant Ones* or the other about the atomic bomb [*On the Beach*], are the work of an ass. Can a white love a black and vice versa? Don't make me laugh! The person who treats a subject like that must not be very convinced himself by the answer; if he were, he wouldn't make the film. I'll go further: to talk about things like that is indecent. . . . Naturally, if the same subject had been done by Renoir, it would interest me.

One can talk about "great problems" only with a terrific sincerity, so that it really stops you from sleeping at night; it won't be decided from the outside. Autant-Lara came back from Yugoslavia, where he made a film on conscientious objection (thanks to me, who proved to him that censorship didn't exist), but he will always be for me the director of *La Jument verte* and therefore an imposter. If he wasn't an imposter, if he was an "auteur" of films, he would have moved away from the nobility in *La Jument verte* and the lewdness in *L'Objecteur* because there is no noble or ignoble genre, there is no genre, I say, as *Shoot the Piano Player* proves, and I'm going to finish by praising it myself even if you spit on it.

Be logical, sir. When you reproach me for making *Shoot the Piano Player* and not some great "generous" film, you are reproaching me for having lacked generosity. But look: if, being what I am, what you see me to be, I had externally taken on a "great subject" as your heart wants me to, I would have been insincere, since I had in my heart a sleeping *Shoot the Piano Player*. Therefore, this general film that I haven't made, wouldn't it be like Kramer's horrible films that I was just talking about: international blablabla, misused cinema? Now you see I was right to make the film I made; in any case that's the one I ask you to judge and not the imaginary one that I hope I'll be able to make someday.

From an Interview with François Truffaut

In one sense, I made *Shoot the Piano Player* in reaction to *The 400 Blows,* because the success of the film, the imbalance that I suddenly discovered [between the sympathy accorded the child and the antagonism toward the parents], so flabbergasted me that I said to myself: "I must pay attention, I must not fall into demagoguery." But I don't really understand very well what happened in *Shoot the Piano Player.* In the final analysis, I had to be too faithful to the book. I was too sure of myself, because of the success of *The 400 Blows.* But I think that's a law of the second film. Thus, *A Woman Is a Woman* (because *Le Petit Soldat* was banned, I consider the other to be Godard's second film) is done in the euphoria of *Breathless. My Life to Live* is a complete recovery.

In a first film, you take the plunge: let's go, I'm risking everything; after this I may not make any more films, but for now I want to see how this will turn out. The reaction to the first film is very important. If it succeeds, one is always astonished. The second shows this. *Last Year at Marienbad* too shows a great self-confidence, born of an unexpected success. All these second films have this in common: they are less complete than the first, in which there was a whole beginning of life to express, when you wanted to say everything. The second film becomes intentionally more modest in design. It's the third that's the most interesting: it's a reflection on what happened in the other two and marks the start of a career.

If you think about *Shoot the Piano Player,* you see the scenario doesn't stand up under analysis. It really lacks a directing idea. There is a directing idea in both my other films. In *The 400 Blows,* it's a question of presenting as honestly as possible a child who has been guided by a moral stand. The same goes for *Jules and Jim:* if you did it this way, it would be porno; like this, indelicate; like this, conventional; so it's necessary to make it in a different way. The mistake in *Shoot the Piano Player* is that you can do anything with it; it's material whose form doesn't impose itself. Aznavour has terrific comic power: I could have made a comic film. He has great authority: the character could have been ferocious. At the start I didn't have any set purpose, only a crazy desire to use Aznavour, because of *La Tête contre les murs;* but it would have been better if I had known him for a long time. The really courageous thing I've done in *Shoot the Piano Player* is to use flashbacks, while knowing that they are never forgiven. I said to Braunberger: "Remember *Les Mauvais Rencontres?* and *Lola Montès?* And *The Barefoot Contessa?* Those didn't work because of the flashbacks. Well, we'll treat ourselves to two of them, one inside the other." In fact, that throws everything up in the air.

Excerpted and translated by Leo Braudy from "Entretien avec François Truffaut," *Cahiers du Cinéma* 138 (December 1962): 49–51.

It's a law: you can't mix things up. You can't be fully in one story and fully in another. If you worked at it a little, *Shoot the Piano Player* could be narrated in chronological fashion. You have to work at it. There are good things in the film, but no one can say: this is the best that's been done on this theme. There is no theme.

What about this one: a man is caught in the gears of life, rejects them, and, at the end, resigns himself to them. Courage, cowardice . . . ?

Even if you accept that, there are parasitic things in the film. And also there's the director who resigns himself to entering the gears of a gangster film! I didn't think of it beforehand, but while I shot *Shoot the Piano Player,* I saw that I abhorred gangster films. Now I wouldn't write laudatory articles about *Rififi.* I believe you don't have to create sympathetic gangsters, weeping truants, or set up the nice people against the nasty ones. If you do that, you get a film in which all the bourgeois conventions are transposed into the gangster world. That's why I decided to make my gangsters comic: it was the only solution if I didn't want to fall into conventionality—and I made fun of them a little. To make up for that, it was necessary that they be a little frightening, an effect I achieved through the boy's kidnapping and the death of Marie Dubois. That reawakened the people who otherwise would have believed that they were dealing with English puppets. But it's dangerous to change ideas in the course of a film. You should have an idea at the start and then strengthen it, as I did in my two other films, where the idea was originally poorly expressed in the scenario. If I had known beforehand that Aznavour and Nicole Berger would make an extraordinary couple (he worked less well with the others than with her), I would have made a film about the two of them.

Another thing must have offended the public in Shoot the Piano Player: *the rupture of tone that characterizes several films that didn't work—*A Woman Is a Woman *for one—and it's something the French public has never accepted.*

Yes, that's the most difficult thing to get by. In any case people in America understand *Shoot the Piano Player,* but differently; they laughed without stopping, even in the dramatic passages. The first song is comic, but they laughed all through the second, which theoretically is not.

Anyway, you can say what you like to me, but *Shoot the Piano Player* still needs a month of work. Mix together two or three reels of film that you like, and you won't get a film that will interest people, even if there are good things in it. It's true that change of tone is a thing to work for; it's a gamble that has to be tried sometimes, and Renoir has succeeded in doing it.

Reviews

The reviews that follow have been chosen from French, British, and American sources and demonstrate that Truffaut's film was widely misunderstood—and widely admired—in all three countries when it first appeared. What struck most reviewers was the film's clash of genre and tone, as well as its other apparent absurdities, and the reviewers' appreciation or dislike of the film seems, to a revealing degree, to have been largely a subjective matter.

Cinéma 60
Alain Vargas

Pierre Braunberger presents Charles Aznavour in a film by François Truffaut, adapted from David Goodis's Shoot the Piano Player.

T hus begin, almost to the last detail, the credits of the second full-length film by the auteur of *The 400 Blows*.

Why *Shoot the Piano Player?* In the first place, by and for Charles Aznavour. When Truffaut had a presentiment of the distinctive character—something between a James Dean and a Charlie Chaplin—that this composer/singer could become, he had not yet abandoned film criticism, that last resort that isn't even a means of subsistence. Truffaut had this vision even though Aznavour was highly controversial and considered incapable of playing comic roles, according to the generally held definition of comedy—an attitude that is really meaningless, since what good is acting, or worse, knowing how to act, when it's essentially a question of being alive?

In the second place, the movie was made for David Goodis, Truffaut's favorite detective story writer. Hardly had Truffaut read *Shoot the Piano Player* than a fantastic runaway car scene seized his imagination, and he thought immediately of Aznavour to play it.

La Tête contre les murs and *Les Dragueurs* thus must have satisfied Truffaut, insofar as Aznavour was a revelation to even the most blasé or skeptical eyes, but they also must have disappointed him insofar as Franju (who nevertheless has the honor of really having helped Aznavour make his screen debut) and Mocky were using him in only one key, hieratic or clownlike, according to the situation. No matter what differences there are between them, there was in some way in Aznavour the material of a Sinatra.

And so it is that "Charlie, 32 years old, a piano player," hard and vulnerable, resembling both a clown and a Franciscan monk, becomes active rather than passive, seduces women instead of being seduced, and drives others to suicide instead of being suicidal. To like an actor is quite simply a matter of wanting to reveal him to himself, while revealing him simultaneously to the public, in an entirely new, unexpected light. The filming of several scenes that I was able to watch, and the rushes I saw, inclined me to think that both of them have already profited. I would bet that words like heartrending, poetic, charismatic, and pathetic will certainly appear again and again in the writings of our high-flown critics as the four qualities that best describe the performance of my friend Charlie, as the father of Zazie would say.

Translated by Leo Braudy from *Cinéma 60* 44 (March 1960): 31–35.

Truffaut initially had hoped to film *Shoot the Piano Player* entirely in the studio, following the example of Visconti's *White Nights,* which had fascinated him so. But he abandoned this idea after seeing the cost of, for example, stage models, scenery, and transparencies triple his projected budget. During the six weeks between Pigalle and not Place Blanche but Place de Levallois, from the Prisunic to the Hotel d'Orsay, all the images of *Shoot the Piano Player* were shot in Dyaliscope black and white by Raoul Coutard, that adventurer in Cameflex who photographed *La Passe du diable* and the newest film of the New Wave, Jean-Luc Godard's *Breathless.*

The script that Truffaut uses here is similar to that of *The 400 Blows:* both have almost no technical directions. Nevertheless one can't totally accept the criticism-manifesto he made about the admirable *Passions Juveniles,* although it's an excellent brief for what he's done himself: "the direction is largely improvised, full of ideas that were unpredictable before filming, and obviously so spontaneous that one wouldn't know how to indicate them in a script." As spontaneous as his improvisations may appear to an unprepared spectator, they are born in the fire of rehearsals or successive takes, and thus frequently at least are very premeditated. Only the person who wishes to be mystified will be.

Truffaut is more relaxed than he had been for *The 400 Blows.* Not that he had been in an impossible mood then, but now he no longer risks his career on a first full-length film; he does not have to direct children in this film; and he has a certain confidence derived from the public and critical success of *The 400 Blows* (acclaimed by people as diverse as Buñuel, Rossellini, Franju, Welles, Gene Kelly, Lang, Resnais, Cocteau, Renoir, Becker), all of which relieved him of certain worries.

But does this mean that *Shoot the Piano Player*—a work of relaxation between *The 400 Blows,* which he had inside him for so long before he unburdened himself, and *Le Bleu d'outre-tombe* [*The Blue Beyond the Grave;* a project that was never completed] (for and by Jeanne Moreau, in June), which is presently his most cherished project—will be more the work of a director than an auteur?

No, despite whatever its . . . auteur may say or think. Truffaut, in fact, will never make anything but autobiographical films. I don't mean films in which he will describe his life—Antoine Doinel/Jean-Pierre Léaud is and is not the adolescent Truffaut was—but films in which he *will speak only about what he knows and likes.*

Thus *Shoot the Piano Player,* like *The 400 Blows* before and *Jules and Jim* later (once again Jeanne Moreau), will exalt a *cult of friendship* under the guise of fraternity—one of the keys to François Truffaut the man in both his public and his private lives, despite the slanderous legend of his unpleasantly careerist nature. His friends would attest to this without any obligation; it wouldn't be the first time that a hypersensitive person was accused of heartlessness, nor would he be the first sufferer to be called cold-blooded.

Nicole Berger and Charles Aznavour relaxing on the set

Thus *Shoot the Piano Player* will demonstrate, with disquieting yet warm insistence, a great truth: Truffaut's inner alliance of intimacy and genuine poetic realism; the *moral* and *epidermal* relations of a timid, unstable, maladjusted (shall I say characterial?) man with several women; the slow and unavoidable disintegration of a couple whose driving element, the man, passes from semipoverty to wealth, from semipenury to opulence, and from semianonymity to celebrity.

You can read in the details of *Shoot the Piano Player* Truffaut's love for music halls. From the Alhambra to the Cheval d'Or, passing through les Trois-Baudets or Bobino, there is no club or bar that he doesn't visit regularly. After movies he loves music halls best in the entire world. He confided in me one day that if it happened for some reason or another that he could no longer be involved in films (either as a critic or a director), he would like to write a music hall column. It was there in a music hall, in a cabaret,[1] that he decided to cast Jean Constantin as his composer (*The 400 Blows, Shoot the Piano Player*). Also from cabarets came the

1. "Formerly, the best school for actors was the café-concert. Today there are no more café-concerts, but it's in the cabaret, the many nightclubs, that you can unearth the stars of the future. And the touring company, with its precarious way of life when it has a young troupe, is the best place to meet the movie stars of tomorrow" [Jean Renoir, recently].

actors Charles Aznavour, Pierre Repp, and Henri Virlogeux (the English teacher and the night watchman in *The 400 Blows,* in which Dufhilo, another cabaret person, had a scene cut out in the editing); and Serge Davri, "Plyne the tightwad," an astonishing character, the counterpart of Jean Hersholt (the informer in *Greed*), and dish breaker emeritus; and Boby LaPointe, whose light and vulgar songs will be hummed all over after *Shoot the Piano Player.*

Also around Charles Aznavour will be Michèle Mercier (Clarisse), whom the former critic of *Arts* [Truffaut] was the first to praise in her first screen appearance (*Retour de Manivelle*); Nicole Berger (Thérésa), shown here as never before; Marie Dubois (Léna), former pupil of Henri Rollan at the Conservatory, discovered on television, named by Audiberti, and a new star people will talk about; Catherine Lutz (Mammy), whom all the BBC projection room regulars know very well; Albert Rémy, Richard Kanayan, and Jean-Jacques Aslanian (Charlie's brothers); Claude Heymann (the impresario); Alex Joffé; and finally, the "American stars," saving the best for last, the duo of killers, Daniel Boulanger, the ubu-esque cop from *Breathless,* the script and dialogue writer for *The Love Game* (formerly *Suzanne et les roses*), the first feature by Philippe de Broca, produced by Chabrol; and Claude Mansard, right now the best French-made actor and the fetish of the new lords, since he's been seen in *The Lovers, La Tête contre les murs, The 400 Blows,* and *Breathless.*

Cinéma 61
Marcel Martin

Waiting now for the reception of his first film since he received the prize for direction at Cannes in 1959 for *The 400 Blows*, François Truffaut risks seeing himself summarily executed with the release of *Shoot the Piano Player*, for good reasons as well as bad ones.

The good reasons, or at least the seemingly good ones, assert that the subject of *Shoot the Piano Player* will seem narrower and more frivolous after *The 400 Blows*. On this point Truffaut explains himself perfectly, and he does it with such evident conviction that no one could think to reproach him with wanting to remain the prisoner of a genre nor force his inspiration and his talent to attack the great problems of the day. It is certainly normal that critics and the enlightened public both want to find in films the reflection of their political, social, and human preoccupations. It's one of the most frequent reproaches that has reasonably been made to the New Wave—that they forget we are in 1960, that grave problems have been posed to us today, and that the cinema must not be only a means of escape, under pain of becoming sterile.

Certainly, with this point of view, there will be a general disappointment with *Shoot the Piano Player*. And yet one has to admit that the universal and unanimous success of *The 400 Blows* has been a little unexpected. It is evident that the film has completely escaped from its director and is repeatedly crowned in private by groups that one does not expect to find so enthusiastic, but who have the habit of "annexation." That the film has had the Catholic International Office of Cinema prize bestowed on it at Cannes, and more recently the Grand Prize of the Week of Religious Cinema at Valladolid, did not fail to embarrass, if not to surprise, those who found in *The 400 Blows* a tone of bruised tenderness and an almost hopeless distress and those who had seen in it, in any case, more a cry of anarchist revolt than a breviary of moral edification.

I don't think that François Truffaut wanted this. You might say that this moving film, once it left him, after a creative act of undoubted sincerity, truly escaped from him and took on an unforeseen importance and resonance. And, therefore, it's not bad that *Shoot the Piano Player* will disappoint all those who burned incense before *The 400 Blows*, and, for the bad reasons I've just pointed out, attempted to imprison the author in a conformist but edifying universe that is clearly not his own.

Be assured that these same people, after they detest his second film because it doesn't correspond to their expectations, will be blind to the unbounded sensibility

Translated by Leo Braudy from "*Le Pianiste* de Truffaut," *Cinéma 61*, 52 (January 1961): 5–7.

and especially the remarkable sense of cinema that it shows. Such a film clearly offers us, by methods far removed from those of a Resnais or a Godard, moments of intense and profound cinematic pleasure. I am not far, myself, from preferring it to *The 400 Blows* for precisely this reason of pleasure, and for something else in addition, which may be surprising but which I hope the spectator will think about: *Shoot the Piano Player* contains fewer commercial formulas and less glibness—"commercial" isn't a pejorative judgment but a statement of fact—than *The 400 Blows*. *The 400 Blows* had everything necessary to attract a vast public; *Shoot the Piano Player,* I'm afraid, will only please the true lover of movies.

François Truffaut says that he wished to make his film an homage to the American B film. And certainly he got closer to those films not only by his subject (taken from a detective novel by David Goodis), but also, on the brilliant and detached side, by his ability to go beyond and transfigure his subject by extremely careful direction, and especially by a sense of cinema that appears in the unusual intensity of his magisterial use of CinemaScope, in the poetry of the camera movement and the dissolves, in the fascinating presences of Aznavour and Nicole Berger—in a word, by a "charm," in the strongest sense of the word, that is freed from any images and situations that deny the lightness and the detachment of his purpose.

Truffaut tells us: "I wished to make a respectful pastiche of the lesser American cinema." He has succeeded perfectly, but it's clear that one must love the "lesser American cinema" if one is to love his film. I mean that one must sometimes look on the screen not for a Cartesian story that leads to a demonstrable conclusion, but for isolation and action, and especially a little dream and fantasy, a little vertigo, and a little poetry.

What I've said here doesn't constitute proper and well-formed "criticism." I have no other aim than to prepare the spectator to sample a film that will not win the Grand Prize at Cannes, but that will delight the real connoisseurs.

The New Yorker
Edith Oliver

I n *Shoot the Piano Player,* a brilliant and original French movie, François Truffaut, who wrote and directed it, uses every conceivable kind of comic idea—human and technical—to tell a sad story about a honky-tonk pianist in a cheap café in Paris. All the jokes and surprises work. Movement is accelerated, then stopped to living statues; a bottle of milk is splashed on the windshield of a car, and we look through it at the white-smeared city streets; a finger on a doorbell, blown up to gigantic size, becomes a surrealist picture; there are photographic puns and Keystone chases. But the real triumph is the irony that pervades the film. An intimate scene is played at an open window, through which pour all the air and sunshine and traffic noises of Paris; a farmhouse that Grandma Moses could have painted becomes the background for gunfire. As you can see, the movie is made of fragments, some dim and mysterious, some sharp. Much in the way of meaning and feelings is hinted at, but little is set down squarely.

Only when the picture is over does the design, and even the plot, become clear. The pianist is a quiet, timid, girl-shy fellow, once a promising concert musician whose career was suddenly cut short. Now he wants only to be left in peace. He is frightened of violence, yet he is constantly being drawn into it, and is himself responsible, directly and indirectly, for several violent deaths. It all may sound very gloomy in synopsis—and, of course, it is—but somehow it is also terribly funny. M. Truffaut, who made *Shoot the Piano Player* after *The 400 Blows* and before *Jules and Jim,* has compounded humor, imagination, logic and illogic, beauty, nonsense, and pain into a completely satisfying piece of work. He handles his actors skillfully, and he has assembled some good ones. All the performances are right, and, as the pianist, Charles Aznavour, who looks like a young Irving Berlin, is just about perfect.

From *The New Yorker,* August 4, 1962, p. 50.

Variety
"Mosk"

rançois Truffaut, an ex–highbrow film critic, was responsible for one of the most touching among the "New Wave" pix with his *400 Blows*. This second film is done with the same freewheeling, inventive quality. But with adult heroes the plot is less clear and has a tendency to skirt its theme; storyline, too, goes off in too many directions and moods.

Truffaut still displays an unusual visual fair. The production is strewn with excellent scenes and revealing, incisive statements. But it floats between a gangster opus and a tale about a timid young man whose inability to act leads to the destruction of the women in his life.

Charlie (Charles Aznavour) is a pianist in a little bar. The waitress, who loves him, reveals she knows he was once a noted concert pianist before his inability to forgive his wife, who had had an affair with his sleazy impresario. He is content to play in the bar until his brother brings in two gangsters whom he has double-crossed.

The gangsters take out after Charlie and eventually slay the waitress. Charlie also inadvertently kills his boss in self-defense. He goes back to his piano and a new serving girl after it is all over.

Truffaut leaves too much that is not clear as he concentrates on individual scenes. Using a CinemaScope-like process, Dyaliscope, he still manages to give this a terse quality in keeping with the hero's own prison he has created within himself. But the meandering script only intermittently makes its point. However, his offbeat technical aspects still give this enough quality to make it a possible arty theater entry abroad. The aimless progression may make it more difficult for subsequent-runs.

Aznavour is excellent as the pianist in making himself felt despite the negative quality of his timidity. Truffaut still seems one of the most endowed among the "Wavers." And when he gets down to more uncluttered plots, he should be an important part of the film scene here.

Technical credits are good with on-the-spot lensing a help.

From *Variety,* August 31, 1960, pp. 4, 16.

Sight and Sound
Peter John Dyer

T he Festival's most obvious disappointment lies in the apparently complete
lack of impact made by *The 400 Blows* on this year's French entries. Like
some stiff and staring corpse, *Moderato Cantabile* has wandered through
the night in search of its cultural burial place—one of those weekend country
houses, last inhabited by *Les Amants,* where chandeliers and conversation tinkle
and Jeanne Moreau displays agonized composure. Chabrol, another night-bird,
has abandoned the idealism of *Le Beau Serge* and the (albeit subconscious)
disclosure of *Les Cousins* for a particularly nasty exercise in True Love pulp
fiction. Truffaut himself has gone dashing back to base and emerged, still fascinating and unnervingly talented, with the freak flop of the year, an archetypal *Cahiers*
antic disarmingly entitled *Shoot the Piano Player.*

It would be much too easy, and absurdly premature, to write off Truffaut purely
on the evidence of *Shoot the Piano Player.* Undisciplined, Hollywood-influenced,
confused to the point of anarchy, outrageously funny ("May my mother drop dead
if I'm lying," a gangster solemnly swears, and, in a funereally framed cut-in,
mother keels over dead as mutton), this infuriating film has two redeeming
features. The first, carried over from *The 400 Blows,* is its unsentimentally autobiographical flavor. Shy, secretive and withdrawn, the pianist hero so touchingly
played by Charles Aznavour has a striking resemblance, in both temperament and
appearance, to Truffaut himself. So that, if one delves a little deeper into the
workings of a typically devious *Cahiers* mind, all puckish iconoclasm and brusque
inattention to conventional niceties coupled with a passion for far-fetched analogy, one could well draw certain parallels. One might even be disposed to identify
the celebrated Truffaut of *The 400 Blows* with Edouard Saroyan, ex–concert
pianist, masquerading through force of circumstances as Charlie the café musician, friend and relative of gangsters: in other words the Truffaut of *Shoot the
Piano Player,* marking time, churning out B-picture extravagances and satisfying
the *Cahiers* crowd.

It would be foolish to try to labor this point (it is, at best, a rationalist's conceit),
but I would seriously suggest that this film's autobiographical hints are encourag-
ing. They would seem to indicate that Truffaut still has much that is subjective to
get out of his system; and I would personally rather see him expending his
obsessions on one (or two, or even three) apprentice, experimental pieces like
Shoot the Piano Player than turning something more ambitious into a technician's
field day. For, at the moment, it is the film's second redeeming feature, its

From *Sight and Sound* 30, no. 1 (Winter 1960–1961), 18.

intense, perfervid feeling for cinema, that strikes me as Truffaut's greatest potential danger. Though *Shoot the Piano Player*'s sheer professional grasp triumphantly extinguishes any lingering suspicions that *The 400 Blows* may have been a
piece of "unconscious" filmmaking (in comparison with *Hiroshima, mon amour*),
it is nevertheless something of a Pyrrhic victory. Sequences of extraordinary
brilliance flash past with a prodigality that soon defeats itself. They simply stick to
the screen. The film ends, and within hours one realizes that nothing has stayed in
the mind but the plot (or as much of it as one has managed to follow), which is
patently rubbish.

Film Culture
Pauline Kael

The cover of David Goodis's novel *Down There,* now issued by Grove Press under the title of the film adapted from it, *Shoot the Piano Player,* carries a statement from Henry Miller—"Truffaut's film was so good I had doubts the book could equal it. I have just read the novel and I think it is even better than the film." I don't agree with Miller's judgment. I like the David Goodis book, but it's strictly a work in a limited genre, well done and consistent; Truffaut's film busts out all over—and that's what's wonderful about it. The film is comedy, pathos, tragedy all scrambled up—much I think as most of us really experience them (surely all our lives are filled with comic horrors) but not as we have been led to expect them in films.

Shoot the Piano Player is about a man who has withdrawn from human experience; he wants not to care any more, not to get involved, not to *feel.* He has reduced life to a level on which he can cope with it—a reverie between him and the piano. Everything that happens outside his solitary life seems erratic, accidental, unpredictable—but he can predict the pain. In a flashback we see why: when he *did* care, he failed the wife who needed him and caused her death. In the course of the film he is once more brought back into the arena of human contacts; another girl is destroyed, and he withdraws again into solitude.

Truffaut is a free and inventive director—and he fills the piano player's encounters with the world with good and bad jokes, bits from old Sacha Guitry films, clowns and thugs, tough kids, songs and fantasy and snow scenes, and homage to the American gangster films—not the classics, the socially conscious big-studio gangster films of the 1930s, but the grade-B gangster films of the 1940s and 1950s. Like Godard, who dedicated *Breathless* to Monogram Pictures, Truffaut is young, and he loves the cheap American gangster films of his childhood and youth. And like them, *Shoot the Piano Player* was made on a small budget. It was also made outside of studios with a crew that, according to witnesses, sometimes consisted of Truffaut, the actors, and a cameraman. Part of his love of cheap American movies with their dream imagery of the American gangster—the modern fairy tales for European children who go to movies—is no doubt reflected in his taking an American underworld novel and transferring its setting from Philadelphia to France.

Charles Aznavour, who plays the hero, is a popular singer turned actor—rather like Frank Sinatra in this country, and, like Sinatra, he is an instinctive actor and a

From *I Lost It at the Movies* (Boston: Atlantic–Little, Brown, 1965), pp. 189–194. This article first appeared in *Film Culture.*

great camera subject. Aznavour's piano player is like a tragic embodiment of Robert Hutchins's Zukerkandl philosophy (whatever it is, stay out of it): he is the thinnest-skinned of modern heroes. It is his own capacity to feel that makes him cut himself off: he experiences so sensitively and so acutely that he can't bear the suffering of it—he thinks that if he doesn't do anything he won't feel and he won't cause suffering to others. The girl, Marie Dubois—later the smoky-steam-engine girl of *Jules and Jim*—is like a Hollywood 1940s movie type; she would have played well with Humphrey Bogart—a big, clear-eyed, crude, loyal, honest girl. The film is closely related to Godard's *Breathless,* and both seem to be haunted by the shade of Bogart.

Shoot the Piano Player is both nihilistic in attitude and, at the same time, in its wit and good spirits, totally involved in life and fun. Whatever Truffaut touches seems to leap to life—even a gangster thriller is transformed into the human comedy. A *comedy* about melancholia, about the hopelessness of life, can only give the lie to the theme; for as long as we can joke, life is not hopeless; we can enjoy it. In Truffaut's style there is so much pleasure in life that the wry, lonely little piano player, the sardonic little man who shrugs off experience, is himself a beautiful character. This beauty is a tribute to human experience, even if the man is so hurt and defeated that he can only negate experience. The nihilism of the character—and the anarchic nihilism of the director's style—have led reviewers to call the film a surrealist farce; it isn't that strange.

When I refer to Truffaut's style as anarchic and nihilistic, I am referring to a *style,* not an absence of it. I disagree with the critics around who find the film disorganized; they seem to cling to the critical apparatus of their grammar school teachers. They want unity of theme; easy-to-follow transitions in mood; a good, coherent, old-fashioned plot; and heroes they can identify with and villains they can reject. Stanley Kauffmann in *The New Republic* compares *Shoot the Piano Player* with the sweepings of cutting room floors; *Time* decides that "the moral, if any, seems to be that shooting the piano player might, at least, put the poor devil out of his misery." But who but *Time* is looking for a moral? What's exciting about movies like *Shoot the Piano Player* and *Breathless* (and also the superb *Jules and Jim,* though it's very different from the other two) is that they, quite literally, move with the times. They are full of unresolved, inexplicable, disharmonious elements, irony and slapstick and defeat all compounded—*not* arbitrarily as the reviewers claim—but in terms of the filmmaker's efforts to find some expression for his own anarchic experience, instead of making more of those tiresome well-made movies that no longer mean much to us.

The subject matter of *Shoot the Piano Player,* as of *Breathless,* seems small and unimportant compared to the big themes of so many films, but it only *seems* small: it is an effort to deal with contemporary experience in terms drawn out of that experience. For both Godard and Truffaut a good part of this experience has been moviegoing, but this is just as much a part of their lives as reading is for a writer. And what writer does not draw upon what he has read?

A number of reviewers have complained that in his improvisatory method, Truffaut includes irrelevancies, and they use as chief illustration the opening scene—a gangster who is running away from pursuers bangs into a lamppost, and then is helped to his feet by a man who proceeds to walk along with him, while discussing his marital life. Is it really so irrelevant? Only if you grew up in that tradition of the well-made play in which this bystander would have to reappear as some vital link in the plot. But he's relevant in a different way here: he helps to set us in a world in which his seminormal existence seems just as much a matter of chance and fringe behavior and simplicity as the gangster's existence—which begins to seem seminormal also. The bystander talks; we get an impression of his way of life and his need to talk about it, and he goes out of the film, and that is that: Truffaut would have to be as stodgy and dull witted as the reviewers to bring him back and link him into the story. For the meaning of these films is that these fortuitous encounters illuminate something about our lives in a way that the old neat plots don't.

There is a tension in the method; we never quite know where we are, how we are supposed to react—and this tension, as the moods change and we are pulled in different ways, gives us the excitement of drama, of art, of *our* life. Nothing is clear-cut, the ironies crisscross and bounce. The loyal, courageous heroine is so determined to live by her code that, when it's violated, she comes on too strong, and the piano player is repelled by her inability to respect the weaknesses of others. Thugs kidnapping a little boy discuss their possessions with him—a conversation worthy of a footnote in Veblen's passages on conspicuous expenditure.

Only a really carefree, sophisticated filmmaker could bring it off—and satisfy our desire for the unexpected that is also *right*. Truffaut is a director of incredible taste; he never carries a scene *too* far. It seems extraordinarily simple to complain that a virtuoso who can combine many moods has not stuck to one familiar old mood—but this is what the reviews seem to amount to. The modern novel has abandoned the old conception that each piece must be in place—abandoned it so thoroughly that when we read something like Angus Wilson's *Anglo-Saxon Attitudes* in which each piece does finally fit in place, we are astonished and amused at the dexterity of the accomplishment. That is the way Wilson works and it's wonderfully satisfying, but few modern novelists work that way; and it would be as irrelevant to the meaning and quality of, say, *Tropic of Capricorn* to complain that the plot isn't neatly tied together like *Great Expectations,* as to complain of the film *Shoot the Piano Player* that it isn't neatly tied together like *The Bicycle Thief.* Dwight Macdonald wrote that *Shoot the Piano Player* deliberately mixed up "three genres which are usually kept apart: crime melodrama, romance, and slapstick comedy." And, he says, "I thought the mixture didn't jell, but it was an exhilarating try." What I think is exhilarating in *Shoot the Piano Player* is that it *doesn't* "jell" and that the different elements keep *us* in a state of suspension—we react far more than we do to works that "jell." Incidentally, it's not completely accurate to say that these genres are usually kept apart; although *slapstick* rarely enters the mixture except in a far-out film like *Beat the Devil* or *Lovers and Thieves* or the new *The Manchurian Candidate,* there are numerous examples of crime melodrama–romance–comedy among well-known American films—particularly of the 1940s—for example *The Maltese Falcon, Casablanca, The Big Sleep, To Have and Have Not.* (Not all of Truffaut's models are cheap B pictures.)

Perhaps one of the problems that American critics and audiences may have with *Shoot the Piano Player* is a peculiarly American element in it—the romantic treatment of the man who walks alone. For decades our films were full of these gangsters, outcasts, detectives, cynics; Bogart epitomized them all—all the men who had been hurt by a woman or betrayed by their friends and who no longer trusted anybody. And although I think most of us enjoyed this romantic treatment of the man beyond the law, we rejected it intellectually. It was part of hack moviemaking—we might love it but it wasn't really intellectually respectable. And now here it is, inspired by our movies, and coming back to us via France. The heroine of *Shoot the Piano Player* says of the hero, "Even when he's with somebody, he walks alone." But this French hero carries his isolation much farther than the earlier American hero: when his girl is having a fight on his behalf and he is impelled to intervene, he says to himself, "You're out of it. Let them fight it out." He is brought into it; but where the American hero, once impelled to move, is a changed man and, redeemed by love or patriotism or a sense of fair play, he would take the initiative, save his girl, and conquer everything, this French hero simply moves into the situation when he must, when he can no longer stay out of it, and takes the consequences. He finds that the contact with people is once again defeating. He really doesn't believe in anything; the American hero only *pretended* he didn't.

Breathless was about active, thoughtless young people; *Shoot the Piano Player* is about a passive, melancholic character who is acted upon. Yet the world that surrounds the principal figures in these two movies is similar: the clowns in one are police, in the other gangsters, but this hardly matters. What we react to in both is the world of absurdities that is so much like our own world in which people suddenly and unexpectedly turn into clowns. But at the center is the sentimentalist—Belmondo in *Breathless,* Aznavour here—and I think there can be no doubt that both Godard and Truffaut love their heroes.

There are incidentally a number of little in-group jokes included in the film; a few of these are of sufficiently general interest to be worth mentioning, and, according to Andrew Sarris, they have been verified by Truffaut. The piano player is given the name of Saroyan as a tribute to William Saroyan, particularly for his volume of stories *The Daring Young Man on the Flying Trapeze,* and also because Charles Aznavour, like Saroyan, is Armenian (and, I would surmise, for the playful irony of giving a life-evading hero the name of one of the most rambunctious of life-embracing writers). One of the hero's brothers in the film is named Chico, as a tribute to the Marx Brothers. And the impresario in the film, the major villain of the work, is called Lars Schmeel, as a disapproving gesture toward someone Truffaut does *not* admire—the impresario Lars Schmidt, known to us simply as Ingrid Bergman's current husband, but apparently known to others—and disliked by Truffaut—for his theatrical activities in Paris.

If a more pretentious vocabulary or a philosophic explanation will help, the piano player is intensely human and sympathetic, a character who empathizes with others, and with whom we, as audience, empathize; but he does not want to accept the responsibilities of his humanity—he asks only to be left alone. And because he refuses voluntary involvement, he is at the mercy of accidental forces. He is, finally, man trying to preserve his little bit of humanity in a chaotic world—it is not merely a world he never made but a world he would much rather forget about. But schizophrenia cannot be willed and so long as he is sane, he is only partly successful: crazy accidents happen—and sometimes he must deal with them. That is to say, no matter how far he retreats from life, he is not completely safe. And Truffaut himself is so completely engaged in life that he pleads for the piano player's right to be left alone, to live in his withdrawn state, *to be out of it.* Truffaut's plea is, of course, "Don't shoot the piano player."

The Village Voice

Andrew Sarris

rançois Truffaut's *Shoot the Piano Player* is a movie most readers of this column should enjoy without any further critical rationalization. Just for the record, this relaxed piece of filmmaking is Truffaut's second feature-length opus, released in France in 1960, a year before *Jules and Jim*.[1] The director's apparent casualness has disconcerted some of our more solemn critics, who would rather suffer along with Antonioni than sing along with Truffaut. The notion that great art can be great fun, and vice versa, has always offended spokesmen for moral sensibility. The argument against humor in what should be serious art has been disguised as an argument over purity of form, the argument advanced for Racine against Shakespeare, Richardson against Fielding, and Mann against Proust. I suppose that Antonioni is purer than Truffaut, but I suspect that cinema, like water, obtains its flavor from its impurities. And what impurities there are in *Shoot the Piano Player!*

To begin with, *Shoot the Piano Player* is adapted from a wildly melodramatic novel, *Down There*, by the relatively unknown American novelist David Goodis. Everyone knows that melodrama is not the stuff of great art. Everyone knows you can't make an important film about a small, homely piano player with a tragic past as a concert pianist even when the piano player is admirably played by Charles Aznavour. You can't have gangsters, chases, kidnappings, murders, and a suicide littering the pristine art-house screen, particularly when you are not indicting society in the process. Furthermore, why is this sad-eyed piano player so irresistible to lovely girls like Marie Dubois, Nicole Berger, and Michèle Mercier? How can you have pathos that way, and since when does a serious film spend so much time in bed? However, if this is not a serious film, how do you explain that strange opening in which a stranger passing down the street talks briefly about the love he feels for his wife and then disappears into the vast conjugal sea of middle-class humanity? What are we supposed to understand when a brutal bartender declares before his death that for him woman was always supreme? Why did Truffaut say in 1960 that *Shoot the Piano Player* was the only statement he could make about the Algerian war?

Shoot the Piano Player reverberates on too many levels to be dismissed as an exercise in escapism. What Truffaut is saying about the nature of love, disengagement, and timidity transforms the incidents of his melodrama into the events of our time. We are all involved, as James Dean cries out in *Rebel Without*

---

1. *Jules and Jim* was released in the United States prior to *Shoot the Piano Player*.

From *The Village Voice*, July 26, 1962.

a Cause, and whatever is done or not done for whatever reason affects us all. Fortunately, the director's ideas are implied rather than inflicted. Truffaut, like Renoir, loves his audience, but some audiences do not want to be loved. They would rather be tortured by Antonioni, bored by Satyajit Ray, or preached to by Stanley Kramer. Nevertheless it is in the tension between self-expression and pleasurable communication that the cinema achieves authentic greatness. *Shoot the Piano Player* may disturb the hobgoblins of consistency as it oscillates between comedy and tragedy, realism and fantasy, improvisation and stylization, but the final image of Aznavour's resignation in front of a tinkling piano will linger in the mind long after the sounding brass of more pretentious cinema has been forgotten.

The New York Times
Bosley Crowther

François Truffaut, the French director who showed in *The 400 Blows* that he had a rare talent for lacing pathos with slapstick comedy, pulled all the stops on that talent and let it run rampant when he made *Shoot the Piano Player,* which arrived at the Fifth Avenue Cinema yesterday.

Nuttiness, pure and simple—nuttiness of the sort that has a surly kidnapper in a presumably serious scene swearing to something on the life of his mother, where-upon there's a cut to the mother dropping dead—surges and swirls through the tangle of solemn intimations in this film until one finds it hard to see or figure what M. Truffaut is about.

Evidently he is asking that the audience pay gentle heed to the significance of the old barroom legend, "Don't shoot the piano player; he is doing the best he can." For his hero is a small piano player in a noisome Parisian bar who turns out to be a poignant victim of fate and his own timidity.

This little ivory-tickler, played by Charles Aznavour with an almost Buster Keaton–like insistence on the eloquence of the dead pan, is more than a tired and pallid jangler of popular ragtime tunes. Oh, yes. He is a former concert pianist with a brilliant and glamorous past. But for some unspecified reason he couldn't get along with his wife, who finally tells him she brought him his big chance with her virtue, and this dumps him into the bars.

Maybe, in this little fellow, M. Truffaut is trying to construct an arch example of a sentimental hero that he is subtly attempting to spoof. But if this is the case, why does he bear down on the little fellow's piety so hard and bring his seriocomic roughhouse to a mawkishly tearful end? Why does he scramble his satire with a madly melo-dramatic plot and have the little piano player kill a man in defense of a girl?

It looks, from where we are sitting, as though M. Truffaut went haywire in this film, which he made as his second feature picture, following the great success of *The 400 Blows.* It looks as though he had so many ideas for a movie outpouring in his head, so many odd slants on comedy and drama and sheer clichés that he wanted to express, that he couldn't quite control his material, which he got from a novel by David Goodis called *Down There.*

Else why would he switch so abruptly from desperately serious scenes and moods to bits of irrelevant nonsense or blatant caricature? Why would he let Nicole Berger play a lengthy, heartbreaking scene in which she boldly explains to her husband how she was unfaithful to him, then turn around a few minutes later and put two gangsters through a frolic of farce?

From *The New York Times,* July 24, 1962.

It is a teasing and frequently amusing (or moving) film that M. Truffaut has made, but it simply does not hang together. It does not find a sufficiently firm line, even one of calculated spoof or mischief, on which to hang and thus be saved.

M. Aznavour is touching as the hero, when he is supposed to be, but his character is much too shallow and vagrant for substantiality. Marie Dubois is appealing as a young barmaid who tries to help him out, and Mlle. Berger is excellent in her brief role as his flashback wife. Several other fellows overact in various roles. The English subtitles do bare justice to the lusty colloquial French.

Esquire
Dwight Macdonald

François Truffaut, the reformed movie critic who made *The 400 Blows,* has done a second film which couldn't be more different from his first, which was simple, direct, and moving. The first two adjectives don't apply to *Shoot the Piano Player* and the third takes a bit of doing. Farce and tragedy are hopelessly (and deliberately) mixed up: the hero's first wife kills herself because of a split-second misunderstanding; he kills a man in an absurd fight; his gangster brothers get him involved in a comic imbroglio with a bungling rival gang who accidentally shoot his sweetheart. It is all brilliant and heartless: "As flies to wanton boys are we to the gods; / They kill us for their sport." It is Gide's *acte gratuit* in reverse: the hero is accident-prone and suffers, rather than commits, senseless catastrophes.

From *Esquire* (March 1961).

Commentaries

The following section begins with essays and excerpts that consider *Shoot the Piano Player* in the most general terms. Pearson and Rhode discuss the film in the context of the philosophical proclivities of the New Wave in a way that is astonishingly up-to-date, despite the difference in the vocabulary they employ from our own. A portion of Insdorf's essay is included to provide background for an examination of Truffaut's treatment of women in this and other films. The three early films—*The 400 Blows, Shoot the Piano Player,* and *Jules and Jim*—are usefully compared by Thiher, who emphasizes Truffaut as a thinker. Thiher's essay has the further merit of placing these films in the context of the absurdist, existentialist aesthetics of the period in which they were made. The selections by Braudy and Monaco discuss the film in terms of genre, convention, and its relation to popular art.

The remaining essays concentrate more specifically on the details of *Shoot the Piano Player.* Crisp offers what is probably the most solid, traditional thematic reading of the film and gives useful details about its making and reception, and its relation to the original script. Allen's encyclopedic knowledge of his friend's films enables him to link this film with the others in Truffaut's canon. Török provides a more typically "French" reading of the film, concentrating on its psychological complexities, its portrait of love and the relations between men and women, and its function as autobiography. (It should be noted in passing that Török wrote this essay for *Positif,* a Parisian journal that fought with *Cahiers du cinéma* for years and that, initially at any rate, was opposed to the New Wave. Thus his praise for the film seems occasionally grudging and guarded.) Petrie outlines the film's recurring motifs, and discusses the use of music and the voiceover in an excellent close reading that seems to me a model of what good formalism should be. Greenspun's essay also discusses the film's motifs (especially blackness versus whiteness), and focuses on the notion of "multiple relations . . . by which ideas, things, and images enjoy equality as phenomena." The section ends with Reisz and Millar's informative technical discussion of the film's innovative editing.

It should also be explained that Truffaut, as the quintessential auteur, has to some extent fallen out of critical favor in this post- or even anti-auteurist age. Hence the relative lack of more recent commentary in the following pages.

Cinema of Appearance

Gabriel Pearson and Eric Rhode

Without doubt, the best films of the New Wave have been associated with a radical change in filmmaking. Though their innovations are often startling, we should not be blinded by this from seeing them as part of a more general revolution in which our idea of art, or consciousness itself, may have been subtly transformed.

Part One: The Humanist's Approach

As humanists, our first reaction to the most extreme examples of this revolution—Godard's *Breathless* and Truffaut's *Shoot the Piano Player*—is as much one of bewilderment as of pleasure; for these films, according to our theories, shouldn't work. They break most of the rules of construction; sequences are barely connected; moods veer violently and without explanation. Like a cat teasing a ball of wool, the thread of a tale may be arbitrarily picked up, played with, and just as suddenly dropped. As for morality (if there is a morality), we are given few indications of how we should understand its alien logic: characters apparently behave without motive, their feelings remain unpredictable. Moreover, we feel that this is a contingent art, created on every level by improvisation—a procedure that affronts our belief in the artifact as a contrived and calculated work. It is as though, having landed on the moon, we were confronted by a lunar art.

For our intensity of response confirms these films as works of art. And here we notice the first of two contradictions. Although apparently outraging every principle of organization, they are not chaotic. On the contrary, they cohere beautifully. And second, though their very being is improvised, they move with a deftness and aplomb that is almost scornful.

The aim of this investigation is to explore these contradictions and try to resolve them, if only partially. This undertaking would be pedantic if it were restricted to *Breathless* and *Shoot the Piano Player,* both of them relatively slight films. What interests us is that these two contradictions, expressed here in their most extreme form, are found to varying degrees in the most recent films of Antonioni, Resnais, Bresson, and Wajda; in such plays as *The Connection* and *Waiting for Godot;* and, moving out into another field, in certain types of nonfigurative painting. To investigate the New Wave, therefore, may throw back an unusual light on what at first seem a number of widely disparate works of art.

From *Sight and Sound* 30, no. 4 (Autumn 1961): 160–168.

The critic must have some basis of understanding with a film before he can analyze it. Otherwise his comments, however intelligent, will be continually off the mark. As in politics, there must be a common language before negotiations can take place.

Jacques Siclier's article on New Wave and French cinema in the summer issue of *Sight and Sound* is a case in point. We have here an intelligent humanist who is unable to come to terms with the new movement. Lacking the vocabulary by which he can both define his response to these films and at the same time make evaluations from a humanist standpoint, his argument, though for the most part logical, remains at one remove from the subject. We see this most obviously in his conclusion: "Progressively this young cinema is losing itself behind a curtain of smoke and dreams; and this cinema, which has been described as representative of its time, is in reality as remote from the actual as anything one can imagine."

In using such phrases as "losing itself behind a curtain of smoke and dreams" and "remote from the actual," Siclier is taking certain assumptions for granted. But this makes his position extremely vulnerable, since it is on just these points that apologists for the New Wave would challenge him. Their argument would be that the humanist approach, though admirably decent, provides us with an unsatisfactory approach to criticism since it presupposes a stable reality (implied in such terms as "actual") that we can no longer believe in. For many reasons, they would continue, reality has become as arbitrary as smoke and dreams. There is no curtain, and there is no "actual" as Siclier would have it.

Faced by this challenge, the humanist critic may at first feel—as perhaps Siclier doesn't—that his position is so inadequate that he must abandon it. If he is more tenacious, however, he may hope to discover a vocabulary to resolve the deadlock between himself and the New Wave without a forced surrender of his position. Before he can achieve this, and in order to discover such a basis of understanding, he would first have to analyze his own assumptions. For the sake of clarity, we are summarizing these in note form.

Assumptions of the Humanist Critic

1. Great art is created out of certain conditions, and these conditions are limited. They are:

   (*a*) That in this art both the inner world of the individual and the outer world in all its totality are stable and continuous; that their relationship is dynamic; and that man is equipped, by his reason and imagination, to understand both this world and himself.

   (*b*) That this inner and outer world remain, despite disruptions, in harmony with each other.

   (*c*) That, most important of all, the greatness of this art depends on the extent to which it illuminates the central human predicaments. This concept of centrality is a difficult one to define; for centrality in art, the critic usually points to such literary models as *The Odyssey* or *Anna Karenina,* or to such films as *The Childhood of Maxim Gorki* and *The World of Apu.*

 (*d*) Finally, that this art matches up, however inadequately, to our sense of continuity in the real world. It achieves this by aspiring toward both maximum inclusiveness and maximum coherence. This is brought about by making connections. (See E. M. Forster's "Only connect.")

2. This stable yet dynamic relationship between inner and outer world can best be conceived of in dramatic terms (i.e., dialectically). Because of this a certain type of plot is most useful, a type of plot that develops from:

 (*a*) *Antagonisms:* the most valuable of these play the stable world against some disruptive force, i.e., order against chaos, moderation against excess.

 Ulysses'

"Untune that string,
And, hark, what discord follows!"

describes the most serious development of that conflict.

 Fortunately, such discord is usually followed by:

 (*b*) A *dénouement* and *resolution,* in which the world returns to its natural harmony.

3. Having consented to this model of reality, we are then forced to accept further steps in the argument.

 (*a*) The artist holds this balance between inner and outer world at his peril, for if he cannot sustain it in his work his vision of reality is impelled to become *either* a riotous, all-embracing fantasy in which his mind is the controlling authority *or* a "scientific" construction of mechanistic laws in which men are seen as no more than biological automata (cf. Naturalism).

 (*b*) Though these two deviations move in opposing directions, they do, when taken to an extreme, merge into each other and unify; for any aspect of reality becomes indistinguishably grotesque and arbitrary when taken out of total context.

The misunderstanding between humanist critic and New Wave apologist begins to make itself clear. It arises, as misunderstandings often do, over a confusion of categories. The deadlock in fact is less over an aesthetic than over the theory of reality on which it depends.

In realizing this, the humanist critic finds himself in an impossible position. If he is honest he will accept his opponent's point: that at our present state of knowledge we can no longer believe in a stable reality, since such a belief supposes a hierarchy of values based on a public morality—and none such now holds. This concession breaks the back of his argument. Without a centrality there can be no "arbitrary and grotesque." Therefore the humanist has no reason to describe the New Wave films as failures: he must indeed accept them on their own terms.

This is the situation—stated too drastically, perhaps. Most humanist critics would probably go as far as admitting that they desired, rather than believed in, a stable reality, and that they willingly suspended disbelief as they went about their work. Unfortunately, this skepticism does not extend to their critical language. If it did, we would be spared such presumptuous judgments as the *Sight and Sound* reviewer's faulting of *Pickpocket* because it didn't make "the necessary connections," or the BBC critic's rejection of *Breathless* ("The best one can say of it is that it stinks") because its plot lacked conflict. Such comments reveal a failure to recognize how far these films have broken from their humanist prototypes in the nineteenth-century novel and play.

It is over this "how far" that confusion has arisen. If the break had been complete from the start, the inadequacy of the humanist's vocabulary would have been obvious. The shift to a completely new kind of film has, however, been a gradual one; and the directors themselves seem to have been barely conscious of it. It is only now, with our complacency disturbed by the New Wave, that we can look back and see the process by which the meaning of such concepts as plot and action has been developed. One can usefully trace such a development from *The Bicycle Thief,* through *L'Avventura* to *Breathless.*

The Bicycle Thief (Vittorio DeSica, 1948) is apparently conceived in terms of the nineteenth-century theater. The plot exposes a typical conflict: a lone man pitted against the injustices of society. As in a Feydeau farce, De Sica uses objects to further the intrigue—the stolen bicycle is no more than an honorable equivalent of the stolen letter or double bed. Yet by the standards of the well-made play this plot is weak; for the intrigue is undermined by a current of aimless and seemingly irrelevant lyricism. The social conflict in fact is not the plot: it is no more than a theme. The true plot, miming the wayward drift of father and son lost in a labyrinth of streets and piazzas, is the futile search for the illusive thief. This search poses strange, unanswered questions: "What do we mean by a thief, and how can we apply moral categories when we know the situation that makes him as he is?" There is an equally strange transference of guilt, by which the father-as-detective becomes the father-as-criminal. Such preoccupations, though never acknowledged fully, disrupt the plot's manifest action.

Yet it is still rewarding to approach *The Bicycle Thief* in terms of the humanist's idea of plot. This is not so with *L'Avventura* (Michelangelo Antonioni, 1960), in which such a plot is both a lure and an irrelevance. Critics have understandably been disturbed by the unexplained disappearance of Anna. As a device this can be justified: it enacts Antonioni's sense of the arbitrariness of experience—the unpredictable workings of memory and feeling. Yet in the last resort the device leaves us uneasy, since the conventions of the film do not prepare us for it. Although Antonioni has moved a long way from De Sica in his discovery of new techniques, he has not come to terms with their similar problem. His plot, too, does not conduct the film's true meaning.

Claudia, the critical and moral intelligence of the film, involves herself with a corrupt society and helps to define it, in much the same way that James's bright young things from America define the corruption of Europe. Yet Claudia, for many reasons, lacks their moral stability; hence the idea of corruption, as exemplified by Sandro and his circle, needs drastic qualification. The conflict is so blurred that moral judgment at first sight becomes impossible. To make sense of *L'Avventura,* in fact, one must initially discard this concept of corruption, with all its satisfying imprecision, in favor of the more neutral concept of failure. For it is surely part of Antonioni's intention, by doing as much justice as he can to the complexities of human relationships, to neutralize such self-approving moral categories.

But first, if only as a form of puzzle about technique, *L'Avventura* helps us to start asking the right questions. What are we to make of Antonioni's camerawork? Those beautiful dolly and tracking shots cannot be understood in terms of the narrative devices of the nineteenth-century novel, upon which so much previous camerawork has implicitly relied. Antonioni's tracking shots do not fulfill any obvious narrative requirement. Yet our aesthetic sense warns us that this ballet of movement is as much part of the film's meaning as the device of Anna's enigmatic disappearance. The difficulty here lies in relating our sense of the "rightness" of these techniques to our general moral sense of what the film is about.

In *Breathless* this difficulty is at its most extreme, and for this very reason it should begin to point the way to a solution. Here there is no gradual shift of conventions to help us to readjust. We are launched immediately into anarchy. We have no apparent choice between blind acceptance and blind rejection. We cannot, as we could with *L'Avventura* and *The Bicycle Thief,* simply go on trying to read the film in our own terms. Here connections are difficult, almost impossible to discover: the camerawork, the editing, and the behavior of the characters appear alike random and unmotivated.

Yet the tensions between apparent plot and what actually happens on the screen are not so different from those of its two predecessors. The plot could best be described like this: Patricia is a Jamesian Daisy Miller involved with what one might quaintly call a corrupt young European, Michel. Here, however, the notion of corruption is not even questioned: it is rendered absurd and irrelevant. Michel's banditry and search for a mysterious colleague who owes him money by no means define what Michel is. On the contrary, the whole notion of corruption is burlesqued, until it ceases to be in any way what the film is about. Hence the apparent plot, of which we could give a clear account in the conventional terms of the hounded thief, is utterly extraneous to the film's action. It becomes indeed what Godard would call *un gag.*

With so little connection between action and plot, all other connections begin to fail us. The usual out is symbolism; but here there is nothing like such a meaning.

Indeed, as soon as we seize on some aspect of the film as containing symbolic significance, we are immediately contradicted by the action. To be symbolically satisfying, Antonio (the man with the money for whom Michel is searching) ought never to turn up. Yet, aping the conventions of the B thriller, up he duly pops with the money in the last reel, although he is too late. This too late evokes no irony, however. That sort of moral is not the subject of the film.

And so our confusion increases. Significance is like a chair continually being pulled from under us. We fall with an absurd bump, victims of *le gag*. The more we probe these films, the more enigmatic they appear. The more we try to penetrate their depths, the more we find ourselves involved in a series of shifting, ambiguous surfaces. We are like Alice, trying to walk away from the Wonderland cottage.

Part Two: The Artist's Approach

The principal reason why the humanist critic has failed to realize the inadequacy of his vocabulary is that the artist himself has been barely conscious of a change in outlook. While ostensibly holding on to the humanist's belief in a stable reality, he has in fact been groping toward an expression that requires a quite different metaphysic.

Pirandello's plays give us a lead. We have here a writer whose artistic insights are ahead of a metaphysic to clarify them. Hence our impression of hesitancy in a playwright who employs many of the modern devices of improvisation. He is hesitant because, despite the utmost skepticism about the notion of centrality, he remains a humanist. Centrality, however illusory, exists for him, though he doubts our ability to recognize it. In his *Henry IV* he is still asking whether the madman is sane or the sane man mad, whether the twelfth century is eternally present or irredeemably past. The most challenging question for a humanist—as to whether a central reality exists or not, whether there is only illusion and therefore an art that can only be illusion imitating illusion—remains masked.

Six Characters in Search of an Author takes us a stage further. One notices here the title's pun: "author" is both desired author in the ordinary sense and "auctoritas"—a coherent metaphysic that can establish hierarchies among the characters' modes of being and so evaluate and dignify their actions. Their terrible predicament, their anguished states of mind, are both heightened and nullified by the ironic framework within which Pirandello sets them. They are no longer figures of tragedy but specimens with tragic potentialities. Inasmuch as the theater has been turned into a laboratory, so they too have been turned into automata, puppets struggling desperately to be human. They protest—too much perhaps. But in this clinic of humanity their anguished clichés are seen to lack meaningful content; only in their enigmatic but terrible cry, in their very desire to become human, do they transcend this sorry state.

All we are left with is a cry, and the debris of a play. Pirandello's achievement is strangely moving; yet we may well ask why such a paraphernalia of construction yielded results so meager and limited. The humanist critic, we remember, fails to account for the new aesthetic because he is blinkered by a theory of reality that cannot make sense of it. In Pirandello's case, the failure works in reverse.

The humanist assumes that (to use Sartre's image) experience is an onion from which one peels off layers and layers of illusion to expose a small white nub of reality at the center. But if we shift to an existentialist view, we conceive of experience as an unending series of appearances, each of which is equally "real." Pirandello fails, then, because his idealist humanism, from which he ultimately derives his sense of form, cannot contain his existentialist insights.[1] We are left in the end with an impression not of controlled irony, but of bewilderment and contradiction.

The best films of the New Wave leave no such impression. Their existentialism may be partial and muddled but it does support their aesthetic. And since it is this philosophy that their language of smoke and dreams enacts, we need to know its main assumptions. Again, we are summarizing these in note form.

Assumptions of the New Wave

1. A world in which all appearances are equally valid is a world of discontinuity. The self is a series of events without apparent connection: its past and future are a series of actions, but its present is a void waiting to be defined by action. The self therefore is no longer seen as stable. It is without an inner core—without essence.
2. Other people are likewise without essence; since they too are an infinite series of appearances, they remain unpredictable. Only objects, i.e., "things" with an essence, can be understood. People remain mysteries.
3. Since there is no longer a stable reality, traditional moralities prove untrustworthy. They seek to essentialize appearances, order them so that they can be predicted, and so conceal from men their true condition in a discontinuous world—utter isolation. Each is responsible for improvising his moral imperatives; to accept any one role (i.e., to fix one's identity as "bandit," "pianist," or "intellectual") is an evasion of responsibility and becomes "bad faith." Such "bad faith" dehumanizes and turns man into an object. Existentially, he dies.

---

1. This failure to embody insights is to be found in a number of directors. In *Rocco and His Brothers,* Visconti fails to find a suitable form for those unmotivated bursts of violence that characterize his anarchistic vision of experience. Since he tries to develop these within the outworn formal husks of nineteenth-century literature, the result is not tragedy but grand opera. Ingmar Bergman, too, cannot find a form for his existentialist insights, and so resigns himself to describing rather than enacting them. His films contain much sophisticated byplay around a philosophy of appearance. They even produce symbols like the clock without hands. Yet the vision remains intellectualized, and the films fail to make their potentially powerful impact.

4. Conversely, to avoid bad faith, morality must be an endless, anguished process of improvisation. One no longer acts to fulfill ideals like goodness and decency, but to initiate one's own self-discovery, the only moral "goal" left. Hence action is necessarily opportunistic.
5. In consequence, each act is unique and without social precedence, and so to others will appear motiveless since there is no stable self on which to pin a motive. From this arises the seemingly absurd notion of a motiveless act (*l'acte gratuit*).
6. Our continuous re-creation in every act is the condition of our freedom. But such a continuous freedom demands total responsibility for all that we are, have been, and are to be. It is only theoretically possible to live up to such a rigorous ideal, so that we seek to flee from it into the passivity of being an object. To the man-as-object the world ceases to be an infinite series of appearances and becomes an infinite series of accidents.

The self is a void. Its past and future are a series of events waiting to be filled in. To take on an identity is an act of bad faith: we become objects to be used by others; we die existentially. The hero of *Shoot the Piano Player* moves uneasily between such self-destructive roles. He can become Charlie, the timid lover; Edouard Saroyan, the concert pianist; or a wild beast like his brothers. Though he knows that each of these choices is false, he is unable to discover the authentic. In *Breathless* Michel has similarly disastrous alternatives: finding himself cast as bandit, callow lover, or son of an eminent clarinetist, he immediately tries to break out into freedom. Identity is a trap; and since sex is identity, he and Patricia try to save themselves by remaining androgynous. In the void of the self, these identities are deceptions; and they can teach us nothing. They are appearances, as "real" only as the actor's role. To ask if Michel's father was indeed a great clarinetist is as naive and irrelevant as to ask the actor if he was "really" King Lear.

To believe we can learn from the past is also bad faith. Memories are as ambiguous and deceptive as identity. So Sandro cannot learn from his previous *avventure,* nor can Charlie make sense of the murder in the snow. Was it a nightmare or did it take place? Such questions are meaningless. If, for the benefit of the doubt, he were to mourn the girl's death—and who knows if she, like Sandro's Anna, ever existed?—he would again be deceiving himself; for to become a mourner is again to take on an identity.

A world of appearances confronts us not with expressive faces and meaningful objects, but with enigmas and indecipherable images.[2] In *Breathless,* Patricia

2. The process by which morality breaks down into images can be traced most interestingly through the films of Andrzej Wajda. In direct relation to the director's increasing skepticism about their ideology, the plots disintegrate, to be replaced by an unaccounted-for lyricism. In *Kanal* plot controls every element of structure, but by *Ashes and Diamonds* it barely contains certain lyrical sequences like the polonaise at dawn. In *Lotna,* his most recent film to be shown here, plot has collapsed completely

seems to conceal her feelings behind her dark glasses, but when she removes them her face is still an enigma. And it is still the same enigmatic face she turns to us at the end of the film—the face of a beautiful sphinx. To all our questions she returns the same answer: her own cool features into which we can read all meaning or no meaning. The face of Charlie at the end of *Shoot the Piano Player* is her male equivalent.

Of all enigmas the most inscrutable is suicide. Because of this inscrutability, and because it is the one act we have no adequate response to, suicide has haunted writers like Fitzgerald and Pavese, film directors like Antonioni and Truffaut. If we mourn a suicide we take on a role, so deceiving ourselves. All we can do is either hastily forget, or answer it with our own enigma. As the hero of *Il Grido* hurls himself down from the tower of a sugar refinery, his wife screams. As with Pirandello's characters, this cry is a last chance to assert her humanity against an inscrutable mystery. She tries to call his bluff by matching enigma against enigma.

In a world of appearances, responsibility lies in discovering one's own morality. Our intention is opportunistic. Since other people are unpredictable, our only chance of survival is to trap them into taking roles. Naturally they will behave in the same way to us. In such a game we can only hope to win by improvising the rules. Our principal trick will be *le gag,* the unpredictable quip or act that turns the tables. So Michel robs people, plays jokes on them, and knocks them down. In each case the result is the same: he turns them into objects. "Have you anything against youth?" says a girl and flourishes a copy of *Cahiers.* "Yes," he counters. "I like the old. . . ." Distinctions between generations, class, or creed must be minimized: they are traps to be evaded by improvisation.

With Patricia this shadowboxing takes on a disinterested intensity. "A girl's a coward who doesn't light her cigarette the first time," he improvises, and waits for her next move. She bluffs him magnificently by *un acte gratuit;* that is, by an act that is an enigma to him, but that is in terms of her own morality quite understandable. "I stayed with you to see if I were in love. Now I know I am not, and I am no longer interested in you." For the sake of her own freedom he must no longer exist; and it is therefore logical that she should betray him to the police and so indirectly bring about his death. As she says, "Elephants vanish when they are unhappy." Too bad that he should hold the last trump in the pack—death, and an inscrutable remark, *"Tu es dégueulasse* [You are disgusting]."

A morality that requires us to be continually free and responsible at the same time is impossible; so we retreat into a passivity one of whose forms is stoicism. The world in this position becomes a series of accidents, and we can do nothing about controlling it. Charlie is resigned to bearing his brothers' guilt; because of their crimes he too has become a criminal. Though this transference of guilt is

---

into a twitter of trivial ironies. The only positive elements left are images—of a white horse, of a flaming emblem—that have no significant connection with the action.

mysterious, he makes no attempt to understand it. He is as stoical about it as he is about the inconsequentiality of life. Somehow for him action and intention never connect. In trying to be kind to the café *patron,* he murders him; respecting women, he kills the two he loves the most. In both this film and *Breathless* there are long sequences shot from within a car. A jumble of lights and scenery whirls past. The characters look out, but they are cut off from this world, this senseless inanimate place. What can they do about it? Nothing. They shrug their shoulders and drive on.

This morality, of course, applies to more than the story on the screen. It conditions, too, the director's own relationship to his material. He no longer uses the film as a means of unveiling the reality behind illusion. Such penetration is out of place in a world of appearances, in which the cinematic shadows are as "real" as the world outside. If there is no "reality" art cannot be an illusion. Further, the director rejects the rules of filmmaking as bad faith. Both morality and aesthetic must be discovered through improvisation, and our interest will lie in this process of discovery. Each director must create his own language of appearances, although his language is not one of shadows and dreams as Siclier would claim; shadows imply a reflecting object, dreams a waking reality; and these are assumptions rejected by the existentialist. The humanist critic should not be surprised if this improvisation fails to create a plot, for the plot is not now found within the film but in the director's relationship to his material. This is where the conflict and drama lie.

   Such an aesthetic is neither new, nor developed to its full extent in the films of Truffaut and Godard. Harold Rosenberg in the *London Magazine* (July 1961) has described how such a theory finds its most extreme form in action painting. The action painter, he writes, does not work from a predetermined idea, but approaches his canvas as he would a person. He sets up a dialogue with his medium, and through improvisation tries to make discoveries about his own mind. "To work from sketches arouses the suspicion that the artist still regards the canvas as a place where the mind records its contents—rather, it is itself the 'mind' through which the painter thinks by changing the surface through paint."

   This is not to be seen as a form of self-expression, "which assumes the acceptance of the ego as it is. It has to do with self-creation, self-definition, or self-transcendence." This art is not "personal," though its subject matter is the artist's individual possibilities. Painting here significantly approaches pantomime and dance.[3]

---

3. The comparison here with the symbolist aesthetic is irresistible. It is only odd that painting and the cinema should have taken so long to develop similarly. The paradox about this art is that the more successful it is, the more it will appear autonomous. Films like *Breathless* are similar to a symbolist poem in that they try to become an image from which one cannot generalize, and which sets up hazards to our doing so by reminding us that we are controlled by the artist's mind.

In light of this we must be cautious of the way in which we consider the "content" of *Breathless* and *Shoot the Piano Player.* We cannot censure them for the banality of their material or the self-regarding nature of their humor. Gags, snippets from the B feature thriller, Cocteauesque surrealism, and so on are used not for their intrinsic merit but as a kind of vocabulary. It is only if they fail to find a diction or a style that one can fault their use. We can talk here of burlesque and quotation but not of parody, for parody implies a "real thing" on which to depend.

Since we are not interested in content but in the mind handling it, the disruptions and disconnections of narrative no longer disturb us; for these features do not signal a failure on the director's part but, on the contrary, a success. Failure would lie in his forgetting this self-exploration and becoming involved in the bad faith of telling a tale. He achieves his success by freeing himself from this temptation, imposing his own mental gestures on us. This can best be contrived through camerawork and cutting. In *Shoot the Piano Player,* for instance, there is a sequence of a girl walking up and down a corridor that is not edited for the sake of narrative economy, but for that of maximum visual brilliance. Not enough that this scene, by the canons of traditional filmmaking, should be excessively obtrusive; but Truffaut must underline his pyrotechnics by developing them against a background of virtuoso violin playing. Cutting, too, is used to set up enigmas of troubling beauty. There is one device in particular which is favored by these directors. In *L'Avventura,* we see it in embryonic form. It begins in the island hut with a close-up of Claudia's face that fades into a shot of the turbulent sea. Before we can shriek pathetic fallacy, however, the camera pans and we see Claudia in long shot looking down at the waves. Since Antonioni makes no clear point with this device, it remains a trick. Godard, however, uses it continually and to a purpose. Michel raises his revolver to the sun. We cut to a shot of the sun, synchronized (apparently) with the sound of a pistol shot. Then Michel's voice is overlaid: "Women," he says, "never drive carefully." The gun shot has become the crash of car bumpers. At another moment Michel, looking ashamed, is seen in the back of a car. Just when we become certain that he has been arrested, he steps out of the car and pays the driver; and we have to reinterpret his expression. In a world of appearances, Godard seems to be saying, we must always be on our guard; for not only are our assumptions a form of bad faith—they also deceive us.

The director is no longer an interpreter; he is indeed a director, a dictator. Though we may be privileged to enter his mind, we must pay a price in obeying its seemingly arbitrary movements. It is as if we too were inside the fast-moving car; for we too have to accept the phantasmagoria outside as the total world. We are all—characters, audience, and film—at the director's mercy. His disturbing treatment of his characters is typical. When Michel turns to us and we see how his dark glasses are without one lens, we laugh uneasily. We are laughing not only at his expense but at the expense of our previous assumptions.

We are not involved in the story, then, but with the director. Each time we try to identify ourselves with the narrative he will deliberately attempt to alienate us.

Naturalistic effects therefore must be limited: the love scene is disinfected of possible associations; blood is conspicuously absent from Michel's death. The messiness of the world, all its pathetic and irrelevant demands on our attention, have to be tidied away. If they weren't, our attention might all too easily deviate from the play of the controlling mind.

Our two contradictions are now resolved. Since films like *Breathless* and *Shoot the Piano Player* enact a philosophy of discontinuity, they can be disconnected on almost every level and yet cohere beautifully. Further, their improvisations do not appear hesitant, since the director, in making his self-discoveries, uses them purposively. If it is bad faith to believe that reality is predictable, improvisation rather dishonestly satisfies our naturalistic habits ("It's so like life!") and so dupes us. Too dazzled to notice the aggressive originality of these films, we watch them without our usual defensiveness toward experiment.

Part Three: The Humanist Position Reconsidered

Despite its many insights, the Cinema of Appearance is inadequate, for reality is much richer than it makes out. To define its limitations we need a humanism reinterpreted by psychoanalysis, in the light of which the existentialist outlook is shown as psychotic and centrality, or the total rich vision, becomes closely linked with an idea of the "integrated self."

We have attempted so far to describe the New Cinema without discussing its own standards of evaluation. How, in fact, would one of its defenders judge the worth of its films, know whether a film was good or bad? Their criteria are threefold: first, they would be concerned with the quality of the director's imagination; second, with his ability to avoid the bad faith of previous conventions, like narrative or plot; and third, with his talent in creating a coherent style.

By these criteria, *Breathless* emerges as a better film than *Shoot the Piano Player,* for Godard avoids bad faith and creates a self-contained style while Truffaut creates a poignant, uncertain style and hints at a lost centrality. By evoking an atmosphere similar to the *apache* world of *Casque d'Or,* Truffaut makes plain his nostalgia for the lost luminous place where all men are brothers, where love is given and received with unselfconscious gratitude. In his film the most haunting image is of people putting arms around each other, helping each other to bear a mutual pain. Behind these images lies a theme of man's desire for centrality, a theme that is established from the first moments of the film as Chico, the amiable gangster, listens to a stranger talking about marriage, and developed through Charlie, his brother, into a formidable criticism of the Cinema of Appearance.

As a great pianist, Charlie is unhappy not because his role is a form of bad faith, but because he knows it hinders him from being a complete man, from giving himself to others both through his talents and, especially, through his love for them. This failure is disastrous. His wife commits suicide when he is unable to give her the help she needs. As an act of reparation he retreats to a café, apparent center of brotherhood, where his failure to be a total person leads to the murder of the *patron* and the death of a second girl he would like to love. Since he cannot be himself, he remains an enigma to others: people therefore try to create roles for him. The girl sees him as a means of escape from the sordid city, the *patron* as a catalyst for lustful fantasies in which all women become prostitutes. Charlie's self-mistrust becomes a denial of responsibility, so that instead of actions he breeds accidents. It is not without significance that he accidentally kills the *patron* at the moment when he embraces him; for to claim brotherhood without responsibility can only lead to death.

In taking refuge from himself in timidity, Charlie condemns himself to failure. Why then has he been forced into such an unhappy position? The two kidnappers supply an answer. "Always prepare for the murderer at your door," they say, "and if it turns out to be only a burglar, you're lucky." In making such a remark, these two clowns cease to be an arbitrary gag and—unlike the shadowy detectives of *Breathless* with whom Michel and Godard merely play—take on a sharp symbolic force. They begin to stand for all that is sordid, stupid, and malignant in society, all that drives Charlie into flight from society and himself. If we accept this motivation, we see that Truffaut's film no longer embodies a philosophy of discontinuity, but has become a film about a man who suffers discontinuity and loss.

By existentialist canons, then, and unlike *Breathless,* this film breaks all the rules and fails. At the same time it approaches more closely than *Breathless* to our own sense of reality's richness. Since in the last resort we must base our judgments on this response, we are forced to question the all-embracing claims of this New Cinema.

The Cinema of Appearance, we see, is a retreat from a total vision of reality. Though this retreat is honest (it takes courage to realize how lonely man is in a disconnected world where traditional consolations are useless), it is unable to articulate our sense of life's richness. Yet to argue failure in such terms is to leave oneself vulnerable to the charge of whimsical subjectivism. We need a public criterion. One of these is indicated by psychoanalysis, though this does not exclude others.

The terms we would use are those of Melanie Klein. According to her, the individual under stress moves either toward integration or disintegration—and this, of course, conditions his perception of the world. To achieve integration, he must work through the depressive (or mourning) phase in which he acknowledges, however unknowingly, the fact that he has destroyed his inner world by envy. By confronting this desolation, he begins to recreate the value and coherence of his inner world, and this in turn begins to give meaning to the outer world. If this isolation is too hard to bear, however, he will defend himself by "splitting" himself, and thus cutting off the consciousness of depression. If he does this frequently he gradually becomes schizophrenic. The inner and outer world cease to relate and each in turn splits more and more.

By this view, *Breathless* exhibits all the symptoms of such a manic defense. It is no more than a splintered fragment of a splintered reality. Its hard, glossy clarity can be seen as an attempt to foil the onrush of reality with all its messy completeness. It constructs a relationship whose sole justification is to deny love, with its mutual knowledge and commitment, and substitutes instead a form of manic defense—narcissism—so that Michel and Patricia see each other as mirrors and not as people. It works toward no release, because it creates no solid, intractable stuff through which to work. The disturbing tensions between youth and age, class and creed, are deliberately excluded. Bodies never sweat. Objects hit, neither crunch nor thump. Hence death is denied its sole human significance—loss. For as there is nothing to lose, there is nothing to gain; as there is nothing to destroy, there is nothing to create. This is the antiart of an antiworld; and all we are left to marvel at is the pyrotechnic flight of intellect through void.

Or so the director would have us believe. Yet even the most extreme manic defense is not impregnable. In *Shoot the Piano Player* there is, obviously, a fumbling attempt to recreate a world where love and the desolation of reality are not feared. In *Breathless* the break in the defense is not so immediately apparent. It only begins to reveal itself when we look closely at its morality, which is a form of stoicism.[4]

Since traditional moralities have lost their sanctions, our only alternatives are either collapse or a manifestation of dignity simply at the process of being. This stoicism finds for itself a weird code of honor that runs counter to the improvised rules of the game. Michel, having murdered, must court death and endure without comment the neon headlines announcing his coming capture. Patricia, having betrayed, must go on betraying. As Michel says, "Murderers murder, informers inform, and lovers love." Michel imitates the tough man ethos—his idol is Humphrey Bogart—and mimes his set of aggressive gestures, which is ridiculous since a shadow world presents no objects. There is no point in being tough if there is nothing to be tough about. If this stoicism is inconsistent with the theory of the world as appearance, why then does Michel subscribe to it?

In Kleinian terms one would say it was a defense against the tragic sense of life, of the fullness that love and gratitude can bring, and with it—since we cannot have one without the other—the desolation of death and destruction. One can only partially realize this knowledge, for a complete realization would require more than human courage. To some degree we all have our defenses; and all our

4. Without a public morality our feelings lack sanction, and we become hesitant about their importance. Consequently we play them down: we develop a morality that is "cool." Our repressed energy, in compensation, finds release in violence, in living for "kicks."

defenses in the light of this reality are absurd. Michel's stoicism, however, is a defense not only against this awareness of tragedy but against the terrifying demands made by an existentialist morality; for this philosophy of appearance is in itself deeply psychotic. Instead of mourning it offers anguish, instead of the integrated self it offers flight from identity, and instead of reality it offers us a reality like a shattered mirror.

Yet Michel and Patricia cannot gag the tragic sense. It is there in the pregnancy they try to ignore, and it is there in Michel's desire to go to Rome, that old center where all roads used to lead. It is even there in his jealousy, which contradicts his "cool" creed of stoic indifference. A sense of loss does issue from this film as a note of wistfulness—the willfulness of world-baffled children. And once we have caught this note, we begin to make sense of the film in humanist terms. However tentatively, the film begins to transform itself and take on the shape of drama. It begins to manifest plot. Up to now we have accepted Patricia's betrayal of Michel on its own terms as an *acte gratuit*. It now exposes itself to a different reading.

Throughout the film Patricia is bombarded with a series of misleading, gnomic, and contradictory statements about the meaning of life. There is a spate of these at her airport interview with a celebrity. Finally she manages to get in her own question, which is both urgent and, in the context, rather stupid. "What is your greatest ambition?" she asks. Though his reply—"to become immortal, and then to die"—might pass as an artist's insolent flourish, it cannot help her; and help is what she needs. Patricia is forced into fabricating naive formulas so that she can cope with life. In order to be independent of men, she claims, she has to earn a living. Yet she is waiting for some lead that she cannot discover. Her American friend baffles her with remarks she cannot understand about books she only boasts of having read. She would like to love Michel, but he makes her play his game, which drains words of their meaning. Perhaps her hand really shook with emotion when she could not light her cigarette for the first time, but the rules force her to "gag" back at the accusation. Michel might be sincere about his Rome invitation, but how is she to judge when he won't allow her to know him? He denies her the full choice of commitment and rejection and uses her simply to explore the spectrum of his own attitudes.

All she can do is retaliate. Her betrayal is a desperate attempt to force him to commit himself either one way or another. But he denies her even this gratification by the enigma of his death. She is left, at last, still unenlightened, still not knowing whether she is a sex machine waiting to be worked, or a woman waiting to be loved. Not knowing who she is, she cannot tell us; and so, in the final shot, she looks out at us enigmatically. Yet in psychoanalytic terms the enigma does betray a meaning. For is this not the face of the seventeen-year-old schizophrenic described by R. D. Laing in *The Divided Self,* in whom, beneath the vacancy and terrible placidity of the catatonic trance, there still lurked the desolation of irreparable loss, and of whom, though she was a hopeless case, the author could still conclude: "There was a belief (however psychotic a belief it was, it was still a form of faith in something of great value in herself) that there was something of great worth deeply lost or buried inside her, as yet undiscovered by herself or by anyone. If one could go deep into the depths of the dark sea one would discover the bright gold, or if one could get fathoms down one would discover the pearl at the bottom of the sea."?

"Are Women Magic?"

Annette Insdorf

To the question posed by numerous males in Truffaut's films, we can add, "are women mad?", "are women vulnerable?", "are women more complex than the men assume?" The answer to all of these is yes, for Truffaut has created a rather bizarre gallery of rich female portraits. It is impossible to generalize about the women from *Les Mistons* through *The Story of Adèle H.*, for they can be as repellent as attractive, as destructive as warm, as absolutist as adaptable, and as inclined toward madness as love. Truffaut's awareness that a multiplicity of selves inhabits even one woman is evident in the "doubling" that is characteristic of his work. There are films that center on a male protagonist, whose own needs lead him to embrace two complementary female figures: Thérésa/Léna in *Shoot the Piano Player*, Franca/Nicole in *The Soft Skin*, Linda/Clarisse (played by the same actress) in *Fahrenheit 451*, Christine/Fabienne in *Stolen Kisses*, Christine/Kyoko in *Bed and Board*, and Anne/Muriel in *Two English Girls*. And there are films that devote more attention to one female psyche with (at least) two manifestations: Catherine in *Jules and Jim*, Julie/Marion in *Mississippi Mermaid*, Julie/Pamela in *Day for Night*, Adèle/"Madame Pinson" in *The Story of Adèle H.*

Moreover, if we see Truffaut's work as a whole, another pair is formed by Julie Kohler (Jeanne Moreau) in *The Bride Wore Black* (1968) and Camille Bliss (Bernadette Lafont) in *Such a Gorgeous Kid Like Me* (1972), both of whom display no less than five personalities—one for each of their admirers. Despite the fact that the films are adapted from different novels (William Irish's *The Bride Wore Black* and Henry Farrell's *Such a Gorgeous Kid Like Me*) Julie and Camille can be seen as two faces of the literal femme fatale that Truffaut often presents: Kohler (colère-anger) killing for revenge and Bliss killing for pleasure. Whereas the former is intensely moral, the latter is amoral (calling her murderous activities "fate-bets"), for Camille takes about as much responsibility for her actions as a "kid"—gorgeous or otherwise. In fact, "kid" is an important term to keep in mind, for the resonances within Truffaut's cinema bring us inevitably to his first film, *Les Mistons*, which can be seen as the foundation for both *The Bride Wore Black* and *Such A Gorgeous Kid Like Me*. All three films explore the adoration of one woman by five males.

Les Mistons introduces Bernadette (Lafont) as the first of Truffaut's beautiful and inaccessible "apparitions" for the male. A group of young boys are smitten with her as she rides around Nimes on her bicycle, her skirt billowing in the summer wind. The narrator who is looking back at this chapter from his past states

Excerpted from Chapter 4 of *François Truffaut* (Boston: Twayne, 1978).

that she was "the wondrous incarnation of our secret dreams." We see the boys worship even her "pedestal," the bicycle whose seat they sniff reverently while she is in the water. They follow Bernadette and her lover Gérard, spying upon them, and their communally thwarted love is rechanneled into hostility. These little voyeurs annoy the pair (experiencing "the vicarious thrill of the interrupted kisses of the lovers") until they learn of Gérard's death in a climbing accident. When Bernadette walks past them in black at the end, they are able to observe her without yearning. Too young to comprehend, they have glimpsed the mysteries of love and death.

The voiceover narration places the emphasis on the boys, and we see the woman uniquely from their eyes. She is the *object* of affection, especially when she plays tennis and the camera participates in the infatuation by whirling around her little skirt and supple breasts. *The Bride Wore Black* picks up where the plot of *Les Mistons* leaves off: what happens to the woman after the death of the man she loved. Julie becomes the *subject* of the film, the active principle, the one whose thwarted love is rechanneled into hostility. The focus shifts to her response to her older (but no less naive) admirers. By the time of *Such a Gorgeous Kid Like Me,* Truffaut permits the woman to tell her own story—as the title makes clear—and she controls all the characters and events. (To take the doubling a step further, Bernadette Lafont gets her revenge on the *mischief-makers* who tormented her in his first film.)

Truffaut's work revolves around the relationship between the adolescent and the goddess, and his treatment of his own female characters in a sense resembles that of the *mischief-makers.* One way of studying his films is in the movement from adoration (Bernadette) to resentment (*Shoot the Piano Player* and *Jules and Jim* kill off the women—Thérésa, Léna, Catherine—and even *The 400 Blows* includes Antoine's lie—and perhaps subconscious wish—that his mother died), to witnessing the death of the hero/rival (in *The Soft Skin, Fahrenheit 451, The Bride Wore Black,* and *Mississippi Mermaid,* the wives destroy the men, although Linda less directly so), to detachment (from the extremes of Camille and Adèle).[1] *The Man Who Loved Women* (1977), however, suggests that Truffaut has come to terms with the opposite sex: the adolescent male is still the focus (Bertrand is "a wolf who has remained a child") but the goddess is redefined into a group of women, each one individuated, sympathetic, autonomous, warm, and articulate.

Shoot the Piano Player can be interpreted as a continuation of *Les Mistons* since Truffaut's second feature presents five older adolescents who are preoccupied with women: the two gangsters Ernest and Momo, Plyne, Edouard Saroyan, and his second self, Charlie Kohler. These males constitute a spectrum of distorted perceptions of women, from the gangsters' coarse remarks to Plyne's "purity of

---

1. See Marsha Kinder and Beverle Houston, "Truffaut's Gorgeous Killers," *Film Quarterly* 27, no. 2 (Winter 1973–1974): 2–10.

womanhood" speech. Truffaut stated that the real theme of the film is love and the relations between men and women.[2] This is evident from the very first scene in which the stranger tells Chico about his marriage and the number of virgins in Paris—and this theme is developed during the subsequent scene in the bar. The perspective is predominantly that of male fascination: one dancing couple consists of a man peering intently down a woman's dress, which he justifies by declaring "I'm a doctor"; Clarisse is dancing with a short man, repeatedly enticing and pushing him away till he slaps her; two awkward young men watch Clarisse, their eyes practically popping out of their heads. Even the song performed by Boby Lapointe, "Avanie et Framboise," deals with sex, in the spirit and actions of the first half of the film. (The song we hear on the car radio in the second half is rather about emotional commitment and love, and is more in keeping with the developments of this part.)

The "kidnapping" scene is primarily a pretext to talk about females. One of the gangsters tells how his father was killed in a car crash because he was looking at a woman; they discuss how women torment men with makeup, brassieres, and stockings; the other thug recounts how he tried on his sister's silk panties; and they elicit from Charlie those famous last words, "when you've seen one, you've seen them all." At the other extreme is the café boss Plyne whose conception of woman belongs in a medieval court rather than a café: "la femme" is "pure, delicate, fragile, supreme, magical." While his position is a bit excessive, it is not totally removed from Edouard's own behavior. Plyne dies because Léna cannot conform to his expectations; Thérésa dies because Edouard expected the fidelity of an idealized love rather than imperfect experience. In his inability to accept his wife's altruistic adultery (she slept with the impresario in order for Edouard to get his break) and to comfort her, he resembles Plyne (as well as Catherine and Adèle) in their demand for an absolute—and therefore doomed—form of love. And like the *mistons,* he destroys what he cannot comprehend, namely the woman he loves. From this perspective, Truffaut seems to be establishing a context of male culpability to which his future heroines will address themselves.

2. Yvonne Baby, "I Wanted to Treat *Shoot the Piano Player* like a Tale by Perrault." In *Focus on "Shoot the Piano Player,"* ed. Leo Braudy (Englewood Cliffs, N.J.: Prentice-Hall, 1972), p. 23; reprinted in this volume.

The Existential Play in Truffaut's Early Films

Allen Thiher

A rt, one might argue, functions in two essential ways. First, it opens our experience, deranges our way of perceiving experience (including the experience of art itself), and changes the space within which experience may be represented or perceived. In this respect art is a form of discovery and a creator of the conditions of experience. It is a kind of knowledge. Second, once art has opened a space of representation or perception, it can become a testing ground, a realm of experiential probing, in which art may receive its informing impulses from other sources than itself and submit them to various forms of trial that allow us to evaluate the experience of these sources. In this function art derives its basic concerns from other realms, but organizes them so that we can understand these other realms in their full import as experience. In this sense art may be a way of appraising experience as it is defined by other modes of discourse. It is, then, a kind of praxis.

In the greatest works of art these two functions seem to condition each other, as, for example, in the early films of the New Wave filmmakers, in which the need to find new means of filmic representation was made imperative by a desire to portray and to probe the modern absurdist sensibility. Particularly important in this respect are the early films of François Truffaut, who, if he has become the exponent of a rather facile classicism in some of his later films, was perhaps the most inventive of all those young filmmakers whose work reflects the prevailing existentialist ideology of the late 1950s. For it now seems clear that the absurdist sensibility conditioned the experiential limits of the early work of those directors—Godard, Chabrol, Rivette, and others—who, like Truffaut, came to maturity in an ideological climate in which the absurd was the fundamental category that conditioned all attempts at representation.

Before turning to examine how Truffaut's early work is informed by what we are calling the then reigning existentialist ideology, it might be well to consider what were the limits that the notion of the absurd imposed on any artist who was open to the dominant sensibility. It seems to us that the absurd imposed three basic configurations that determined the limits of representation in both formal and thematic terms. First, the absurd was construed as a form of mere presence beyond which there could be no transcending telos or other types of motivation. The notion of absurd presence finds its classic expression in Sartre's vision of being as superfluous, gratuitous presence, as well as such notions as dereliction, fallenness, and alienated being. A second configuration is given by the notion of rupture and

From *Film/Literature Quarterly* 5 (Summer 1977): 183–197.

divorce. Camus's view of the absurd as the divorce between the cosmos and man's desire for a rational understanding of it is one example of the absurd as a form of rupture. But this notion is also at work in the existentialist view of man's radical freedom, by which he can constantly break with his past, or in the idea that man's identity is essentially a discontinuous series of assumed roles. The notion of rupture undermines all rational principles of representation, especially causality, and leads to a third configuration that we might call disfunctionality or the lack of congruent relations. A locus classicus for an expression of this kind of absurdism is Beckett's entropic world, in which all the old modes of representation fail to function, as they, in effect, come to represent the disfunctionality of all attempts at representation. The notion of disfunctionality leads in turn to various forms of self-referentiality by which the work designates its own consciousness of its incongruity, and irony thus becomes one of the fundamental modes of absurd consciousness.

These three configurations established the possibilities of representation for Truffaut's *The 400 Blows* (1959), *Shoot the Piano Player* (1960), and *Jules and Jim* (1961); at the same time they demanded the formal inventiveness that constituted the New Wave's rejection of classical cinematography. Consider in this respect the very beginning of Truffaut's first feature-length film, *The 400 Blows* (or *Les 400 Coups,* a bit of colloquial French that should be translated as "raising hell" or "going on a spree"). The mobile camera in the title sequence, going around the Palais de Chaillot—the home of the Cinémathèque—capturing the Eiffel Tower as it goes down tree-lined streets, denotes Paris as the film's dramatic locus. But its very mobility, "read" against the canons of standard cinematography, designates the film's self-conscious quest for significance. Moreover, this aimless mobility, within the film's specific context, is converted into a metaphor for the indeterminate freedom that the film's hero, Antoine Doinel, enjoys. The camera's gratuitous movement thus foreshadows Antoine's ramblings in the film as he goes on sprees. The absurd, as designated by the camera's very movement, finds an analogous expression in the music played in this sequence. From the outset the music establishes an ironic tension between image and sound, for the music is incongruously lyrical. And this incongruity is another way by which the absurd is signified.

Thus the presence of a camera aimlessly set in motion, breaking self-consciously with the canons of traditional filmic representation and setting forth a world that has no rapport with the film music, seems to confirm immediately our assertion that the absurd informs Truffaut's early work in its most basic formal aspects. It is, of course, at the most primary level of mimesis that these absurdist configurations are most evident, since Truffaut's representation of episodic experience is grounded in plots that are essentially discontinuous series of non-causally related events that reflect the radical, if often incoherent, freedom that Truffaut's characters enjoy. This discontinuity is grounded in an existentialist sense of human liberty, and it is also an expression of the absurdist view that holds that man must live experience as a series of ruptures for which no definitive account can be given until man's flight into the future meets death. And death is the real or metaphorical terminus of all these early works.

In *The 400 Blows* episodic experience springs from the boy Antoine's choices, fortuitous or intentional, that result in acts whose consequences ultimately go far beyond those that a child might foresee, but for which he is entirely responsible. Antoine Doinel, conceived by accident out of wedlock and thus forced into a world that is indifferent to his existence, is something of a prototype of the existentialist hero, especially as he comes to discover that he must bear the responsibility for the least of his caprices. Whatever may be the autobiographical element in Truffaut's portrayal of Antoine's being branded as a delinquent, it is clear that his manner of depicting how the boy stumbles into crime and incarceration is grounded in both an absurdist sense of fortuitous being and an existentialist view of the radical responsibility that is the converse side of freedom. Sartre's description of our helpless dereliction and our paradoxical responsibility in the world gives a special insight into understanding how Antoine is a victim of his own freedom:

> Someone will say, "I did not ask to be born." This is a naive way of throwing greater emphasis on our facticity. I am responsible for everything, in fact, except for my very responsibility, for I am not the foundation of my being. Therefore everything takes place as if I were compelled to be responsible. I am *abandoned* in the world, not in the sense that I might remain abandoned and passive in a hostile universe like a board floating on water, but rather in the sense that I find myself suddenly alone and without help, engaged in a world for which I bear the whole responsibility without being able, whatever I do, to tear myself away from the responsibility for an instant.[1]

It is this tension between the boy's abandonment and victimization, on the one hand, and his free, if unenlightened, choices, on the other, that explains in part the extraordinary power that *The 400 Blows* has. Unwanted by his parents, a superfluous child in a world where no adults will or perhaps can help him, Antoine is none the less the author of a fate that is all the more cruel because it could not be predicted.

In *The 400 Blows* the rhythm of episodes does follow a regular pattern. The boy's activities, his accidental faults or spontaneous caprices, set up situations that result in his punishment. Each of these situations is in turn followed by a spree, a period of seemingly indeterminate freedom, during which Antoine plays, or, as the title suggests, raises hell. The film begins on a humorous note as we see Antoine in a lycée or a secondary school that appears to have been borrowed from Vigo's

---

1. Jean-Paul Sartre, *Being and Nothingness,* trans. Hazel E. Barnes (New York: Citadel Press, 1964), pp. 531–532.

Zéro de conduite. Antoine, now at the age where eroticism is as much a subject of mirth as a mystery to be explored, looks at a pinup photo the boys are passing around the drab classroom. The consequences of this bit of schoolboy rowdiness set the pattern for the rest of the film, for it leads to Antoine's grammar exercise punishment and to his decision, at his friend René's urging, to go on a spree and to play hooky the next day. The pattern continues when, on returning to school on the day after his spree with no excuse for his absence, Antoine blurts out to his teacher that his mother died. This bit of spontaneity results again in punishment when his mother and adoptive father arrive at the school. Antoine again goes on a spree, feeling he can no longer live in a home where he is no more than a tolerated burden. The episodic rhythm finally results in Antoine's expulsion from school when, encouraged by his mother to do better in school, he reproduces in a school composition a passage from a Balzac novel he has read with such fervor that he has unconsciously, it would appear, memorized it. Expulsion is immediate, as is Antoine's decision to go on what becomes his longest spree when he goes to live in secret in an abandoned room in René's house.

This pattern of acts and consequences has thus prepared the viewer to accept that Antoine's petty thievery, his attempt to get some money by stealing a typewriter from his father's office, could result in the child's incarceration. One might construe the disparity between the child's act and its consequences as an indictment of those societal conditions that so easily allow parents to divest themselves of their child and which then offer no better way of dealing with the boy than imprisoning him, forcing him to consort with adult criminals, and finally interning him in a prison camp whose name of observation center seems to be the most cynical of euphemisms. This indictment is undoubtedly present, but beyond this Truffaut has shown how the concatenation of rather innocuous acts can lead to an absurd catastrophe in which there is no congruity between intent and consequence. And beyond societal deficiencies—though the bureaucratic order is replete with them—it is the structure of freedom itself that somehow seems deficient. The boy is free to choose his acts, but these acts can turn against him and ultimately destroy his freedom. There is, then, more than a little romantic fatalism in this rather nihilistic vision of freedom. This paradox is, however, one of the defining features of this kind of existential nihilism, according to which freedom appears inevitably to turn against itself in self-destruction.

This nihilism seems to lie behind the film's final spree, Antoine's escape from the observation center. The final shots are a powerful visual translation of the frenzy of flight, of an explosion of indeterminate freedom, as the continuous tracking shot rushes forward with Antoine through the anonymous landscape. This is another visual metaphor for freedom. The child's flight is a desperate but gratuitous act that leads him to the sea, to the vast, mythic expanse that he had never seen before. In its limitlessness the sea appears to be the antithesis of all the constraints—school, family and prison—that had limited the boy's freedom. But in itself the sea is also a limit to the boy's flight, an absurd barrier not unlike the wall in Sartre's short story of the same name. It is an absurd presence marking the limits of freedom.

The film's final freeze-frame presents a still image that recalls the mug shots the police had made of Antoine. In this respect the still image, in the cinematic context, designates itself as an image and denotes the inconclusiveness of the cinematic quest for significance. It, too, has seemingly run up against this absurd presence. Moreover, the image, insofar as it recalls the police photo, seems to offer a kind of summing up, a résumé that might attempt to fix the boy's identity, though in an absurd world of radical freedom this final résumé could be fixed only by death. And so the final image perhaps connotes death, the final absurd limit of all freedom. In this respect we again see another aspect of the fatalism that decrees that the boy's acts can only generate an ever-increasing crescendo of catastrophes whose logical conclusion could be his death. When one turns to *Shoot the Piano Player* and *Jules and Jim* death is, in fact, the explicit limit that terminates each film.

In *Shoot the Piano Player* Truffaut has recourse to one of the more classic cinematic narrative devices, the flashback, in order to break up his linear narrative and to create a sense of discontinuity in the narration of episodic experience.[2] He first presents his piano-playing hero as Charlie, the barroom pianist who beats out his popular tunes, before portraying him as Edouard, the successful concert pianist whose wife commits suicide. Normal linear narration might have imposed what could be perceived as a causal framework on the character's development, but the flashback, by its very rupture of the narration, forces the viewer to perceive the relation between Edouard and Charlie as a kind of hiatus. Through the flashback Truffaut thus succeeds in portraying the discontinuity that underlies the absurdist view of the self. It also produces a fracture in the narration that nothing can join together. Events are thus related as a disparate series of acts springing from a self fragmented in time. Perhaps nowhere does Truffaut more beautifully portray this fragmentation, however, than immediately after the flashback when we find Charlie and Léna now in bed. The repetition of shots of the couple, breaking their lovemaking and sleep into a mosaic pattern, seems to convey at once an image of their newfound joy and its fragile dependency on this single moment in time, isolated from all those that came before or might come after it.

In *Jules and Jim,* on the other hand, absurd chance is incorporated into the very fabric of the plot itself in such a way that not only does the plot set forth the dramatic action, but its very structure also connotes the arduous difficulty of choice in a world given over to absurd hazard. Consider, for example, the film's pivotal choice, Catherine's decision to marry Jules. She makes this decision, as

2. On the notion of discontinuity one can read with profit Gabriel Pearson and Eric Rhode's "Cinema of Appearance," in Leo Braudy, *Focus on Shoot the Piano Player* (Englewood Cliffs, N.J.: Prentice Hall, 1972), pp. 25–45, reprinted in this volume.

Truffaut stresses by the long scene set in the café, only after she misses a rendezvous with Jim. Later in the film Jim tells her, admittedly while under the influence of his own desire, that he would have counseled against the marriage; and thus it appears that the turning point in the life of these three is due, in part, to mere accident. In the first part of the film Truffaut stresses how sudden, seemingly gratuitous decisions shape his characters' lives, as when Jules and Jim suddenly go to the Adriatic island where they see the mysterious female statue, the incarnation of the eternal feminine, that Catherine represents; or when the three decide with no forethought to go on vacation by the sea together, where Jules finds himself drawn closer to Catherine. These ruptures, predicated on the characters' total freedom, place in relief how much all choice, no matter how premeditated, is ultimately an absurd leap in which one encounters chance.

In the second half of the film, after the war has separated the Frenchman and the German, breaks in the narrative underscore how episodic experience is the product of chance encounters. Jim's return to Germany, for instance, might have ended with his sudden departure, had not Catherine returned at the precise moment he is walking out the door—a coincidence that seems to be ironically reflected in her facial expression as she peers through the window pane. Later, in France, they again come together through pure chance. Truffaut ironically emphasizes the role of chance in the final sequence by introducing it with a title, "Some Months Later," a narrative device that in this context can only signify the arbitrary workings of hazard. It hardly seems to be an accident, however, that Truffaut should place this final encounter in a cinema, for this oblique form of self-reference is another ironic foil by which film designates itself as the locus of chance encounters. Moreover, the newsreel the three see in which the Nazis burn books also reveals how their encounter is due again to those historical vicissitudes that separated them during the war. For it would appear that it is Hitler's seizure of power that has forced Jules and Catherine to come to France and thus cross Jim's path once more. Chance thus leads from burning books to the flames that consume the remains of Jim and Catherine.

In *Shoot the Piano Player* the absurdist configuration that gives rise to narrative ruptures also lies behind the gags and parodistic devices that constantly rupture the film's tonality: a gangster's mother falling dead because he tells a fib, an absurd song that needs subtitles even in French, Charlie's telling his prostitute girl friend to cover her breasts because the censor will not accept the shot (as indeed happened in the American version)—these and many other examples immediately come to mind. In fact, from the film's first sequence Truffaut establishes how he wants to use ironic ruptures to redefine our way of experiencing film so that we come to it as a locus of indeterminacy. In the first scene we see a character, pursued by a car, running in the dark, in a nearly total blackness that is clearly an exaggeration of the tonality that is coded as a sign of mystery or danger in a conventional Hollywood film. The flight we see sets up automatically the expectation of a chase that must be motivated by a crisis. We would then expect the narrative structure to resolve eventually this opening crisis. But Truffaut shows our expectation to be a product of conditioned response, stemming from a desire that film characters be determined in their conduct by fixed narrative codes that govern their responses in accord with the conventions of genre.

In Truffaut's absurdist world characters are governed only by the dictates of ironic self-consciousness, and thus his fleeing character can, in the most improbable manner, run into a street light, knock himself down, get up, and then begin a long conversation with a passing stranger who explains how he found marital happiness. Then the character resumes his flight with all the speed he can muster. This break with the codes of psychological verisimilitude and of standard narration signifies, from the film's outset, that we must read the film in terms of new codes predicated on those absurdist configurations that set the limits for representation at the end of the 1950s. Moreover, Truffaut's parodistic use of codes derived from Hollywood films and the film noir underscores how one, perhaps inevitable, consequence of an absurdist viewpoint is that the work comes to designate itself and to call into question the very possibilities of the medium.

In this respect, it is more than a little revealing to note that Truffaut has been a very harsh critic of *Shoot the Piano Player,* perhaps in reaction to its failure to receive wide public acclaim. But *Shoot the Piano Player* is Truffaut's most difficult film, much like many works of Godard, insofar as it demands a constant recognition of its use of filmic codes and conventions and its parodistic break with them. For it is a film that constantly tests the conventions of representation and their adequacy for representing what we might call conventional life.

The film begins and ends with the image of Charlie Kohler seated at his piano as he grinds out popular tunes for the motley crowd that gathers to dance in this down-and-out bar. The film thus fails to go beyond its opening situation, which is another way of designating a kind of absurd stasis in that the film cannot progress beyond this circular movement. This structural circularity suggests the film's failure to advance beyond the conventions it uses for representation, just as it narrates Charlie's failure to overcome his passivity, or more precisely, to engage himself in a project, or to acquire a self. Yet the film is full of action in a conventional sense. The film first appears to be a gangster film as we now see Charlie help his brother Chico escape from the pair of pursuing crooks, Momo and Ernest. It then appears to borrow the conventions of boy-meets-girl romance as Charlie courts, in his fumbling way, Léna the barmaid. The film's flashback, portraying Charlie/Edouard's conventional success as an artist, recalls the typical Hollywood newspaper tragedy: headlines proclaim that the concert artist's wife has committed suicide—and we know it is because Edouard, in another conventional response, rejected her when he learned that she had slept with his impresario and thus launched his career. The film then borrows from the hero-as-tracked-man genre, the sort that Prévert and Carné perfected in the 1930s, when Charlie interposes himself between the barman Plyne and Léna, and, after using a telephone speaker to duel with this sentimental idealist, is forced to plant an enormous knife between Plyne's shoulder blades because the barman is slowly strangling him to death. And, finally, *Shoot the Piano Player* draws upon the western, to which, after all, it owes its ironic title. When Charlie retreats to the family cabin, where his brothers await the gunslinging gangsters, it is at the beginning of the prolonged shoot-out that Léna is gratuitously gunned down, the victim of the only accurate shot in the otherwise absurd gun battle.

It is this mixing of conventions and resulting multileveled parody that has undoubtedly been responsible for the rather hostile reception that was once given to *Shoot the Piano Player.* The mixture of lyricism and parody, of gags and tragic seriousness, must be envisaged as another form of representation that signifies the absurd, the loss of certainty, the sense of discontinuity that underlie Truffaut's early work. The image of the gangster who twirls the pistol about his finger appeals to the western convention that designates sure-fingered accuracy. In the narrative context, however, such an appeal is a gag that does not seem consonant with the irrevocable death that follows, with the slow slide of Léna's body down the snow-covered hill. But it is precisely this rupture between cause and effect that signifies the existential gratuitousness that informs *Shoot the Piano Player.* The gag, and this film is filled with them, is raised here to the level of a mimetic mode that signifies a metaphysical vision. If we may borrow an expression that is usually applied to Ionesco and Beckett, *Shoot the Piano Player* is often a metaphysical farce.[3]

The absurdist configurations that lie behind the shaping of episodic experience and the parodistic devices in Truffaut's early work also seem to determine his choice of themes. In this respect we can consider a privileged theme in these three films for an understanding of how the absurd orders the representation of character: throughout these films the theme of the characters' identity appears to be a key motif. It is a theme to which all the others are related and from which the other themes derive their full significance. Antoine's freedom, for example, derives in one sense from his identity as a legitimized bastard. To be a bastard is, in effect, to exist free of a determining heredity, absolved of familial and social ties, capable of realizing oneself in complete liberty. Antoine does not, of course, have the maturity to think of his fate as that of being condemned to choose his own form of self-realization in an indifferent world. Yet as a bastard he is, like Stendhal or Sartre's heroes, the prototypical free hero for whom there exists no predetermined structures of identity because there exists no father ready to emasculate him if he does not accept the ideal identity that the father would impose on him. Such seems clearly to be the sense, for example, of the shots presenting Antoine's "father" in the kitchen, a weak cuckold at whom Antoine can only laugh as the apron-wearing man prepares supper while his wife "works late" at the office.

---

3. Rosette C. Lamont, "The Metaphysical Farce: Beckett and Ionesco," *French Review* 30, 2 (February 1959): 319–328.

The bastard's accidental presence in the world is thus a metaphor for man's presence, though the child can enjoy this gratuitous existence as a form of play until he must pass into the world of adults and assume their identity. Truffaut brilliantly contrasts the world of children's magical freedom and the adult world of consciousness when he shows Antoine and René at the puppet show. Here the little children are enraptured, even terrified, by the magic presence of the theatrical world of play, whereas Antoine and René, in the not-so-innocent company of the little girl, are rather indifferent to the spectacle, already too much adults to give themselves over to the puppets' illusory world of magical presence. Truffaut further shows during the theft how the child's assumption of adult identity leads to the assumption of radical responsibility for one's existence. Antoine attempts to change his identity by transforming himself into an adult, and the slouch hat he wears during the theft is thus a sign of his seeking to change his identity. In a sense, of course, he does succeed in assuming another identity, but it is a catastrophic one since it leads to imprisonment and expulsion from society. One can see then that the child's changing identity ultimately gives expression to Truffaut's fatalism, for the child's attempt to be an adult can only result in a form of fall—the fall into adulthood—that leads to dereliction and abandonment.

In *Shoot the Piano Player* Truffaut pursues this vision of absurd dereliction even further in his portrait of Charlie/Edouard, the piano player whose two names point to the discontinuous identity he lives as he seeks to deny the past. Charlie today, Edouard yesterday, he seeks to live the present as a rupture that refuses any existential weight to that catastrophic past in which he sought his identity as a public image. In this sense Charlie has chosen to be the existentialist bastard who refuses all familial and hereditary links, though the film demonstrates, from beginning to end, the impossibility of escaping those ties. We first see Charlie when his brother Chico runs into the bar and, immediately drawing Charlie into his family's imbroglios, calls him Edouard as he asks for help in order to escape from the gangsters. Charlie's angry but comically incongruous response, "Call me Charlie," underscores how difficult it is, in effect, to live one's identity as a negation of one's public image, or, in existential terms, to deny one's being-for-others.

In the existentialist's world of gratuitous presence we can thus see that the converse side to one's radical freedom is the way in which one must exist for others. There is a public dimension of identity over which one has no control insofar as it is determined by the other. The absurdist man is therefore free to choose any identity, and yet tied paradoxically to a being-for-others, an identity he cannot choose and cannot even really know.

Charlie/Edouard's dereliction thus turns on his impossible impasse: as Charlie he attempts to deny his being-for-others and, as Edouard, he tried to exist only as a being-for-others. The first is, as the film demonstrates by the way the family clings to him and by the way others impose identities on him, a hopeless task, whereas to seek to exist only for others is a catastrophically inauthentic mode of being. The episode narrated by the flashback shows this inauthenticity from the very beginning. At the outset of this sequence Truffaut shows Edouard acting out a role with Thérésa as he plays at being a customer before a third party, who is, most appropriately, his future impresario, Lars Schmeel, the promoter who will in effect grant Edouard his future identity as a public figure. This initial scene is emblematic of how the couple lives its relationship as a form of public ritual, even when they think they are playing roles for themselves. Indeed, Truffaut's iris shot that closes this opening scene, isolating Schmeel's head over the couple's bed for a brief moment before the shot fades to the new scene, shows not only that the impresario has infiltrated their relationship in erotic terms, but how his presence as a third party invests their relationship completely, granting them their identity as the publicly known couple.

In their bedroom the other or third party is also present in the mirrors on the bedroom's walls, for it is against these mirrors that they project their image as they act out roles in so-called privacy. The mirror seemingly can embody the presence of the other and, perhaps, allow us some knowledge about our being-for-others. In the case of Thérésa the mirror is the source of an identity that she cannot abide, as she reveals when she confesses her infidelity to Edouard: "Only you know, it's strange, what you did yesterday remains in you today. I look in the mirror, what do I see? Thérésa? Your Thérésa? No, no Thérésa, nowhere, just a filthy rag. . . ."[4] The mirror offers Thérésa an image of what she takes to be her being-for-others, her image as degraded flesh, for her body continues to have a public existence that no act of contrition can change and that no act of denial can overcome. The mirror forces an enduring identity upon her, and it is only through suicide, through the destruction of her body, that she can bring about the rupture that will deny that humiliating image of herself.

Thérésa is perhaps a victim of her own projection, for it seems that it is really quite impossible to ever coincide in any sense with one's public image. One view of this split between Edouard and his public image is given when Truffaut shoots the bedroom scene during which the couple quarrel and Edouard expresses doubts about his identity as a public success. The viewer first sees an image of Edouard that he takes to be the "real" image of the pianist, but the camera then moves, and the spectator discovers that he has been viewing a mirror image of Edouard. This split between the man and his double seems to signify the gap that always exists between a man's knowledge of his identity and his knowledge of that identity as it exists as his being-for-others.

Truffaut uses a number of ironic and sometimes comic devices to show how Edouard's being-for-others takes on multiple forms. Lars Schmeel, for instance, has a portrait made of Edouard so that through this image he can, as he says, possess the piano player. Léna keeps a large publicity poster in her room, which

4. My translation from a screening of the film.

seemingly allows her, too, to possess an image of the piano player, the public image of the conventional success that she wants to admire. Edouard also tries to create publicly verifiable images of an identity, such as when he poses for photographs in the hope of creating a new image as an aggressive public figure who has overcome the timidity that has been offered to him as his essence. These multiple images are ironic doubles of the multiple identities that Charlie/Edouard has for others, and their very multiplicity points up the difficulty of ever knowing what one's image in the world might be.

Yet, in anguish, Edouard/Charlie seeks that knowledge and acts upon what others tell him. It is Lars Schmeel who tells Edouard that he is timid, which sends him comically scurrying in search of images of the non-timid so that he might correct his identity. Plyne, the barman, tells Charlie that he is fearful, which, in one of the more amusing ruptures in the film, leads Charlie to try out various ways of saying "I'm afraid," as if he might hear in his own ears a public intonation that would give him a sense of what he is. Happy to welcome Charlie/Edouard back into the family, his brothers offer him a hereditary identity—that of a born criminal, a true Saroyan—and with it a gun that seems necessarily to accompany his new role. It is revealing, too, that Léna/Héléna, the bastard orphan whose name reflects her own uncertain identity, also wants to force Charlie/Edouard to act in accord with the identity she has determined to be his, that of a great pianist. The final result of this profusion of identities and the mishaps that result from them is that the piano player withdraws from the world, determined to have no being-for-others, desiring to commit no act other than that most derisive non-act of beating on his tinny piano. Aznavour's stoical face, as he pounds on the piano keys, seems then to signify directly a loss of self in this world where act and identity refuse to congrue.

Perhaps the most powerful ironic representation of this loss of self is given near the film's end, when the viewer sees that Charlie, trapped in his parents' house by his accidental crime, must confront the futility of his attempt to change his identity. But now, having assassinated Plyne, having thus committed a disastrous act by having intervened in Léna's quarrel, he has acquired another public image that should somehow be visible to him. He is, after all, a criminal. With unwanted gun in hand, he looks twice at himself in mirrors, as though looking for some sign of an identity, but all he finds is a cracked image of himself reflected in old broken glass. The cracked double is an ambiguous sign, for it seems at once to set forth Charlie's loss of self, the destruction of any identity, and the impossibility of finding an affirmation of one's identity in the world. Moreover, the circular tracking shot that follows Charlie around the room where he keeps vigil, leading him from his cracked image and then back to it, seems to stand in an analogical relationship with the film's circular movement, that leads from the opening image of the piano back to the final shot of the piano. The circular movements designate how the piano player is trapped in his own immobility, incapable of going beyond the search for an image, gratuitously derelict in a world of absurd presence.

The antithesis to this kind of immobile presence, lived as a refusal of one's being-for-others, is of course to be found in the way Catherine seeks, in *Jules and Jim,* to renew her existence and invent new values at every moment. The absurdist configuration underlying this attempt at permanent creation is again that of rupture and discontinuity, as we clearly see when Catherine, dressing in a manner that recalls the boy in Chaplin's *The Kid,* can seemingly change even her sex at will. The question of Catherine's identity determines, in fact, the way Truffaut constructs his representational space throughout the film, for it is she who defines the limits within which the others attempt to find their own roles. This is evident from the very beginning when Jules and Jim, attracted by the image of a statue whose enigmatic face is shaped like Catherine's, go to the Adriatic in pursuit of this mystery. In a sense they are drawn there by the power of eros, of the eternal feminine, of physical forces that are beyond their control and all of which seem to be part of Catherine's identity. In this respect Truffaut has modified his filmic axioms insofar as Catherine deprives Jules and Jim of their freedom. As in Goethe's *Elective Affinities,* that classic study of passion's magnetism that Truffaut posits as an extrafilmic parallel to his work, Jules and Jim must contend with affinities that they are powerless to control.

Like the heroine in the Scandinavian play that neither Jules nor Jim cares for, Catherine refuses all permanence and sees herself, as she says, "inventing life at every moment."[5] When Jules quotes Baudelaire's definition of women ("Woman is natural, therefore abominable."), Catherine's leaping into the Seine is a gratuitous act by which she shows that no label can be imposed upon her, no simplistic formula can give a résumé of her being. Like the water into which she leaps, she sees herself as one and yet ever different. This leap signifies a form of rebellion against all conventional restraints, including reason itself, and thus represents a kind of triumph over the absurd in which the irrational is held up as in itself a supreme value. In this respect Catherine seems to be quite close to certain of her historical contemporaries and in particular to the Gide of *Les Nourritures terrestres,* who, in proclaiming his hatred of families, sets forth an ethic of readiness, of willingness to try out all forms of experience. For in this post-Nietzschean world of nihilistic gratuitousness the maximization of experience, as Camus described it for his "absurd man," becomes the only form of redemption.

Catherine is allied not only to water, but also to fire, as we see when, immediately before the three go on their vacation by the sea, she decides to burn her letters and in doing so sets her robe on fire. It seems to be an ironic foreshadowing that it should be Jim who is there to put out the flames, for the film's dénouement reverses, in metaphorical terms, this gesture when it is Catherine who drives Jim into the water and finally quenches the flames of desire that have burned in them. Catherine's burning her letters is again a sign that she is another of Truffaut's

5. François Truffaut, *Jules and Jim,* trans. Nicholas Fry (New York: Simon & Schuster, 1968), p. 36.

characters who deny the value of the past, for, as Catherine says of the letters that contain her past, they are merely a matter of lies. But flames also burn those who live in them, and it would appear that Truffaut in this scene sets forth an implicit critique of that ethic of freedom that refuses all limits in the name of intensifying experience.

This critique is even more evident as one notes how Catherine's refusal of a fixed identity and her pursuit of freedom resolve themselves into a series of fetishes and rituals by which she constantly seeks to affirm her power of inventiveness and to prove her power over others. One might consider, for example, how Catherine refuses to allow Jim to place his hat on her bed, first when he comes for her baggage before their vacation, and then later when he takes possession of the room in the chalet in Germany with Jules and Catherine. Or, to cite only a few other examples, Catherine's resolution to use only the same bottle of vitriol wherever she may be, the search for rubbish she undertakes with the two men while on vacation, her refusal to speak on the telephone with Jim, or even her notion of "equilibrium" in sexual matters. This kind of constant ritualization and fetishism has no psychological significance in any conventional sense. Rather these games and prohibitions are so many signs of how Catherine gratuitously converts objects and acts into rites endowed with an arbitrary taboo value. In his third film, then, Truffaut seems to present a rather direct critique of the absurdist view of identity. The quest for total inventiveness, denying any continuity in time, only results in a disparate series of gestures and disconnected rituals, until finally Catherine has no identity except that of an aging woman who has accumulated a repertoire of roles that are no longer adequate or even amusing.

The gratuitousness of man's presence in the world and the discontinuity of identity that underlie these films' vision give rise in turn to another essential motif. This is the motif of play, for it can be maintained that all of Truffaut's characters are essentially players and that the space of representation here is a ludic or play space. With the advent of the absurd, play becomes a privileged activity precisely because it needs no exterior or transcendent goal to give purposiveness to human action. Play is a self-contained activity that justifies itself by its very nature. As we see in the early films of Chabrol and Godard as well as Truffaut, absurd man is almost obliged to be a player, for not only does play endow his being with at least a temporary justification, but, in a second and related sense, the disparate identities that he chooses to embody condemn him to be nothing more than a player, or an actor whose identity is nothing more than a series of roles.

In *The 400 Blows* periods of play alternate regularly with periods of constraint and confinement. Constraint takes place in those enclosed spaces, such as the schoolroom, the dank apartment, the wire cage, or the observation center, that are so many emblems of societal efforts to repress the child's desire. They are also so many emblems of absurd enclosure that stands in opposition to the child's freedom, to his play instincts, to his sprees. Every time Antoine can escape from one of these places of confinement, he immediately begins to play. By himself, or in the company of his friend René, he uses his spree time as a playtime in which going to the cinema, stopping traffic, playing pinball machines, or simply exploring Paris are moments of a ludic freedom that allows acts to be gratuitously organized for their own sake as play. The tension between enclosure and play is present throughout *The 400 Blows,* though perhaps this tension finds its most revealing expression during the series of shots in which Antoine is in the amusement park rotor. The machine begins to spin and, as the centrifugal force pushes the riders to the wall, the floor falls away, leaving the riders pressed against the ride's inner walls. Here is an image of play in one of its purest states, for, as we see on Antoine's face, the apparent suspension of normal physical laws sets up a new state whose ludic justification is the pure exhilaration it offers. Yet Antoine also struggles against the forces that literally pin him to the wall, and the strain his face expresses shows us that the image is ambiguous. For he is pushed against the wall, forced into an immobility that seems to foreshadow the final freeze image in *The 400 Blows.* Within play itself, it would seem, are forces that threaten the child, for, as we see here, play can result in a kind of oppressive confinement at the same time it remains an exercise in spontaneity.

What we have called the fall into adulthood marks for Antoine the loss of magical purity that play offers. In *Shoot the Piano Player* Truffaut next portrays an adult player's failure to play in any authentic fashion. It hardly seems an accident, moreover, that Charlie/Edouard tries to define himself by playing the piano. As Edouard he attempts to use his playing to give himself a public role, whereas, as Charlie, he uses it as a defense against the world, as a way of isolating and protecting himself. But in both cases it is noteworthy that Truffaut frames all shots of the piano player playing so that the piano is a barrier between the player and the world. Charlie's use of the piano in this respect is fairly obvious, but there is little difference when we see Edouard at the piano. The piano, in one shot hemmed in between large columns, gives the impression of creating a kind of cell in which Edouard is locked. The piano player has thus perverted play, and what should be a form of affirmation in an absurd world becomes instead the walls of a prison house in which the self dies. Music—the purely ludic organization of sound—becomes for Edouard a means to an end, to the creation of an inauthentic social self, whereas for Charlie it becomes the means to the opposite end, the creation of a barrier around the self. Play has turned against itself and, perhaps as in the case of Antoine, become a form of confinement.

It is in *Jules and Jim,* however, that Truffaut has developed his most complex testing of the notions of play in a world without constraint that seemingly allows the invention of any game one is audacious enough to contrive. Jules, Jim, and Catherine's attempt to redefine human relations and perhaps invent new values is undertaken in fact as a form of play, and the way they invent new rapports must be likened to games for which they invent the rules as they proceed. Before Catherine's arrival in Paris, we see that Jules and Jim are free spirits for whom life consists of nothing except games. The remarkable variety of shots at the film's beginning are so many images of play and play freedom.[6] As the credits are given, for instance, we see a quick series of shots in which Jules and Jim entertain themselves with various games—the mock duel, playing dominos, racing, etc.—that are a prelude to the games they play after their encounter with Catherine. It is, of course, Catherine who insists on defining the rules of those games. In the first part of the film this is perhaps most evident when Catherine, after making a series of jokes that do not succeed in disrupting Jules and Jim's chess game, slaps Jules for a casual remark. On one level, she is merely petulant because the two men refuse to pay her any attention. But on another level, she is demonstrating her power to define all relationships, or the rules for the games they play. Truffaut stresses this aspect with the series of freeze shots that follow the slap, portraying Catherine's beautiful face in different expressions. Frozen, statuelike, each expression is like a different mask she wears for each play role she commands. And, appropriately enough, it is at this moment that Catherine decides their vacation is over, for the game of vacation has obviously run its course when the two men have found other distractions than Catherine's games.

In the second half of the film Jim's decision to come to Germany to visit Jules and Catherine opens up a new period of play, for Jim comes to see if he, too, should marry, or, in other words, give up the bohemian rules of the game that do not allow him to live with his mistress Gilberte (though he spends each night with her). Jim finds that he is still magnetically attracted to Catherine. Since Jules, in a gesture of near monastic renunciation, has given up all hope of making Catherine happy, the trio tries to find a modus vivendi through play, through inventing new rituals that will allow them to come to terms with their desire with self-given rules. We see this play in all their activities, in the games Jules and his daughter Sabine enjoy, in their cavorting in the countryside, or in their cycling with Catherine's sometime lover Albert. After Jim and Catherine consummate their desire, directly under the sign of Goethe's *Elective Affinities,* it seems most fitting that the group invents a new game, "the village idiot," in recognition of how the conventional local villagers consider this household to be full of lunatics. This also points up, however, how they are aware that the illusory harmony they institute is the play harmony of an arbitrarily accepted order that, so long as it remains confined to the play space—the isolated Rhine Valley chalet—is self-sufficient.

When Jim leaves the play space, he is forced to confront choices, to commit himself to acts that have consequences that play acts seemingly do not. Or, more precisely, Jim's flaw is that he can neither commit himself to the given rules for societal games nor accept the games that Catherine proposes. When he returns to Germany, he wants to leave as soon as he has arrived, but Catherine's arrival, after she has spent the night with Albert (Albert equals Gilberte, according to her rules), merely starts the game again, with Catherine once more determining the rules.

---

6. Cf. Graham Petrie, *The Cinema of François Truffaut* (New York: A. S. Barnes, 1970), pp. 13–14.

The stakes of the game this time are a child, for it is apparently only by Catherine's conceiving that a play equilibrium can be established in Jim's favor—for Jules has already shown his capacity for paternity. Yet one also feels that the child would be a symbol of the plenitude that their game playing has not achieved. Jim again vacillates, for he has no heart for the kind of inventiveness Catherine desires, and when he learns in Paris that the child they finally conceived was stillborn, he can only conclude: "It is a noble thing to want to rediscover the laws of humanity; but how convenient it must be to conform to existing rules. We played with the very sources of life, and we failed."[7] Having lost at this game, Jim does take refuge in the safer conventions of the life he leads with Gilberte. Given Truffaut's near-obsessive concern with the family, however, their failure to create a child should be seen as a sign of the sterility of the gamesmanship, the inventiveness, and the desire for total freedom that has characterized their relations.

The rest of the film is then given over to portraying how Catherine's attempts to be an inventive player degenerate into neurotic compulsiveness, and, finally, catastrophe. When, some time later, Jim encounters Jules and Catherine and they go for a drive in the country, her repetition of the adventurer's game (she remains at the inn with Albert, the man who has "played the part" for her so many times before) is a humorous but rather mechanical performance. When she later drives her automobile wildly about the square beneath Jim's window, careening about and honking in the early hours, it seems clear that she is using her auto as a toy to express her freedom, as a toy in a new game to entice Jim, though this is as childish a gesture as it is neurotic. And when, in the mill house that spans the river, Jim then confronts Catherine with her failure to "invent love from the beginning," her menacing him with a revolver shows that she is now a desperate player who will stop short of nothing to impose the games she desires. The film's dénouement, then, is only the film's final confirmation that in her playing Catherine has not triumphed over the absurd, but rather, in Camus's terms, that she has chosen to collaborate with it.

In conclusion, it is important to stress how *Jules and Jim*, in differing in one important respect from *The 400 Blows* and *Shoot the Piano Player*, points beyond the New Wave toward such works as *The Wild Child*, *Two English Girls*, and *The Story of Adèle H*. This difference is, in the simplest terms, that *Jules and Jim* is a historical film. *The 400 Blows* and *Shoot the Piano Player*, like most New Wave works, set forth experiential situations that are contemporary with the aesthetic axioms—and the absurdist configuration—that inform them. They are, moreover, works that are, in an existential sense, to be experienced as a radically present world: open, unordered, and gratuitous in its lack of determination. In *Jules and Jim*, on the other hand, the film's experiential space is self-consciously given as a world past, and we are thus invited to make use of our knowledge of that past in

---

7. Truffaut, *Jules and Jim*, p. 92.

experiencing the film. It is perhaps a bit ponderous to say that Truffaut, like many other French artists at this time, encountered history in this film, but it is true that the historical dimension suggests an understanding of art and experience that points beyond the reigning absurdist ideology. To view experience with its historical dimension is to view it, potentially at least, in terms of a rational ordering, and one might well maintain that the sharpness of Truffaut's attitudes toward absurdist notions is heightened by his historical sense in *Jules and Jim*.

This historical dimension is present not only in such shots as the documentary footage Truffaut uses to depict the rupture between the two friends that the war brings about or in the shots of Nazi book burning that they see in the cinema toward the end of the film. It is also present in the way the film develops certain historical motifs that are, in fact, analogous to the absurdist motifs that run through the work. In more precise terms, the work begins during the heyday of modernist experimentation and shows how the modernist quest for the transvaluation of values ends, for Jim and Catherine at least, in the absurd plunge into the river. It is thus not at all an accident that Truffaut first sets the film in the belle époque, during those "banquet years" before World War I, when artists and poets believed, with a naiveté that the war was to dispel, that they were capable of inventing new values and a new civilization. That Jules and Jim are to be viewed as part of the modernist movement is clear in a number of details, such as, for example, the way that Truffaut gives to Albert certain traits that recall the poet Apollinaire. Albert, like the poet, recognizes the great artists ten years before anyone else. Moreover, Jim evokes Apollinaire—the "impresario of avant-garde"—when he describes a soldier who deflowered his fiancée through the mail. Apollinaire's importance in this context is that he was the central figure in the struggle between modernism and traditional values in Paris before World War I, and his struggle to balance invention with an understanding of the past stands in direct analogy with the struggle that Truffaut portrays in the film.

It is with this historical dimension in mind that we can clearly see that in *Jules and Jim* Truffaut sets Goethe against Picasso, or an understanding of the limits of human possibilities against a belief in man's capacity to displace the values of the past—or, to return to the historical analogy, against the absurdist notion that man's radical freedom reduces the past to nothingness. But the only real survivor in any of these three films is Jules, and it is perhaps most significant that it should be the only father in the film, the only man to assure continuity, who can walk away from the crematorium. Moreover, he is the German whose renunciation, as Nietzsche said in thinking about Goethe, is perhaps to be seen as the only way to triumph over the absurd. In this case the final image of Jules walking through the cemetery is, then, as much Truffaut's way of presenting an image of the death of modernist and absurdist hubris as it is an image of dereliction and isolation.

Truffaut, Godard, and the Genre Film as Self-Conscious Art
Leo Braudy

After the 1950s the various genres of film no longer inhabit the same isolated worlds they had before. Instead of being relegated to the periphery, genre films in the 1960s enter the mainstream of film history. Truffaut and Godard considered film to be a total aesthetic world—with a definite influence on the experiential reality of the audience—rather than a world with artistic parts (the "serious" films similar to other types of great art) and unartistic parts (the genre films). The locus classicus of the New Wave interest in genre is Godard's dedication of *Breathless* to Monogram Pictures, an act meant both to outrage the highbrow critics and to assert the one source of film craft—the self-consciously conventional—that the New Wave believed was the most neglected aspect of the art and the history of film. The power of these early films rested in their ability not only to pay wry homage to a purely cinematic tradition of genre narrative and convention, but also to express the way these fables had influenced and shaped what the audience considered reality to be. Realism was only another set of conventions, irrelevant as an absolute standard because of the actual interplay between the world of normally unorganized experience and the world of genre fairy tale, the paranoid hyperorganization of art. Europeans were less surprised than most "cultured" Americans, and the reaction to Truffaut's *Shoot the Piano Player* is indicative of the disruptive effect the New Wave attitude had on the understanding of film in the United States. The greatest producer and developer of genre films in the world— the United States—which for years and years had looked down on its native products and looked up to European film as the only serious expression of the art, suddenly was being told that its most neglected and critically patronized movies were its greatest contribution to the art of film, perhaps greater than the classics that had been revered in the art houses for so many years. Critics as disparate as Bosley Crowther and Stanley Kauffmann complained about the seeming haphazardness and incoherence of *Shoot the Piano Player.* But what actually is so disruptive about the film? It begins with a man running down a street, being chased by someone we don't see—the kind of *in medias res* beginning that had been a staple of American action films in the late 1940s—the way, for example, we first see Burt Lancaster in Norman Foster's *Kiss the Blood Off My Hands* or Cloris Leachman in Robert Aldrich's *Kiss Me Deadly.* The question for the audience is "Why is this person running?" and what better way to draw an

From *The World in a Frame: What We See in Films* (1976; rpt. Chicago: University of Chicago Press, 1984), pp. 164–169.

audience into a film? Truffaut's abrupt beginning to *Shoot the Piano Player* attacks the elaborate narrative exposition (derived from the novel), which had been the hallmark of serious films from Griffith and Eisenstein through Welles, and replaces it with a more oblique, allusive narrator. Renoir, Rossellini, and many of the more open-form directors had also used such a juxtapositional, rather than causal, narrative in their various films (compare the beginning of *Shoot the Piano Player* with, for example, the beginning of *The Rules of the Game*). But Truffaut's story didn't seem to be serious enough to hold together the fragmented and associative narrative. It was a crime film, with murders, greed, petty gangsters, and bantering dialogue. Instead of being economical in the fashion of the enclosed urban crime film, it focused on the variety of the city, a long opening dialogue with a character who never reappears, comic turns, and songs. Inspired by the American film noir in tone and convention, it, like *The 400 Blows* and Godard's *Breathless,* was held together by character as much as by style. As Truffaut said in an interview at the time, "Because spectators see the same scenario in so many films, they have become good scenarists and can always foretell what's coming and how it's going to end. With *Shoot the Piano Player* I would like them to go from surprise to surprise." Truffaut defined the genre conventions as a frame within which he was free to do as he pleased, at the same time that he could ironically reflect on the reasons the conventions existed. The critics who were upset at his film had either, like Crowther, grown up in a tradition in which popular and serious films occupied different compartments in their heads, or, like Kauffmann, considered film to be aesthetically interesting primarily when it was thematically interesting. Those who appreciated it, like Pauline Kael, had no rigid line to draw between varieties of film seriousness, and no inherent prejudice against American films for their mass appeal. That an audience could respond to *Shoot the Piano Player* or *Breathless* in a way that critics often could not indicated that not all film aesthetics were defined by the great tradition of "classic" films. The film audience's experience of all films was aesthetically continuous; films by Renoir, Nicholas Ray, and Stanley Donen could all be alluded to in *Shoot the Piano Player* because all had contributed to Truffaut's sense of the possibilities of film.[1]

The genre film, most markedly in the New Wave's use of it, asserts that there is a normal film aesthetic that is unobtrusive and yet complicated, hardly visible if one looks for technical flash on the screen and yet perfectly understandable to the audience. Genre art, they implied, is the art we learn when we are unaware we are

1. I have discussed *Shoot the Piano Player* in more detail in *Focus on "Shoot the Piano Player"* (Englewood Cliffs, N.J.: Prentice-Hall, 1972), an anthology that includes interviews with Truffaut as well as contemporary reviews of the film. The American film audience had already been prepared for the New Wave self-consciousness about film history by television reruns. Truffaut and Godard may have spent their days in the Cinémathèque, but the average American filmgoer was being exposed to the growing film repository of television.

learning it. It is no less important than the art we learn at the height of our intellectual awareness, and it may be more influential, since its power is frequently unmediated by the detachments enforced by the "art"-perceiving mind. The old distinction between the serious and the genre film could never be the same. If what the New Wave brought into film can be described in one word, that word might be "self-consciousness" at all levels: a self-consciousness about film history and tradition, a self-consciousness about the act of making a film, a self-consciousness in the audience that approaches the film more as a cultural artifact than as an entertainment for which the mind was turned off, and, perhaps the most important aspect, a self-consciousness about the role of the director, matched with the audience's increased awareness that the director is a "star" too. Inspired by the sense of tradition and formal self-awareness that marks genre films, the New Wave at its best treated convention seriously, as it treated technical devices seriously. Some of the effects of the self-consciousness have been negative, or have had negative aspects, as interest was displaced from the film to allusion, director, or anything but the experience of the film itself. . . . Many directors tried for easy brilliance by self-reference and self-mockery. The seeds are already there in *Breathless* and *Shoot the Piano Player*—the allusions to friends, to other films, the awareness of being inside a film, the role of the director in putting the film together—a centrifugal allusiveness that threatened to make the audience forget the main point of being there, a film story and its characters. Although the New Wave shed much light on the previous history of genre films and exposed their aesthetic tenets, its polemic therefore often produced films that were less interesting or moving than the old "classics." The self-consciousness that existed within genre film found it hard to retain its innocence in the face of the self-consciousness that referred to the act of filming itself. Every young director out to make his name in the 1960s believed that his work was automatically intellectually and artistically respectable if he included a camera or a scene from the production of the film. A director like Fellini, who added fuel to the trend toward directorial self-consciousness with his film *8½,* could, because of the theatrical roots of his realistic method, move from literal exposition to dream exposition without obvious halts and stops. But when realistic directors whose roots were in documentary, like Lindsay Anderson, attempted such external references, the result was more often incoherence than extension of the possibilities of film. *If . . .* and *O Lucky Man!* try to use frame-breaking, illusion-shattering devices to convey a Brechtian thematic seriousness. But, without genre, or some other implied order, the breaking of the frame has no context and becomes merely fragmentary and disruptive. Particular sequences may work, but the film as a whole is too easily dismissible as an arch and unnecessarily allusive joke. An effort to go beyond the inherent aesthetic bounds of film comes off as a self-consciously "arty" playing with those bounds, with little enrichment in the play.

Complexity for the New Wave was not only a matter of themes and visual style, but also an effort to treat film conventions in an explicitly self-conscious manner.

Playing on the mythic interactions of the implicitly self-conscious genre films, they told stories in which the moral judgments implied by the aesthetic pattern were inadequate to judge the actual events and characters. Instead of calling on dramatic irony or the bathetic happy ending, they trusted the audience's ability to know the conventions of various forms and the openness that results when forms collide. This active manipulation of film tradition and the new star status of the director as self-conscious artist might recall the relation between Lang and Rotwang in *Metropolis* or between Renoir and Octave in *The Rules of the Game.* At the same time that, outside the film, the creative strength and power of the filmmaker is being celebrated, within the film the main character, usually a man, often an artist of some sort, is presented as a basically weak, self-involved, often impotent figure. Charlie Kohler in *Shoot the Piano Player* thinks of taking a course in daring, falls in love, kills, but finally withdraws again; Michel in *Breathless,* living as he imagines Bogart would, dies because his girl friend wants to play Bogart as well. Sandro in *L'Avventura,* a failure as an architect, continually fails in all his human relations; David in *Through a Glass Darkly* and Elisabet in *Persona* use and almost cannibalize others for the purposes of their art. Charlie Kohler, in flight from his celebrity as a concert pianist and what it has cost him personally, stands in contrast to his creator Truffaut, able to distance his own confusion about the virtues of fame and anonymity by embodying them in a character. Michel, who tries to escape his problems by fitting into Bogart's image, stands in contrast to Godard his creator, who in the film appears as a bystander who recognizes Michel and turns him in to the police. The failures of Sandro, David, and Elisabet as well are the material for the success of Antonioni and Bergman.

In the period of the 1960s and 1970s, therefore, the exploration of genre structure necessarily intersects the exploration of character. The old genre forms are no longer substantial enough to express fully and satisfactorily the themes that now most attract the film audience. Without tradition, the directors must create their own forms, one hopes with more success than that with which their characters explore their own psyches and shape their lives. The New Wave helps mark the way in which films, with their mixed art and their ability to manipulate and transform conventions, have helped free us from the outworn aesthetic distinctions of the past. The end of the 1950s begins the first new era since the introduction of sound in the late 1920s and early 1930s, coinciding with the decline of studio power and the rise of a more independent kind of director in Hollywood itself. The characteristics of that era are not yet fixed. . . . The essential element that concerns me here is the refusal of the new filmmakers to make any absolute or even partial distinction between the methods and techniques of "serious" films and the methods and techniques of popular, genre films. Like the Elizabethans, who could take high tragedy and low comedy, often in the same play, the same film audience can appreciate both serious and popular films and find within them explorations of the issues that equally animate their feelings and their intellects.

The Statement of Genres

James Monaco

The basic structure of *Shoot the Piano Player* comes from David Goodis's novel *Down There* (1956), a standard "gangster" book. It is not a detective story . . . , but a rather straightforward narrative about a former concert pianist who now bangs an upright in a South Philadelphia gin mill.

Onto the basic Gangster structure Truffaut grafted the love story of Charlie and Léna (Marie Dubois), the flashback love story of Edouard (Charlie) and Thérésa (Nicole Berger), the antagonism between Plyne and Charlie, and the relationship between Charlie and his younger brother Fido (in order to provide a role for Richard Kanayan). Most of these elements exist in embryo in the novel, but Truffaut has amplified and refined them so that—in the film—they take on greater significance and disrupt the unity of mood that the novel has. Whereas the novel is cold, straightforward, linear, the film is a mélange of cold and warm tones, sometimes deviously elaborate.

Take the first scene. The action of the first shots of the film is parallel to the first paragraphs of the novel: Chico (Albert Rémy) runs into a lamppost and falls down. But the rhetoric contrasts sharply with Goodis's. Truffaut's Chico is helped to his feet by a stranger and the two—without skipping a beat—launch into a pleasant philosophical discussion of marriage. Truffaut has injected an element of community that is quickly followed by some thoughts on relationships between men and women, two themes that will thread their way through the films to come; the spare, cool, tough milieu of Goodis's novel is transformed into a more human atmosphere.

Truffaut's Charlie Kohler is just as isolated as Goodis's Edward Webster Lynn, but whereas Lynn is pictured as a relatively strong, self-confident guy who has chosen his solitude, Truffaut's Charlie Kohler has found his isolation almost inevitably: he was always shy, withdrawn, reclusive. "My characters are on the edge of society," Truffaut has explained many times; "I want them to testify to human fragility because I don't like toughness, I don't like very strong people, or people whose weaknesses don't show."[1]

Charlie's affair with Léna, short though it is, is fraught with ambivalence. He wants her very much, as we know from the early scene in which he walks her home, agonizing over whether and how to make an advance. When he finally gets up the courage, Léna has disappeared. From that point on the affair is controlled

---

1. Quoted in Sanche de Gramont, "Life Style of Homo Cinematicus—François Truffaut," *New York Times Magazine,* June 15, 1969.

From *The New Wave: Truffaut, Godard, Chabrol, Rohmer, Rivette* (New York: Oxford University Press, 1976), pp. 42–47.

by Léna. Indeed, it is she who narrates the flashback in which we learn of Charlie's earlier life as Edouard Saroyan, concert pianist, and the melo-dramatic death of his wife Thérésa (which, Truffaut notes, is his homage to Nicholas Ray and Samuel Fuller). Practically, it is necessary for Léna to narrate the flashback since we could never conceive of Charlie revealing so much about his past life, but the effect is also to distance further the life of Edouard Saroyan for us. What Léna tells us (and she tells us more than she could possibly know) is her version of Edouard, someone whom, from the evidence of the posters that plaster her wall, she has studied with a special fixation for quite a while. Charlie has been driven to reject the life of the successful Edouard not out of any particular existential scruples but because that life, or at least the success that colored it, was the literal creation of a woman, Thérésa. If she had not slept with Lars Schmeel there would have been no Edouard Saroyan, famous concert pianist. And, with perfect irony, if she had not told Edouard that she was responsible for his career in this way, she would not have been driven to suicide and Charlie Kohler would not have materialized.

From another perspective, it was the magnitude of Edouard's career that drove the wedge into his marriage to Thérésa, so it was only fitting that that career be sacrificed as a memorial. What Léna sees in this story is further evidence of the romantic ideal that Charlie represents (not only to her but also to the denizens of the café for whom he effortlessly grinds out music). But she also should see that she is in the same relationship to Charlie that Thérésa was to Edouard. She doesn't know, however, that she will meet the same end. What is fascinating about these twin love stories is the unusual imbalance of the relationships. Charlie/Edouard truly plays a passive role in each and becomes, therefore, an embodiment of the romantic fantasies of both women. This double triangle is a pattern that will become quite familiar in many of Truffaut's succeeding films—as will the shy, isolated hero.

It should be remembered, however, that Charlie is not entirely alienated: he demonstrates a real concern for his kid brother Fido, to whom he is a surrogate father. This makes him rather more interesting than the relatively wooden pro-tagonist of Goodis's novel, or than a classic existential hero like Camus's Meur-sault. It is Fido's kidnapping that provides the impetus for Charlie's flight, even if it is Charlie's accidental murder of Plyne that finally forces the issue. Léna, as well, has a role to play in this chain of interlocking responsibilities: it is she whom Charlie and Plyne fight over. As so often in Truffaut's films it is the woman who controls the relationship and, thus, the story.

Yet the women are not the focus of *Shoot the Piano Player* as they are in other films. The film is a portrait of Charlie Kohler. His face dominates the screen as Truffaut tries to capture the weary, thoughtful, introspective, frightened, persistent character he divines in Aznavour. Once again an actor has dominated the film and changed its nature. "Aznavour gives the tone," Truffaut explained. "What hit me about him? His fragility, his vulnerability, and that humble and graceful figure that made me think of St. Francis of Assisi."[2]

As with Léaud, Truffaut was extraordinarily lucky with Aznavour. The great paradox of the New Wave is that the critics who had championed the author of a film—the director—had such tremendous assistance from a broad gallery of talented actors when they began making films themselves. Aznavour, Léaud, Belmondo, Brialy, Moreau, Deneuve, Dorléac, Karina, Blain lead the list of remarkable talents. Strangely, Truffaut never again used Aznavour after *Shoot the Piano Player,* and the adult male protagonists of his succeeding films never quite catch the full flavor of Aznavour's fragility, vulnerability, and grace. As the films become narrower in intent, so do their protagonists, it seems, and Truffaut chooses actors more professional than Aznavour (who had been and remains a singer) but less striking, less precise.

In fact, of the succeeding films only *The Wild Child* and *Day for Night* give so large a space to male heroes (we are excepting the Doinel films for the moment) and, significantly, Truffaut chose to play the main roles in both of those films himself. For the rest, from *Jules and Jim* through *The Story of Adèle H.,* the focus rests more often on the female protagonists. Having caught the substance of the particular kind of male character he finds fascinating in his first two films (especially *Shoot the Piano Player*), Truffaut seems to have turned his attention to women, who remain even today vaguely mysterious. ("Are women magic?")

In a small book, *L'Existentialisme est un humanisme,* published just about the time *Shoot the Piano Player* was released, Jean-Paul Sartre defended that nebulous philosophy against the charges of pessimism and quietism that were so often leveled against it. The book announces the changes of mood and direction that were taking place at the time in existentialist thought, as the possibility of action became more attractive. Truffaut's Charlie Kohler is an existential hero who seems carefully balanced between the relatively passive philosophy of the 1950s and the more active mood of the 1960s. He is still unable to take control of his life, yet far more able than existential characters of the past to understand the dimensions of it. He has already made the Camusian choice when we meet him: Edouard Saroyan has rejected his own existence and built another, considerably more isolated. He now exists almost outside of everyday reality and has only one strong connection with another human being—his brother Fido. His life is as close and circular as his theme song. But just as the melody of the song repeats itself, so will the pattern of Charlie's life. A new woman begins the whole intolerable business of feeling all over again; and the tragic conclusion is parallel. It is Charlie's terrible burden that his simple story always ends in someone else's death, not his own. The pattern is Sisyphean. There is no resolution for Charlie's dilemma, but there is some relief in his art. At the end of the film he has retreated once more to

2. "Aznavour donne le 'la,'" *Cinémonde,* May 5, 1960.

the comfort of the piano, as he is introduced to the new waitress and the story begins again.

In a way, Charlie is a surrogate for Truffaut at this point in his career, for both have rejected the world of "serious" bourgeois art in order to make genre art: Charlie for the people in the bistro, Truffaut for the "film nuts." Any conscious genre filmmaker has made a commitment to popular art similar to Charlie's, and we may surmise that some vague, unexpressed political sentiments lie behind Truffaut's decision to devote himself to genre films, just as such sentiments seem to support Charlie's own choice.

Nevertheless, despite the wealth of hints we receive in *Shoot the Piano Player* as to Truffaut's political world view, the complex narrative structure of the film makes it difficult to draw conclusions. Charlie abstracted from the film may very well fit these developing theories. But Charlie inside the film is a creature of his women. Our point of view is Léna's (and Thérésa's), strictly speaking, and the subtle narrative tension between the audience's analysis of Charlie and the women's is what makes the film still intriguing. Charlie's is a life overheard, not boldly offered. And it is grudgingly given up to us in fractured pieces. Mirrors play an important part in the narrative: we are introduced to Charlie through a mirror, we most often observe him at the piano through the overhead mirror, he stares at himself in a fractured mirror at the climax of the film in the little house in the mountains. Posters and paintings of his face are important as well. We get bits of his life in almost random order and have to piece them together. It is the mosaic approach again.

There are notably fewer long and inclusive pans in this film. The wholeness that such pans convey in *The 400 Blows* (and the other Doinel films) is not part of the gestalt of *Shoot the Piano Player* (nor that of most of the other genre films). The technical metaphor that *is* common in Truffaut's second film is what we might call the "edited zoom," a series of three or four quick shots of a detail in which each shot successively magnifies the image. This device is jarring, explicit, and introspective, and it fits Charlie's fractured story well.

In the standard text on editing, Karel Reisz and Gavin Millar describe a classic example of this device. When Charlie goes to Schmeel's office for an audition, he doesn't enter right away. He hears someone playing the violin and, not wanting to interrupt (or simply because he is too timid), he is left standing in the hall, caught in the midst of one of the miniature dilemmas of everyday life that has suddenly become unbearable. At this point Truffaut inserts a quick series of shots of Charlie's finger poised above the doorbell button, each more magnified than the one that preceded it. For Reisz and Millar,

> The shots provoke a whole string of reactions: (1) They are funny. (2) They
> are menacing, as all moments are when the action slows up, or the cutting
> begins to go into a great deal of detail. . . . (3) They are psychologically ac-
> curate since they represent his timidity. (4) They draw attention to a notorious

temps-mort, that time that we all spend standing outside doors that won't open. . . . (5) Charlie is a protagonist who embodies the philosophy of discontinuity.[3]

A heavy freight of meaning to load upon such a simple metaphor? Perhaps. But the sequence stands as classic Truffaut. It is concrete, evocative, and self-effacingly edited, and it speaks volumes. Charlie eventually does ring the bell and enter. But Truffaut, with what will become characteristic reserve, chooses not to follow him into the audition. Instead, we watch the woman who had been playing the violin a bit earlier leave Schmeel's, walk down the long corridor, and leave the building, while we hear the stirring strains of Charlie's melodramatic audition on the soundtrack. The sequence emphasizes and respects Charlie's privacy at the same time that it unites him with the violinist—a woman whom he'll never know, but with whom he at least has shared both a moment and a way of life.

This sequence could stand as an emblem for the whole film: it is dialectical (this time in a specifically Eisensteinian sense, through the montage that opposes characters, sentiments, and shots); it gives us two characters alone and isolated—strangers in fact—and manages cinematically to unite them in community; and finally it also carries some of the feeling about art that Truffaut always injects into his films, for it is the music—first the violin, then the piano—that speaks in the scene, not the people. (Is *music* more important than life?)

---

3. Karel Reisz and Gavin Millar. *The Technique of Film Editing,* 2nd rev. ed. (London: Focal Press, 1968), p. 333. The section dealing with *Shoot the Piano Player* is reprinted in this volume.

Tirez sur le Pianiste
C. G. Crisp

The Cannes Film Festival of 1959 had been a triumph for young directors and established the New Wave both in France and internationally. But this very popularity was disconcerting for Truffaut, who had believed that he was making a film for a small group of enthusiasts. Instead he found that his film had been taken up by the mass public "who only go to the cinema twice a year to see fashionable films." Interpretations were distorting it, and it began to seem very remote to him. Success had other effects, too: "What is important, now that I come to think of it is that after Cannes I bought a car. One day I said to myself 'Well, well, it's six months since I took the Metro.' And that's serious. But if I took the Metro 'just to see,' that would be even more ridiculous. . . . In four years I will be incapable of making another film like it because I'll have forgotten that sort of flat, and how it feels to put out rubbish bins, and so on."

Even his intolerance of films that didn't meet his high standards was becoming modified, as he admits with disarming frankness: "After a few years of criticism, I felt I had the cinema at my fingertips. I could distinguish the good from the bad and understood it all. Now that I'm making films myself, I no longer know anything about it: I haven't any criteria or any principles left, I haven't the slightest idea what I'm talking about." And elsewhere: "I've become more indulgent, lost all intention to reform the cinema. Bad films don't arouse my indignation as they once did. I'm simply left with the determination to make good ones. I've lost the purism of the true cinemaniac; I've become an egotist, like all directors."

Truffaut was well aware that his second film was a perilous undertaking. For all the group, their first films had been a natural choice, for economic or personal reasons, but, with producers now ready to back any film they might choose to make, the question was what direction their development should take. "Everything is said in the first film; after that, all you do is embroider it." Truffaut had, in rough form, several other scenarios about childhood and his own experiences, but decided not to persevere with them in case he seemed to be exploiting a success. Besides, he was by nature reluctant to let himself be categorized, and wanted his next film to be as different from the first as possible. He also began to feel that it was bad to be too sure of what one was going to do next: better leave it to chance and the inspiration of the moment.

In this case, the inspiration was provided by one of Marcel Camus's statements after the success of *Orfeu Negro,* also at the Cannes Film Festival. Camus claimed

From *François Truffaut* (New York: Praeger, 1972), pp. 43–57.

that, in order to make the film he wanted, he'd had to hold out against fifteen offers of gangster films. The implied slight on gangster films infuriated Truffaut, who once estimated he had seen about fifteen hundred of them. He had also been disconcerted to see how thoroughly French his first film had turned out to be, when his film background was mainly American. Now he acknowledged this debt by adapting a gangster story to a French setting. There was a precedent in the prewar gangster films of Marcel Carné and Jacques Prévert, which he had admired precisely because they used the genre as a medium for a new type of realism and to express Prévert's personal preoccupations. More recently he had praised *Touchez pas au grisbi* for similar reasons. Noting that Jacques Becker was forty-eight when he made it, and Simenon forty-nine when he wrote it, he suggested that the true subject of this apparently straightforward gangster film was "the feeling of approaching the age of fifty." Becker had played down the violence and the more sensational aspects of the underworld, stressing instead the themes of friendship and aging. Truffaut proposed to do something similar, and offered Pierre Braunberger a film based on David Goodis's *Down There*.

Truffaut felt this was a natural reaction after making an intensely personal film. His impulse to retreat into anonymity was heightened by the flood of "personal" films in 1959, sparked off by *Breathless* and *Hiroshima, mon amour*. This alteration of autobiographical scenarios with adaptations was later to become almost a matter of principle. Besides, he said, "if I made a film each year from an original scenario, my films would all be too French, too full of nuances, too much a collection of little things, with not enough action; so with my taste for filming events which, important or not, are dramatic, I turn to books. I feel like filming their dramatic events, but would never have the courage to invent them."

Goodis had long been one of his favorite Série Noire authors, and Truffaut had already been struck by the cinematic possibilities of the overnight car journey into the snow-clad mountains, which was to remain the central image. The hero is a musician of Armenian extraction, which immediately suggested Charles Aznavour. Truffaut had wanted to use him since seeing him in Franju's *La Tête contre les murs,* which he named the best film of the previous year. He was later attacked for building a film around such a well-known personality, going back, it seemed, on principles that had led him to deride the "star system." For him, however, stars (like big budgets) had never been bad in themselves, but only insofar as they tended to undermine the director's control. He would never make a film with Michèle Morgan, Fernandel, Gérard Philipe, Jean Gabin, or Pierre Fresnay because they saw films as vehicles for projecting their own image, and would "correct" anything in the film that didn't correspond to their inclinations. Aznavour's attitude was entirely different; he was willing to abide by a director's decisions. Because her attitude was similar, Truffaut chose to work with Jeanne Moreau in his next film. Besides, Renoir—his guide in so many things—had often built films around stars, though usually the more attractive female ones. Perhaps not the least important reason for wanting Aznavour was the curious physical resemblance between him and Truffaut. Just as Léaud was to grow to resemble Truffaut to a disturbing extent, Aznavour already looked like a slightly more careworn version of him.

The preparation and shooting of the scenario did not proceed entirely smoothly. Truffaut could not take seriously, or commit himself to, the fundamental situations of the genre. It began to seem to him that underworld conventions and attitudes were simply those of any bourgeois society, very slightly modified—"gangsters who are fathers, and who gasp 'look after my kids,' or 'see that my wife gets the money,' etc. I quite like people in society, provided they are alone; not if they organize themselves into a gang. . . ." In fact he was becoming aware of an attitude that was to unite all his films: the protagonists are brought into conflict with the existing order of things and were to be outsiders who champion a society in which the individual is more free to express himself. He said, possibly exaggerating a little: "I'm interested mainly in thieves, beggars—and prostitutes, the asocial people of whom I should least like to see society cleansed. Anyway, would it want to be. . . .?" As a result, during shooting he emphasized more and more Aznavour's solitude. Léna remarks, "Even when he's with other people, he's alone." Conversely, he treated those gangster scenes that remained in a slightly jocular fashion: "I got out of the problem not by parody but by a sort of drollery. Really I was very ill at ease making it."

His gangsters are highly original creations, slightly grotesque yet also disarmingly human and down-to-earth: whoever saw gangsters dancing around flapping their arms to keep warm, whoever heard of a gangster's car breaking down, or saw them struggling to push it to a garage while the kidnap victim steers, bouncing up and down with excitement? Ernest can scarcely drive, and Chico knocks himself out running into a lamppost. And surely the slang is a bit too colorful, as if the scriptwriter had been more intent on amusing himself than on creating characters? It all reveals a desire to break out of the genre, too constricting for Truffaut; it was neither as amusing nor as appropriate to his personality as he had thought. Even the gun battle at the end, the inevitable showdown, is distinctly grotesque, distorted, so that the gangsters appear fallible and slightly ludicrous human beings trying desperately to act out traditional gangster situations in a convincing manner.

And yet these purely burlesque scenes are juxtaposed with moments of pure pathos. Immediately after the comic gun battle Charlie and his young brother bend over the heroine, poignantly closing her eyes. Intercut with the comic kidnapping trip is Charlie and Léna's overnight journey to the snow-clad mountains. Burlesque alternates with solemn moments of tranquility and beauty. It is presumably the element of beauty that tempted Truffaut to say that his treatment of the story was like a *Conte de Perrault,* that is, a sort of fairy tale, raising Charlie's vain search for love to the level of a fable.

But the result is a "shocking" and quite deliberate confusion of genres: "I know there seem to be four or five films crammed into this one, but it's deliberate, as I strove above all to shatter the idea of genre. I know there is nothing the public detests so much as changes of tone, but I've always had a passion for them." Elsewhere he adds, "the tone of the film resembles a hot-and-cold shower. This is its experimental aspect. I've tried a few risky juxtapositions, alternating passages of riotous fun with others that are disgustingly melancholy. I don't think I could ever make a film all on the same level." It is probable, too, that Truffaut got a certain malicious pleasure out of confusing the spectators, by changing the rules in midgame, for one of his principal complaints about the previous generation had been that they made the same film over and over again, with the result that the audience could read scriptwriters' minds and foresee the next scenes. Here was his chance to catch them out with the unpredictable, to lead them up the garden path.

Revolting against the finished perfection of the "quality" French tradition, Truffaut asks for the same grainy, gray, deliberately ugly image that Godard was to give to *Les Carabiniers* and *Bande à part*. On the other hand, the photography in the mountains is suitably poetic, with clear images and splendid black patterns on the snowy landscape. This recalls the contrast between the seedy, gray, slum-like appearance of the city on the plains, symbolizing hopelessness, and the purity of the mountains, symbolizing fulfillment, that Rohmer later used in *My Night at Maud's*. It also recalls the end of *The 400 Blows,* except that here the snow has replaced the sea as a symbol of liberation. We find that Antoine was justified in feeling ill at ease and uncertain on reaching the sea, for in the present film Charlie's similar hopes of reconciliation with life—through the "love of a good woman"—are totally shattered; he is doomed to return from the heights to his seedy bistro and, by implication, to relive with the new waitress the same hopeless dream he has lived out with the first, and with his wife, who was also a waitress. The message is even clearer than in the previous film: ideals are illusory, and entertaining them can only be harmful. But whereas *The 400 Blows* embodied this message in a basically optimistic form, the overall tone of *Shoot the Piano Player* is pessimistic.

The black and white of the photography is used to reinforce the latent meaning. In *The 400 Blows,* Antoine had 'happened' to drink his stolen milk in front of a winter sports poster and another one advertising Chaplin's *The Gold Rush,* a combination suggesting his youth, innocence, and idealism. In *Shoot the Piano Player* it is a milk bomb, not a water bomb, that Fido drops on the gangsters' car; and the forces of evil, normally associated with black, are hampered by this whiteness, which prefigures the snow at the end.

A discussion of love and friendship is also central to the film; it forms, in fact, a "third film" imposed on the two already described. The preoccupation with individuals and their relationships is as typical of Truffaut's private life as of his films. Antoine and René portrayed an existing friendship, as had *Les Mistons;* and, in *Shoot the Piano Player,* we again find the protagonist involved in a series of close personal relationships—three are with women, and one is with his younger brother. They don't constitute any deep analysis of affection: Charlie's marriage to Thérésa and the collapse of their relationship contain nothing original, and the ideal she represented in his intensely romantic imagination can be defined in simple terms. He sees in Léna the hope of realizing the same ideal. Based on abstract concepts, these relationships don't lend themselves to psychological complexity. Truffaut is less interested in psychology than in noting external behavior, and his attempted psychological explanation at the close of the flash-back is no more convincing than the flashback itself, which is too long, and unrelieved by the burlesque treatment we find elsewhere in the film. It is as if Truffaut were trapped by some private significance into taking seriously material that doesn't merit it. The third variation on this theme is Charlie's relationship with Clarisse, the prostitute with a heart of gold, a stock situation.

But the subject's importance for Truffaut is shown by the introduction of Fido, who didn't appear in the book. Played by the boy in *The 400 Blows* who kept having to tear smudged pages out of his notebook, he becomes the pivot of the action: affection for him has kept Charlie going after his wife's death, and through him the gangsters trace Charlie's mountain hideout. It may reflect the relationship between Bazin and Truffaut, which was originally to have played a much larger part in the film.

Even more remarkable than these instances are the occasions when one of the characters pauses almost in midaction to deliver an impromptu and apparently gratuitous aside on the subject. The casual meeting at the beginning between Chico and the stranger is used to introduce a charmingly irrelevant discussion of married love, the proportion of virgins in Paris, and the possible effects of a first child on a marriage. Truffaut and his wife had had their first child earlier that year. Similarly, Plyne, while trying to strangle Charlie, delivers himself of thoughts on ideal love and the Purity of Womanhood—ludicrous in context, but not fundamentally different from ideals that Charlie seeks in his women. The mysterious stranger makes the same kind of declaration at the end of *Stolen Kisses*. A final variation on the theme is provided by Ernest's lecherous soliloquy during the drive, beginning with his father who had been run over through watching women instead of cars (and had died through trying to grab a passing nurse), and passing on to several dubious puns and cynical epigrams. Truffaut pointed out that love was the one unifying element of the film—"the men in it speak of nothing but women, and the women of nothing but men. At the height of the payoff or the kidnapping the only thing they speak of is Love—sexual, romantic, physical, moral, social, conjugal. . . ."

Reluctantly the focus of all these relationships, Charlie is a typical Goodis hero and has particular relevance to Truffaut. Goodis's novels reveal an obsession with moral culpability, a certain masochism, an awareness of original sin and a puritanical distrust of physical love; his ill-fated heroes aim at escaping the world of action and achieve a state of passivity, or solitary indifference. The pianist is no exception, but the interest lies in Truffaut's modifications. Although he jokingly admits to being puritanical, he makes love to no less than three women in the course of the film, and with enthusiasm. None of these scenes is taken from the book, and they are regrettably trite, especially that in which Charlie goes to bed with Léna.

Truffaut also used the analogy of Charlie's musical talent to speak of his own artistic hopes and fears. He mentions his newfound wealth and success, and continues: "Probably I'm not a great artist, but I need someone to believe I am." His wife replies: "I'd prefer you to be pretentious, and certain of your genius. The least criticism makes you ill, but after all why should you worry, and anyway you weren't any too gentle with others, not so long ago. . . ." This obviously refers to Truffaut's career as a critic, and it's amusing to hear Charlie reply, "Exactly: I rather regret all that!" "Ah, ah," she says, "regrets; too late, my man!" This all corresponds to Truffaut's own admissions of critical humility at this period.

Charlie's lack of self-confidence is another theme contributed solely by Truffaut. The original Eddie was a tough character with strong masochistic impulses. Charlie is quite the reverse. Plyne recognizes his timidity, Clarisse thinks him timid (at least until the episode under the sheet), and it is the timidity of his joke rather than the joke itself that makes gangsters laugh. His hesitation in taking Léna's hand confirms all this, and our later discovery that Léna was equally anguished at the time does suggest a world peopled with tentative, uncertain individuals wanting simply to make contact but seldom daring to try. The feeling is reinforced by Charlie's nervous hesitation at the impresario's door. The camera suddenly retreats to the other end of the corridor, from which point Charlie looks small, trapped, and very much alone.

He overcomes his timidity twice. In a scene improvised during shooting, the impresario advises him that shyness is an illness and should be treated as such: Charlie buys books on the subject and we see him facing journalists with newfound confidence. The second occasion is the psychological climax of the plot: he has walked to the piano to avoid getting involved in a confrontation with Plyne. It looks as if his defeatist impulses will win out: "You can't do anything for Plyne or for anyone. You're not in the race, nothing matters any more. Well, so what? Not your concern, nothing to do with you. Just be so good as to sit down where you belong, at the piano." But finally the threat to Léna jolts him out of his inertia and he accepts his new involvements and responsibilities. Because they undermine all this, the last scenes represent the triumph of mediocrity, of isolation, and of resignation.

The material, strictly speaking less autobiographical than *The 400 Blows,* is nonetheless a logical extension of the director's autobiography. It is not by accident that the gangsters, abducting Charlie and Léna, find themselves driving along behind a van advertising *Cahiers du Cinéma;* that Charlie's brother is called Chico after one of the Marx Brothers; or that Charlie himself should have been so called, because of Aznavour himself, but also because the character in the book was compared to Chaplin. Truffaut's well-known attitude to censorship gives point to Charlie's covering of Clarisse's breasts, because "in films, that's how it has to be." The censors took revenge by prohibiting the film to people under eighteen.

And if the sheet scene and probably the car ride recall *Breathless,* the ending in the snow is strongly reminiscent of the end of Lewis Seiler's *The Big Shot,* with Humphrey Bogart, whom he had already written into the scenario of *Breathless.* Even the phrase *rentrez chez vous, c'est un accident* "was a key phrase for me: in almost every American film someone says it. That phrase had to go in there."

One of the aspects of Truffaut's character we meet for the first time here is his taste for cabaret, with its typical songs, music, and dances. His knowledge of the Paris music hall was second only to his knowledge of the cinema, and he visited cabarets and music halls almost as regularly. Aznavour, too, came from this background, and something of the atmosphere is recreated in the music he is given as well as in the night club numbers. Philippe Repp and Henri Vigoureux, respectively the English master and the night watchman in *The 400 Blows,* had come from the music hall; so does Serge Davri, who plays Plyne; and of course the marvelous song "Avanie et Framboise," which Truffaut lovingly allows to be sung in full, was part of the singer's current cabaret act. Similarly, one of Truffaut's favorite songs by Félix Leclerc, "Dialogue des amoureux," happens to be on the radio during the overnight car journey, and helps to create a feeling of stillness and tranquility at this point.

As before, the fact that people, incidents, and settings are present because of their appeal to the author rather than for their value in the plot helps to create an atmosphere of unpredictability. Truffaut was pleased that he had not included a single scene of which the sole function was to render the plot more credible. On the other hand he included many that willfully interrupt and sidetrack it. The stranger, Plyne's thoughts on women, Boby Lapointe's song, all interrupt the story and remind us of Truffaut's interest in people whose mannerisms he is pleased to record. Even at the climax of the gangster story our attention is drawn away from the battle toward the touching death scene, and we never find out what happens to the loot: Truffaut lets the gangsters roar off, happy to be rid of them at last.

Shooting started on November 30, 1959, at Levallois on the outskirts of Paris, and finished in mid-January with the mountain scenes shot near Grenoble. At first, Truffaut thought of shooting the interiors in a studio, but found that they would cost three times as much as the same sequences shot in natural settings. Probably the real reason was a fear of the unknown. Nervous of dealing with organizations, and conscious of his years of criticizing the studio-made, quality tradition, he had, on the other hand, confidence gained through experience in his ability to use natural settings. Discussing Autant-Lara's claim that he couldn't work outside a studio, he says, "It's not true: he's afraid. Myself I say I don't like studios. In reality I'm scared stiff. We pretend. I'm scared; he's scared; we're all scared."

Again, he used Dyaliscope and postsynchronized sound. Even with sound added later it is usual to record the background noises direct, which involves following the action with a microphone suspended just outside the frame, and the consequent danger of its silhouette or its shadow being recorded. Truffaut bitterly contrasted the perfection of photography with the primitive sound systems. In this case, however, a certain crudity in both was considered acceptable, as conveying an impression of a documentary authenticity. He used two cameras (and later three) to record each take—one for general shots, the other hand-held by Raoul Coutard for close-ups. Truffaut wryly observed that the weight of the camera gave the operator a vested interest in getting the scene right the first time. Multiple cameras make for fluent editing. Truffaut almost certainly used the system in imitation of Renoir, who the previous year had made *Le Testament du Dr Cordelier* for television (where multiple cameras are the norm) using as many as eight or ten cameras to record one scene.

Also from Renoir comes the tendency to modify the scenario drastically during shooting. The shooting script of this film gives only perfunctory stage directions, which disappear after the first few pages, as does the script itself after scene 69, Charlie's arrival at the family hideout. The last sixth of the scenario probably existed only on scraps of paper. Those directions that do exist include such phrases as "Depending on how I feel on the day, Fido will appear at this point or not." Nevertheless, the changes are not as radical as those in *The 400 Blows:* Truffaut now had a clearer view of the form he wanted the film to take.

As with all his films at this period, his first inclination seems to have been for an extensive commentary that would introduce the film and explain several purely visual scenes. The fragments that remain jar with the sections of internal monologue from Charlie, and later from Léna, and give an impression of inconsistency. The script began by casually introducing Charlie, then deserted him to relate Chico's arrival. The film version is therefore more inherently dramatic in building up characters. Truffaut seized any opportunity to push the film toward burlesque. The comic breakdown was originally simply a petrol stop, and the exaggerated shivering of the gangsters was probably spontaneous, since it was being shot in midwinter. Equally, the autobiographical aspects were strengthened during shooting by the last-minute addition of some of the timidity scenes, and also by all the indications of literary or cinematic taste. But most important, the original script had a long monologue in which Charlie pays homage to his old music teacher. This section bears a strong resemblance to Truffaut's accounts of his own relationship with André Bazin. Clearly, when it came to shooting, this testimony, written so soon after Bazin's death, seemed unacceptable.

The flashback, the central section of the film, was much longer in the scenario, with memories within memories, soliloquies, and further commentaries. That he was rather self-conscious about this section is shown by the phrase appended to it: "FLASHBACK (the first in my work, as yet somewhat insubstantial)." Extensive cuts were made during shooting, but it is still unsatisfactory. Much better is the brief flashback in which Plyne is seen betraying Charlie. This was reduced to the time required for Ernest's description of it by dividing it into three and having the end of each shot overlap with the beginning of the next.

Finished in January, the film was not shown to the French public until the end of the year. It met with a curious reception. Critics praised it highly, and almost unanimously, as better than *The 400 Blows* and with *Breathless* the most important film of the New Wave. Possibly forewarned that it was not conceived for the general public, but rather for the initiated, they were better predisposed toward it than it deserved. Despite this praise it was not a popular success, though the producer did not lose money on it. For Truffaut, however, "of those who saw it, eight out of every ten walked away disappointed. So for me it was a failure. There's no point in wasting people's time." This sensitivity to implied criticism is as strong in him as it is in Charlie. He wants to combine the desire to express himself with the desire to entertain. When one critic remarked that he seemed to look on his films as a sort of circus spectacle, he was delighted:

> Precisely. My films are circus shows, and I'm glad of it. I never put on two elephant acts together. After the elephant, the juggler, and after the juggler, the bears. I even allow a sort of intermission toward the end of the sixth reel, because by then people's attention is flagging. At the seventh reel I take them in hand again, and try to end with a flourish. . . . I swear I'm not joking: I think of the circus while working. I'd like to see people hiss and boo the unsuccessful sequences and clap at those they liked. And since in order to see my films people have to shut themselves up in the dark, I never fail, toward the end of a film, to take them out into the countryside, beside the sea, or in the snow, so they'll forgive me. . . . I've created certain laws for myself, often quite naive, but they mean a lot to me and I try to improve them from film to film.
>
> If you like, it's a cinema of compromise in the sense that I think constantly of the public, but it's not a cinema of concessions, because I never use a comic effect I haven't myself laughed at, or a sad one that hasn't moved me. That said, I'm not completely satisfied with any of my films; there's always something important that didn't come off. It's very hard to bring off a really good circus show.

Not only was the cool reception a severe blow to him, but it came at a crucial time for the group as a whole. Chabrol had attempted, in *A Double Tour,* to do something similar to *Shoot the Piano Player,* but it had met with similar coolness. As well as dividing its characters evenly into "beautiful" and evil ones, like *Shoot the Piano Player, A Double Tour* had a similar symbolic subject underlying the murder mystery. Chabrol said that for him it depicted "the massacre of beauty." His *Les Bonnes Femmes* was proving equally unsuccessful, and *Les Godelureaux* was to consign him to several years out of favor. Godard's second film had just been banned, and the first films of Rivette and Rohmer, promised to the public for nearly two years, were still not available and proved disappointing when they did appear. For over a year, no New Wave film had been a commercial success and producers and public alike were beginning to lose faith in them. Truffaut admitted that he and his friends were going through a bad time, and attributed it to the fact that, in attempting to emancipate themselves from the industry, they were making comparatively unsophisticated films on simple subjects. The qualities they aimed at—grace, lightness, elegance, discretion, rapidity—were dangerously close to the faults of frivolity, naiveté, and superficiality.

If he was shaken by this criticism, there were others that he was confident were unjustified. Accused of mixing genres, he said the whole concept of genres was out of date; accused of producing a parody, and therefore a parasitic film, he protested that he detested parody: what had guided him was the concept of affectionate pastiche. In particular, he brushed aside the accusation that he and his friends were basing their films on minor social or personal problems in a world where bigger issues were at stake. Basically he was being called on to justify an apparent lack of political awareness at a time when France was involved in extremely violent postcolonial conflicts. He refused his critics any right to pre-scribe what films he should make; their job was simply to judge the ones he did make. "When a journalist asks why we younger directors aren't making films about Algeria, I feel like replying, 'Why aren't you writing a book about Algeria? Because you wouldn't know what to write. . . . Well, I wouldn't know what to film.' The reality is too complex and foreign to me. I only film things I know thoroughly." Not that politics didn't interest him: on the contrary, he consumed all books and films available on contemporary history, once called Resnais's *Night and Fog* "the greatest film ever made," and admired him enormously for being able to make such an influential gesture. But he himself was always too ready to see all sides of a question, too capable—like the pianist with Plyne—of under-standing even the enemy's point of view, to be able to assert and persevere with one particular line. Rather than documentary or cinema verité he always preferred fiction, based on his own modest experience. "This doesn't exclude ideas on life, the world, society. But I like anything that confuses the issue, that sows doubt; my bedside reading is 'La Séquestrée de Poitiers'; I only like unexpected details, that prove nothing; I like all that reveals the vulnerability of man. . . . Why exalt workers, who hate what they're doing? During the period of my life when I was a welder, I would escape from my work by reconstituting mentally the three or four films I had seen the previous Sunday. And believe me, for nothing in the world would I have gone to see a film about workers."

Despite his protestations, Truffaut's final feeling about the film seems to have been one of regret. By March 1961 he could say: "Perhaps Chabrol shouldn't have made *A Double Tour* nor me *Shoot the Piano Player*. These were detective novels we'd liked long before becoming established, and when you're in a position to realize an old dream you say, 'I'd certainly like to make that thing I read years ago.' At the last minute you realize it wasn't worth the effort." These mistakes were rendered all the more critical by the general context of uncertainty then prevailing in the French cinema. Attendances had fallen to their lowest level since the war, largely due to the spread of television and the steady drop in the real value of workers' wages. People could no longer afford to go to films, especially when they were paying off hire purchase on a television set which showed them five films a week. Producers who had never loved the younger directors, but only their sudden success, had been further hit when Malraux removed state aid to the industry on the grounds that other countries of the newly-formed Common Market didn't have it. It was imperative that the New Wave directors, and Truffaut in particular, should reassert their ability to combine the expression of their personal preoccupations with a wider popular appeal.

Truffaut and Bazin

(a) *As in the scenario (cut from the film)*

CHARLIE: You see, if it hadn't been for Zélény, I'd never have become a pianist; he's the only bloke that ever helped me; he was a father to me; he not only taught me to play the piano, he taught me to be a man. He was a remarkable fellow, and I owe him everything worthwhile that ever happened to me; to speak to him was like bathing in the Ganges for a Hindu. He was far from well, but his moral health was impressive. He borrowed money openly, and lent it discreetly. With him, everything became simple, clear, and frank. When he went away for a few days, he always looked for a friend to lend his house to, and another to lend his car to.

THÉRÉSA: He must have loved you a lot.

CHARLIE: He loved everyone without exception; people are always asking, is the world just or unjust, but I'm certain that it's people like Zélény who make it better, because from believing life worthwhile and acting as if it was, he did good to all those that knew him; you could count on the fingers of your hand the people who wronged him. In his presence, in contact with him, astonished by so much purity, it was impossible not to give him the best of oneself. His secret was goodness, and goodness is perhaps the secret of genius.

(b) *Truffaut's official memorial to him, published in* Arts *no. 697, November 19, 1958*

André Bazin, who has just died at the age of forty, was the best writer on the cinema in Europe. Since the day in 1948 when he got me my first job connected with the cinema, working alongside him, I became his adoptive son, and thus owe him everything happy that ever happened to me thereafter.

He taught me to write on the cinema, correcting and publishing my first articles, and it's thanks to him that I managed to graduate to directing. He died a few hours after the first day's shooting of my film. . . .

André Bazin was, like Giraudoux's characters, a man from "before the days of original sin." Everyone knew him to be honest and good, but his honesty and goodness always surprised one by their richness; to speak with him was like bathing in the Ganges for a Hindu. . . .

André's poor physical health was only equaled by his always astonishing moral health: he borrowed money openly and lent it discreetly: with him, everything became simple, clear, and frank. As he considered it immoral to travel alone in a four-seater car, he would often stop at the Nogent bus stop to give three commuters a lift into Paris; when he was away from home for a few weeks with his wife and little boy, he would see if there was, among his innumerable friends, someone in need of a house to whom he could lend his, and another to whom he could lend his car. . . .

I don't know if the world is vicious or just, but I'm certain that it's people like Bazin who make it better, for believing life worthwhile and acting as if it was, André did good to all those around him; and you could count on the fingers of one hand the number of people who wronged him; every single person who ever spoke to Bazin, though it be only once, can call himself his "best friend," since in contact with him, overwhelmed by so much purity, it was impossible not to give him the best of oneself. . . .

Tirez sur le Pianiste
Don Allen

Shoot the Piano Player takes us back eighteen years to resume the chronological thread interrupted by the Antoine Doinel cycle. The transition is not
as abrupt as it seems. Despite the fact that Truffaut's second feature is an
adaptation of an American novel (*Down There* by David Goodis), it is as much
a vehicle for personal expression of his recurring themes as any of the more
obviously individual statements in the Doinel films. From the point of view of
the film's overall tone, however, with its affectionate comic pastiche of the
Hollywood B feature and its deliberate playing on audience reaction, it can
perhaps best be appreciated in the historical context of the New Wave. A
helpful yardstick for comparison might be Godard's *Breathless,* with its similar blend of melodrama, jokiness, and love story and its capacity for swerving
off in unexpected directions. The total effect of *Shoot the Piano Player* is
achieved by an unlikely mixture of genres and moods that, against all the odds,
results in a quirky, offbeat masterpiece ahead of its time. The essence is
elusive; the effect is invigorating.

Truffaut, whose criteria for judging his own films tended to be overly influenced by their box office performance, rated *Shoot the Piano Player* as a failure
simply because it did not enjoy great popular success. Yet many would see it as his
most idiosyncratic work and wish he had continued in the same vein. Truffaut
criticized the very qualities of "self-indulgence" and "self-assurance" that are the
film's strengths and give it its freewheeling exuberance and bite. For once he
believed in himself and had the courage to make the film he wanted to make: not
exactly without regard to audience reaction, but rather with the deliberate intention of frequently disorienting and misleading his audience, Hitchcock-fashion.
The film was made in the winter of 1959, in the afterglow of the dramatically
unexpected success of *The 400 Blows,* and Truffaut's change of direction, as often
happens with a director's second film, was striking. The film's appeal is particularly to the sophisticated cinephile, that is, to a minority audience. Truffaut
was so disillusioned by the poor financial returns that he never again risked such
bold experiment or allowed himself such untrammeled freedom.

Truffaut's first feature-length adaptation (Marcel Moussy collaborated on the
script) from a literary source must obviously be judged as a film in its own right.
But it is important in passing to compare it with the Goodis novel. Truffaut selects
details of characterization, notably in the person of the pianist—Eddie in the

From *Finally Truffaut* (New York: Beaufort, 1985), pp. 79–91.

novel, Charlie Kohler in the film[1]—according to his own criteria for male "heroes." He avoids, for instance, any mention of Charlie's hereditary violent streak in his "wild man" past, just as he neglects much of the hardbitten poetry of the novel. Yet he retains such aspects of the original as Charlie's sexual timidity and wish for noninvolvement, perfectly captured by the inspired device of using as soundtrack at key points Charlie's "stream of consciousness" monologue, delivered in a fast, self-mocking monotone, and gently spoofing the melodramatic commentary of many a Hollywood gangster film (as Godard did in *Alphaville* with the character of Lemmy Caution, secret agent). Given the transposition of the setting from America to France—and particularly from Harriet's Hut in downtown Philadelphia, where the novel's hero is "a two-bit piano player with a past," to the sleazy Parisian bistro where Charlie plays—Truffaut is remarkably faithful to the atmosphere and climate of the original, and also to the general framework and even many of the incidents. Again, the influence of the American films that Truffaut and the *Cahiers* critics saw after the war is clearly visible in this evocation of the idea of America as filtered through the B films of the period.

After the opening close-up of the inside of a piano with the hammers pounding out the insistently rhythmic and melancholy theme tune, the first sequence plunges us at once into the atmosphere of the gangster chase. A man is running at night down a dimly lit street, pursued by a car with dazzling headlights and screaming tires. Suddenly he slumps to the ground—hit by the car, or perhaps riddled with bullets. Actually, he has run into a lamppost. Our instinctive identification with the victim and our acceptance of the chase scene at face value have been mocked. This is only a spoof of the Hollywood production-line thrillers that formed Truffaut's staple film diet in postwar Paris. The action is then suspended as a complete stranger comes up, helps the man to his feet, and begins to recount his marriage— how he once thought of getting rid of his wife, but then two years after his marriage fell in love with her. A comic insert: skepticism about marriage; "*les gens sont formidables* [people are great]" again: familiar Truffaut attitudes all. The two men part. Then the first man, remembering he is in a gangster film, runs off again at breakneck speed as the narrative thread is resumed.

The next sequence, in the bistro where the man seeks asylum, packs in a lot of information and concludes the exposition. The man's brother, Edouard, greets him laconically: "Call me Charlie and wait there." Charlie's role-playing is even more conscious than that of other Truffaut heroes. He does not want to know about the pursuing gangsters, double-crossed by a brother he has not seen for years. The affectionate reference to the Marx Brothers—this brother is called Chico, there are four brothers in all—is the first of many cinematic in-jokes and allusions in the film. The introduction of the middle-aged bouncer barman, Plyne (Goodis's

---

1. To avoid confusion I refer to him as Charlie throughout, even after the revelation of his real name in the flashback sequence.

Harleyville Hugger, who "has it bad for the waitress," who in her turn is "strictly solo—she wants no part of any man"), shows his pathetic attempt to assert his authority—to play out *his* role—by threatening Chico, who is loudly informing the customers that his brother, Charlie, should be in a concert hall and not in this dump. Plyne is coldly deflated by Charlie, who rejects his familiarity: "Call me *Mister* Kohler."

Charlie thumps out mechanical rhythms at the piano, while the attitudes of the people dancing before his neutral gaze constitute an amusing microcosm of sexual behavior. Chico attempts a cheerfully blatant pick-up ("You are very desirable. That's why I desire you.") and proposes marriage. A generously endowed woman, disconcerted by her small dancing partner's frank interest in her bosom, is told not to worry because he is a doctor. And the comic patter is reinforced by the visual demonstration of the sex theme, as Clarisse, the archetypal big-hearted prostitute, amuses herself by temporarily deserting her role as a plaything for the customers and performing a comic dance with a little man whom she alternately playfully entices toward her and then physically repels, the whole performance watched by two connoisseurs of form whose simulated world-weariness ill conceals their own inexperience. All good, jokey fun, with Truffaut's habitual serious undertones, until the chase is resumed with the sudden arrival of the two gangsters, comic cutout uglies of laughable inefficiency. Their efforts are easily foiled by Charlie, jerked from his inner reverie and thus involved by chance, despite his desire for isolation, in the affairs of others.

A shot of the singer, frantically jigging up and down as he delivers at amazing speed—in an effort to distract attention from the manhunt in progress—a song about avanie and framboise being the teats of destiny, shows his bobbing head juxtaposed in the frame with the faces of Victor, the constantly grinning drummer, and Charlie, looking deadpan and gloomy. The gap between public performance and private reality is succinctly revealed. The show also announces the persistent melancholy of Charlie's character and situation, which tends to get lost among the film's plethora of snappy comic effects.

Plyne is revealed as simply a wreck, further down the human scrap heap than Charlie but engaged in an equally painful identity quest. In this he is hampered by limited perceptiveness and infantile illusions about the world and women, which result in a disastrous inability to make contact with anyone, including Charlie, whose soured lucidity and self-containment insulate him in an equally sterile existence. Charlie offers only mockery in return for Plyne's admiration of him and his power to attract the waitress, Léna. He rebuffs Plyne's friendship-seeking lament about being unattractive to women with the usual Truffaut flippancy that it may be gland trouble (a remark made about Antoine in *The 400 Blows*), and takes jokingly the suggestion that his own problem is timidity; though the idea intrigues him enough for him to repeat to himself "I am afraid" in a semimocking, quizzical tone that debunks Plyne, amuses the audience, and suggests his vulnerability despite his smokescreen, all at the same time.

The poignant woodwind theme that Truffaut often uses for its emotional effect and especially to highlight a gentle "true love" scene is heard now as Léna, taking the initiative, waits for Charlie, borrows money from him, and asks him to see her home. The mood anticipated by the music is enhanced by the soundtrack (Charlie's inner monologue as he rehearses subtle ways of asking her for a drink, finally blurts out a direct proposal, and finds she has slipped away) and brilliantly emphasized by the camerawork: medium close-ups of the couple's head and shoulders, then a series of close-ups at waist level from the rear, stressing Charlie's tentative hand movements behind Léna's back as, fists clenched, he plans his campaign and, Julien Sorel–style, begins to count on his fingers. Truffaut's use here of the camera's capacity to create a mood, in this case humor, prefigures a similar example in *Stolen Kisses*. We see a rear view of a woman's head in close-up, then a shot of her head and shoulders, then the camera pulls back to a medium long shot of the woman with Antoine walking beside her—revealing what it has previously concealed, not merely that she is not alone but that she is taller than Antoine by at least a head. The significance of Antoine's earlier interest in special techniques for very tall girls becomes clear.

Charlie's wry acceptance of the comic anticlimax of his maneuvers—"Perhaps it was better that way"—indicates a man more accustomed to the consolations of stoical resignation than confident of his sexual prowess. The film, not for the first time, then swerves off in an unexpected direction as Charlie switches off the emotional intensity that exposes his vulnerability and enjoys a relaxed, uncomplicated, quipping sexual encounter with his neighbor Clarisse, the prostitute, in which audience involvement is again deliberately shattered by a distancing device. Truffaut mildly upbraids the arbitrary prudery of the censor, and also reminds us that we are in the cinema, as Charlie covers Clarisse's breasts with a sheet and says, "At the cinema it's always like that."

The reappearance of the gangsters (Ernest and Momo) next morning, heralded by a burst of melodramatic suspense music, points up again their role as comic characters, as Fido, Charlie's younger brother, bombs their car windscreen from on high with a carton of milk—another example of the consciously incongruous interpolation of gratuitous humor into an otherwise plausible love story, and typical of the film's abrupt switches of tone.

The ensuing abortive abduction of Charlie, then Léna, by the crooks, with Ernest twirling his revolver and trying to act tough (he has seen too many gangster films), offers scope for another burlesque spoof on the theme of sex. First a split-screen triple iris shot shows Plyne in three consecutive stages of betraying Charlie and Léna to the crooks, another Truffaut homage to the silent screen and in particular to Abel Gance. Then, in a pastiche of standard demonstrations of twisted criminal motivation, Momo reveals his life's quest for revenge on all women because one of them inadvertently caused the death of his father, knocked down by a car as he stared at her in the street. The sexual frenzy into which Ernest and Momo work themselves merely by talking about women as sexual objects who "only want one thing, but expect to be spoken to as well" is temporarily interrupted by Charlie, quoting a familiar Truffaut comic maxim (used also in *The Bride Wore Black*): "When you've seen one, you've seen them all." Their obsession with women's clothing designed to attract men, particularly underwear and stockings, verges on fetishism, and establishes these gangsters firmly in the mainstream tradition of the Truffaut male victim.

Léna and Charlie escape, and his awareness of the danger of falling—metaphorically as well as literally—if he looks at her legs as she precedes him upstairs to her room provides the run-in to the extended flashback sequence introduced by Léna's "Formerly it was different." The idyll of Charlie and his wife Thérésa in bed together is disturbed by the superimposition of an iris shot of the evil impresario Lars Schmeel; the shot, interposed between the couple, is soon faded out, but it leaves an impression of menace, like a fairy tale ogre. Three shots, in progressively increasing close-up (and accompanied by a disorienting long shot), of Charlie's finger nervously approaching the bell-push at Schmeel's door illustrate what Schmeel calls his "illness" of timidity. The impresario later tries to eliminate this flaw in his protégé's public image by subjecting him to a course in personality projection, at the end of which Charlie resembles the required posturing stereotype (foreshadowing Antoine's mouthing of disconnected English phrases in *Bed and Board*), though his real identity remains resolutely enigmatic. His career as an international pianist, pounding out the classics in the world's concert halls, produces in him both total egocentricity and at the same time doubt about his talent, and puts intolerable strain on his marriage. A sad near-embrace at the end of one sequence fades out, suggesting perhaps that the couple are doomed not to complete it. And when Thérésa's burden of guilt drives her to talk to Charlie, it is too late.

Thérésa's confession is prefaced by an ominous silence on the soundtrack. The camera crosscuts between husband and wife, then pans from face to face as she spells out the details of the love or lust dilemma involved in her sacrifice of herself to Schmeel in furtherance of Charlie's career. Charlie's tortured inner monologue reflects his own dilemma: his realization of the need to go to Thérésa and comfort her and his inability to do so. He walks out, hesitates, runs back; but the message implied in the increasingly urgent tension of the music is confirmed as the camera seems to rush past him into the room and on to the balcony, and plunges giddily down to reveal Thérésa's body on the pavement below—followed, as in *Les Mistons,* by a shot of newspaper headlines announcing the tragedy. Léna's voice then takes the narrative up to the present, and the image fades from a poster of Edouard Saroyan, concert pianist, to a succession of superimposed embraces between Léna and Charlie in bed, whose tenderness, heightened by the death scene and its accompanying sense of loss, is also reminiscent of *Les Mistons*.

But even at this time of burgeoning love, the danger signs are there to remind us that in Truffaut's world happiness is transient. Léna takes over Charlie, organizing him into going out to buy her a pair of stockings (the same fate befalls Pierre in

Truffaut and Marie Dubois

The Soft Skin) and trying to resuscitate his sense of identity by telling him to resume his career and his real name. She counters the nihilism of his "Pourquoi?" with the pragmatism of her "Pour qui?," but realistically asks him to have the courage to tell her when he no longer loves her. Then the comic kidnapping (comic in action, but with serious consequences) of Fido by the gangsters, and their naive attempts, like little boys, to impress him with their musical cigarette lighters, new snorkel pens, alligator belts, and other toys, allows Truffaut a moment of joyfully gratuitous farce, unthinkable in any other film, as one of the gangsters swears on the head of his mother and an iris insert shows a little old lady keeling over stricken, legs in the air.

Typically, the climax of the film—the confrontation between Plyne, Charlie, and Léna—is placed within this comic sequence. Charlie's solitude is threatened, despite Léna's view that "even when he's with somebody he is alone." He tries his usual remedy of immersing himself in his music as Léna demolishes Plyne and his pretensions to masculinity. Charlie muses, "Even now, when she's calling him names, he can't take his eyes off her. She's overdoing it, but what can I tell her? That Plyne isn't as bad as she paints him? He's a poor slob who hoped to be somebody and didn't make it." Forced to intervene to save Léna, Charlie is exposed to the full violence of Plyne's anger and sudden disillusionment that this woman, his idol, has been "sullied" and that she no longer conforms to his ideal. "Woman is pure, delicate, fragile; woman is supreme, magical," he informs Charlie, gripping him tightly round the throat in a last desperate effort to assert his masculinity, and refusing Charlie's peace offer (in what might almost be an alternative ending to *Stolen Kisses,* with Plyne as the stranger and Charlie as Antoine). Charlie, on the point of choking to death, finds his discarded knife and, as in Hitchcock's *Dial M for Murder,* stabs Plyne, aiming for his arm but accidentally killing him—the culmination of the note of fatalism that runs through the film. Plyne's concept of the purity of woman, though expressed in this incongruous context, is in the best tradition of declarations by dying gangsters, and also of Truffaut's misunderstood heroes.

"At last, after many adventures" (for this is a kind of fairy story), including Charlie's rescue by Léna and their escape by car, the setting changes from the lights of the city to the blinding snow of the Alps. During the journey a singer on the car radio has proclaimed, "When I don't love you any more, I'll wear my cap," a somewhat unsubtle touch to remind us that this *may* be a fairy story but that it is also set in a world where love ends. Charlie, "despite himself, despite herself," sends Léna away and joins his brothers, Richard and Chico, in their hideout—actually the parental home, from which the parents have been banished.

The final gun battle with the gangsters, prefaced by a combination of the woodwind theme and the gangsters' own suspense music followed by an ominous silence, and by Léna's return to take Charlie back, epitomizes the disturbing clash of tones that has characterized the film. First, comedy—the ease with which Fido escapes from the crooks as they slip on the ice; then burlesque of the gangster film's traditional finale—gun butts shatter windows, one of the gangsters twirls his gun again, but it still looks like a toy gun. We have been manipulated into identifying with Charlie and Léna. We have been willing a happy ending, ignoring the carefully planted omens of tragedy—the song, the suspense music, the gun. The crosscutting between Léna, Charlie, and the gangsters has given us the scent of danger. But the continuing aura of comedy surrounding the gangsters has cushioned us in our expectation that the situation cannot be unhappily resolved. Then suddenly Léna is hit by a bullet, and in an agonizingly prolonged shot her body slides down the slope, insistently proclaiming the reality, and the finality, of this moment. A briefly frozen close-up of her face confirms that Charlie need not have bothered to run frantically to her. Another Truffaut idyll is over, destroyed by chance.

Charlie returns to his piano in the bar. He pounds out the haunting theme, and his bleak, mournful stare as the intensity of the music increases gives way to the opening shot of the piano hammers. The circle is complete. There is a new waitress in the bar; but Charlie's solitude is unassailable and his nihilism intact. The attractive possibility that the film might at any moment lurch in a new direction has been preserved until the end. This capacity to surprise (and mislead) the audience is what distinguishes this from every other Truffaut film. True, anything might *happen* in a loose, episodic structure such as that of *Stolen Kisses*. But it is the unexpected switching of *moods* that gives *Shoot the Piano Player* its particular, elusive quality.

The Sensitive Spot

Jean-Paul Török

Incidentally, the same David Goodis who wrote *Dark Passage* has also written a very beautiful novel, which it's not necessary to have read. It would, however, be necessary to stop those who didn't show up with *Down There* in hand from seeing *Shoot the Piano Player*. This precaution would save having to see the film more than twice. Relieved of the worry of transposing to the screen a story he certainly liked reading, François Truffaut would be allowed to move immediately to the main point, in company with the small number of viewers who are concerned with the things that concern him.

But at the outset there was David Goodis's really beautiful novel, which Truffaut really had to adapt, and adapted faithfully, to make a film whose major part was necessarily devoted to a persistent destruction of the novel. And it has been destroyed so well that *Down There* retains little more than an "accompanying" relation to *Shoot the Piano Player,* a curious state of affairs, since they do tell the same story.

In the suburbs of a large city, in a shabby little bar, a man plays the piano. He's a former virtuoso, an idol of the music-mad public, who mysteriously disappeared one day, changed his name and personality to strand himself in this suburban cabaret, unknown to anyone else. He appears very concerned with not attracting attention, to obliterate himself as much as possible. One night his brother, a low-grade gangster he hasn't seen for many years, bursts into the bar. Hunted by two killers, he's come to ask for help. The piano player refuses. He doesn't want to get involved in anything. However, at the last minute, in spite of himself, he makes up his mind and by a ridiculous but effective action saves his brother from his pursuers. The pursuers notice the complicity of the two men, discover their relationship, and beat up the piano player so that he'll reveal his brother's hiding place. Understanding that the musician is in trouble, the waitress at the cabaret, who secretly loves him, joins up with him, and the two of them find themselves caught in the usual gears of this kind of novel. The piano player will commit a murder; the waitress will be killed in the final shoot-out.

Truffaut has repeated enough times that the scenario had no importance. Nevertheless, Goodis's novel being what it is, any director who would have been satisfied with translating it into images with a minimum of ambitions could have brought off a very good film. That's a very obvious proposition that a first viewing of *Shoot the Piano Player* immediately challenges.

Translated by Leo Braudy from "Le Point Sensible," *Positif* 38 (March 1961): 39–47.

First Viewing

The remaking of a "thriller"-type film today is of interest only as a retrospective. In spite of some rare American survivals, the genre is quite dead, and commendable efforts—Cornfield, Lerner—to renew it by reducing it to its essence result only in fastidious exercises in style, in the functioning without surprise of a skeletal mechanism. With rare exceptions—Ralph Habib's admirable *Escapade,* which only *Positif* noted when it came out—the thriller could never adapt itself to France, that bastion of antiromanticism, except at the price of sacrilegious distortions that resulted in the proliferation of "the detective story," good of their kind, characterized by the loathsome uniformity of the family table, where the cops and the baddies swill beer between two disillusioned shootouts. Nevertheless, let's do Truffaut the favor of believing that he could have, if he wanted to, produced an arresting stylistic exercise, an homage to the American authors of the great period. Whatever you say, you have at least to recognize his courage to have preferred a solution of continuity to one of facility: *Shoot the Piano Player* is not a film noir any more; the rules and conventions of the genre are systematically destroyed, not with the casual contempt of the man who is very high-handed with his subject (Chabrol and Stanley Elkin's *A Double Tour*), but destroyed from the *inside* by a director who first wants to free himself from anything that could tie him to a subject he knows is a fine one, but from which he must nevertheless break loose so he can do *something else,* so he can say freely what he wants to say. Truffaut doesn't play at the cultivated aesthete who, annoyed at having to "deliver a message" by using a "popular" novel (movies are an industry, aren't they?), and wants above all to show he isn't a dupe, hurries through the plot and generally ruins the film. On the contrary, if Truffaut judges it necessary to destroy the original work, he does it honestly, in complicity with his author, scrupulously adapting the novel, keeping the special natures of the characters, the greater part of the dialogue, the feeling of the situations, and even the part-tender, part-ironic "tone" of the description. But he recaptures them *on his own terms* by so subtly bending the narrative that, by an artifice worthy of Borges, even David Goodis's text becomes François Truffaut's text. Insidiously substituting himself for the American writer, Truffaut accomplishes the exact opposite of an adaptation: he lives in the heart of the novel and "possesses" it (in the magical sense of the word). For him the novel has become above all a state of soul.

So, since the "letter" of *Down There* has been loyally respected, it's not so much the "spirit" that's been modified, as the principal characteristics of the "genre noir," particularly its efficiency. Truffaut shifts and disorients the perspective, and puts the viewer in an uncomfortable state where the usual points of reference have abruptly vanished. *Shoot the Piano Player* begins traditionally: a man flees in the night; there are automobile lights, moving shadows, panting. But he unluckily bumps his head into a streetlamp and falls stunned. An honest bourgeois (Alex Joffé), who is passing by, a bouquet of flowers in hand, charitably helps him up, and chats with him a bit: he is married, loves his wife, has three kids—and the fugitive, visibly moved, waits very politely for him to finish before beginning to run again. A "strong" situation in the traditional style has been set up, and then destroyed in the midst of its development by a desire for demystification that uses every possible means to make its way: banality, the grayish humor of everyday or common life, and some not very elegant methods—jokes that are stupid and in bad taste, and inflated stories. The same procedure is used throughout the film and constantly brings into question the dramatic economy by which the viewer has risked allowing himself to be taken in. For example, in David Goodis's work, the two killers are members of an awesome organization; they represent an insidious and terrifying menace that expresses itself through these two shabby characters, who aren't menacing in themselves but in what they represent. Truffaut carefully preserves the ludicrous aspect of the two gangsters, their stupidities, their clumsiness, while at the same time he still accents the demystification of the killer already palpable in Goodis. Truffaut's crooks are more true than life—therefore, they are tinged with unreality. They are not gangsters, but mediocre men playing at being gangsters, and playing poorly. Ludicrous and ineffectual, they barely know how to drive. They are unaware of the ABCs of their trade and are as obsessed with women as schoolboys. They are fond of baroque gadgets (musical cigarette lighters, scarves made out of Japanese metal) and are at ease with no one but the dreadful boy in the film, in whom they find an interlocutor worthy of them. All in all, they would be absolutely inoffensive if they didn't have a pistol that they use more willingly as a calling card—the tangible symbol of their function—than as a weapon.

The detective story background is more effectively undercut by the staging than by the witticisms of the scenario (like the mother who dies because of her son's false oath); with the greatest detachment, the staging presents all the scenes of violence and action with a destructive irony. To make this point I must, of course, cite the final sequence of the grand reckoning, filmed with a long shot in a Christmas card setting, where the combatants stamp in the snow and exchange badly aimed shots, chasing each other all around the house like kids. The site chosen for the camera, resolutely withdrawn from an action that it seems to film as if by chance dissociated from it, is exactly the place where Truffaut places himself in relation to the apparent line of his film, to the "plot" he pretends to allow to unfold all by itself (to prevent the viewer from being too concerned with it), so that he can suggest that the essence of what he's doing is always somewhere else, and to invite the viewer to look for it off-screen, and—why not?—outside the film. Now, with this first destructive enterprise carried out so well, you could think about going and finally penetrating deeper into this secretive work with the certainty of finding the thread of connection. If Truffaut expended all his energy to convince us that *Shoot the Piano Player* isn't a "black" film, we can now expect to discover its true face: the efforts of the director and the spectator will finally be repaid. Meanwhile, a little patience.

Second Viewing

When the new superimposes itself on the old, the French cinema splits under the double weight of false legends. While we wait for the necessary publication of a book about "subrealism" in the cinema, almost entirely devoted to French cinema, with an additional chapter on neosubrealism, *Shoot the Piano Player* already presents us with a repertoire sufficiently stocked with the characteristic traits of the new school. If Truffaut so effectively resists making a film in the tradition of the "old-time movie," could it be that *Shoot the Piano Player* is a New Wave film? At first everything seems to confirm this hypothesis: from the casualness of the treatment of the scenario to the occasionally fuzzy shots of Raoul Coutard and the encroaching, haunting, and enticing influence of Godard, the hateful details settle in with great authority. The gigantic motorized *Cahiers du Cinéma,* the love scene under the sheets, the disrespectful allusions to the great masters (Gance, Vadim), the barely audible dialogue, the private jokes for little pals, the hustling style of directing—all place the film in too precise a context for it to be argued that Truffaut simply wanted to renounce a contemporary taste that elsewhere he had strongly helped to create. Why not disengage yourself to go take the air of another time, that of Autant-Lara—Truffaut's hearty beast from whom he has taken so much—no one would reproach you for going to pay your visits to the Bois des Amants. Well, yes, *Shoot the Piano Player* is precisely placed in 1960, at a moment in French cinema that we have little reason to like. Perhaps the flourishes of the modern style will seem as delectable to future generations as those of the Modern Style are for us. Let us age quickly.

Third Viewing

With *The 400 Blows,* a film shot in the first person, Truffaut gave us (no one is unaware of it) his autobiography, very edifying besides. Since movie criticism is almost a century behind criticism in general—it's had its Sainte-Beuve and is waiting for its Baudelaire—it may seem original to point out that an artist exposes himself with more abandon in an apparently objective work than in pretended intimate journals, which are generally fraudulent. To give an example: there are strong reasons to think that David Lean's *Summertime* is a greater revelation of its director's personality than *Breathless* is of Godard's (to speak of that film again, even by passing over it)—and so much the better or worse for him. I think it's striking to rediscover in certain films this curious mimesis between an actor and his director; to see, for example, at the end of *White Nights* Jean Marais's head resembling Visconti's, to see this ghostly resemblance spread itself over the features of Visconti's actors, to read what Saura said about it to Marcel Oms, and then to see the hero of *Shoot the Piano Player* incarnated in Aznavour, to think of Truffaut and his biography ground out by publicity—an upward mobility like

Vadim's—and to listen to Edouard Saroyan, who, on the screen, speaks of the feelings you have when you become rich and famous. And the names of Charlie and Saroyan are not chosen by chance. It's Charlie certainly because Goodis writes that Eddie the piano player looks like Chaplin, and because Charles is the first name of Aznavour, who is so like Saroyan's characters, with their openness and simplicity. That Truffaut enjoys himself and amuses or doesn't amuse us by his quotations, pastiches, or irreverences shouldn't encourage similarly superficial thoughts in us—from "What a sympathetic boy" to "I find him irritating." There is an otherwise serious sequence in *Shoot the Piano Player,* with an exceptional and at first very obvious gravity of tone, in which Truffaut, taking his distance at the same time that he ingeniously reveals himself, invites us to take our distance, to leave boyishness to the kids (when you've seen one film, you've seen them all), and suddenly sweeps away our reservations. I'm talking about the flashback sequence, carried out with the greatest seriousness, which forms within the film a short film sufficient unto itself and so totally ruptures the tone that, stuck onto the rest like a collage, it profoundly modifies its meaning. Think, for example, of the dream sequence that brightens certain mediocre films; the difference is that in this film, where all conspires to make it unrealistic, this backward glance discovers nothing more than reality itself. The tragically sentimental deception of Edouard Saroyan, betrayed by the woman he loves (and it doesn't matter that it was a good motive, that she betrayed him through devotion) kills Saroyan as surely as if he threw himself out of the window with her as Raymond Rouleau did at the end of Becker's *Falbalas.*

It's all to Truffaut's credit that he dares to shout in 1960, when others shame-facedly invite us to observe the wantonness in the upper class (with a suspicious interest in only the eroticism of the body), that love doesn't work without an absolute demand for fidelity, that the agreement tacitly made between two beings who love each other is so serious that a single betrayal calls for nothing less than death, and a despair worse than death. Edouard Saroyan chooses a more insidious kind of suicide, and perhaps a more efficient one, the *lived* destruction of his personality. After the betrayal and death of his wife—he did nothing to prevent it; he was already detached; and since a woman has betrayed him, what's left but to die?—what can Edouard Saroyan become? The little mechanical piano player of Harriet's Hut? But Charlie has so little existence. He is only the ghost of Saroyan, and the world in which he scarcely lives is beyond reality, beyond the grave, a half-sleep wrapped in cotton (I want to sleep, sleep rather than live . . .).

But this dream refuge is actually a door that opens into nightmare, and it will be enough that a stack of empty boxes collapses for the logic of the dream to open up a series of events all the more frightening because they are a caricature of reality, impossible to question, that you can only submit to like a set of dissolving fantasies. All depersonalization, imaged in the little death of sleep, is accompanied by a radical "derealization" of the external world, and by an oppressive feeling of strangeness, a lack of familiarity with real life. In this subjective upset, born of depressed states, the emotional self relaxes its relationships and breaks all contact with the world around it. But the world continues to exist, to unfold its long chain of derisory events, until the death of a young girl, who ought to have been loved. Charlie must let her die without being able to prevent it (or wishing to) because he is outside the world, an accursed being who can cause only the unhappiness of those who get close to him. *Shoot the Piano Player* bears witness to the impossibility and horror of living on the sidelines. This is an apparently detached film, overwhelming in one's first viewing of its shame and morbid timidity (because isn't timidity here the symptom of a secret culpability?), that nevertheless confesses everything. It is a neurotic work, which multiplies the detours and recesses of repression, yet in which the triumphant obsession finally comes out. You have to be singularly gifted, or similarly obsessed, to follow the unconscious drama of the piano player's libido from your first sight of him. But once you find the thread, everything becomes clear, even the obscurities, hesitations, failures, and self-destruction of a work that presents itself with all the disturbing evidence and discomfort of a stillborn action.

First the anguish, the fear of living. After twenty admirable reverse angle shots (the faces in close-up of Plyne and Charlie), fear appears in Aznavour's face. "It's true, I'm afraid. . . . I'm afraid. . . ." A fear of the world, already perceptible in the famous interview [with the psychiatrist] in *The 400 Blows;* a desire to see things coupled with an impotency to attain them; a false lucidity; and especially a fear of women, a fear of everything the other sex has of the mysterious, the foreigner, and the enemy. Here Aznavour's popular character is invoked like a quotation, his "sexual obsessions" that have been popularized by songs that Truffaut (it's said) scarcely appreciates, although many sequences would suggest a musical commentary in which the "fans" will recognize in passing "Ce sacré piano" and "Après l'amour" obviously, but also "Comme des étrangers" and "Mon amour protège-moi." The atmosphere of Aznavour's songs, so close to that of the film, contributes still more to make this privileged actor into the twin and brother of Truffaut. But in different degrees all the characters carry within them this Baudelairian obsession with Woman, and all are brothers in this morbid impotency to understand her, to understand the movers of this disconcerting merry-go-round, the meaning of this existence.

As fundamental and sordid as the reflections of the two killers seem, they make us think. Why do women have naked legs under their dressing gowns? Why do their uncovered legs disturb us so much? The whole scene in the car intrigues the viewer, because he is worried about avoiding his own embarrassment in order to find out where it ends: the beautiful and mysterious smile that plays over Marie Dubois's lips when Charlie says: "When you know one woman, you know them all" (a very revealing phrase for an analyst), the girl's great burst of laughter, the worried looks of the hooligans. Do we have to look too hard for this kind of thought in the most unexpected character, Plyne, in the astonishing sequence of his death? Isn't the troubling nostalgia for women he expresses the same as

Charlie's before his wife's betrayal? Isn't it also the nostalgia of François Truffaut, in spite of and perhaps because of the extreme derision with which he emphasizes it? The waitress has just attacked Plyne in particularly insulting terms. He has been in love with her for a long time, in "romantic" love. She is the image of the ideal woman for him. He doesn't understand. "Such gross words in such a pretty mouth. She's not a real woman. She isn't a Woman. Woman is pure, Woman is sublime, Woman is a magical being."

At this moment Plyne's voice strangely resembles the voice at the end of Preminger's *Laura* that proclaims from the radio both the impossibility and the absolute necessity of love. Even when certain words are tainted by a modern derision, it is comforting that they be resaid, that a certain sensibility that one has thought lost forever could be dimly retrieved. Of course, it can't be denied that the fringe of uncertainty and confusion that obscures Truffaut's film reduces this interpretation to a kind of light-headed criticism. Yet it is rare in our time that a film can still make us dream. Why should we refuse this pleasure while we wait for the reinvention of a cinema that we used to love, a cinema that doesn't have to be "modern," so long as it again finds the roads of the heart?

On *Shoot the Piano Player*
Graham Petrie

Shoot the Piano Player is a gangster story that refuses to behave like a gangster story, a love story that refuses to behave like a love story, a film that refuses to conform to our assumptions about what a film can and should do. Its unsettling and disorienting quality, however, comes less from unusual or experimental camera techniques than from bizarre and unexpected juxtapositions of mood, setting, and action, from constant and sudden alternations between farce and tragedy, and from the nature and behavior of the characters involved. The tone is established in the opening sequence, which presents us with the totally unexplained situation of a man fleeing from unseen pursuers (represented only by the sound and headlights of their car). We are forced into automatic identification with him, partly by his situation, and partly through repeated close-ups of his anxious, hunted face. While we are busy on the intellectual level trying to work out the mystery of the situation, we are further unsettled visually by the circumstances of the filming: normally a night scene of this kind, even if shot (like this one) in real streets, would be artificially lit in such a way that we could follow the characters clearly. Here, however, only available light is used, with the result that Chico (the man being chased) moves abruptly and disconcertingly from the full glare of a streetlamp into complete darkness, then back into half-light again, and into shots of this kind are intercut jarring flashes of the headlights of the pursuing car. A sudden long shot abruptly distances us from Chico: we see him stumble and hurtle, in almost comic fashion, into a lamppost; laughter at the awkwardness of his fall is stifled by our realization that he seems to be hurt. He lies there moaning, we hear footsteps, we see someone bend over him ominously and slap his face. The newcomer helps him up; we expect him to be an enemy and are prepared for violence, but Chico simply brushes himself off, thanks him, and the two walk off together like old friends. They begin a conversation which quickly takes a very personal turn and Chico's helper takes the opportunity to tell a perfect stranger details of his private life that he could tell no one else. He talks about love, sex, the disillusionments and compensations of marriage as they walk on through patches of light and darkness, his voice competing with the sound of their footsteps and the roar of traffic. They stop at a corner and say goodbye, the other leaves, Chico looks round and abruptly begins to run again—we are suddenly reminded that the danger to him was neither imaginary nor forgotten.

From *The Cinema of François Truffaut* by Graham Petrie (New York: A. S. Barnes, 1970), pp. 23–27, 82–85, 119–121, 127, 143–144, 148, 161–164, 176. Excerpted and edited by Leo Braudy.

Almost every feature of this sequence is designed to disorient the audience: Raoul Coutard's deliberately rough camera style, the lighting (or lack of it), the total absence of background music that might help the audience to develop an appropriate emotional response, and especially the confusion as to whether and when we should experience fear, relief, or laughter, and to what extent we are intended to identify with the characters. This uncertainty continues through the film: in the sequence that follows in the bar where Charlie works, the violence of the gangsters' pursuit of Chico and Charlie's intervention to foil them is followed by the inanity of the waiter's ridiculous song—ridiculous in both its nonsense words and the jerky, puppetlike movements of the singer (yet the words, emphasizing the incongruity of sexual relationships, relate to a major theme of the film). Other scenes inside the bar have a strange, unsettling quality—Chico seizes, dances with, and propositions the barman's mistress all within the space of a couple of minutes; Charlie's prostitute girl friend is seen conducting a strange dance with a young man in which she lures him to her then pushes him contemptuously away, finally provoking him to violence; we are given brief glimpses of background conversations about sex and of tentative sexual advances between people dancing. All these scenes are thematically viable, but the way in which they are presented causes us to start questioning actions and responses we had previously taken for granted.

The film is full of incidents in which serious actions are shot in a comic way: Charlie is abducted by having a quite monstrous gun pointed at his nose in the middle of the street and Léna is bustled into the gangsters' car while passersby look calmly on (this scene may well have been shot with a hidden camera); once in the car, however, captors and captured get on well together, joke and reminisce about their childhood. This approach is crystallized in the scene of the killing of the barman, which begins with the quarrel between Léna and the barman, from which Charlie attempts to remain detached, but which reaches a pitch of virulence that forces him to intervene. A ridiculous yet potentially dangerous duel of telephone receiver against carving knife follows, the absurdity of it being heightened by wildly overemphatic music; Charlie chases his opponent outside but throws down his knife and attempts reconciliation; there is a moment of relief and exhaustion, till the apparently friendly gesture by the barman of putting his arm around Charlie's shoulder turns into attempted murder as he tries to choke him. This scene is shot in dispassionate close-up as the expressionless barman talks (as does every character in the film once given the opportunity) of his life history and the misery of his sex life, while Charlie gasps helplessly for breath beside him. Then comes the struggle for possession of the knife and the ambiguous stabbing, in which Charlie seems to use rather more force that he later claims he did or intended to. In this scene, as almost everywhere else in the film, camera virtuosity is secondary to abrupt changes of mood established by cutting or juxtaposition within the frame, together with brusque transitions in place and action. The two most pervasive stylistic features—the handheld camera and the relentless use of available light, which often leaves the screen in near-complete darkness (elements which are combined in the long sequence of Charlie's arrival at the farm and walk up the hillside with his brother Richard)—create a deliberate visual roughness, a lack of normal technical polish, that, by breaking down our stylistic preconceptions about film, enables us to accept more readily this world where farce, sadness, violence, death, and laughter clash and coincide. We are not, of course, being shown a new world; we are simply seeing our own world, as though for the first time, with unprecedented spontaneity, freshness, and vitality. By breaking down our accepted notions of cause and effect, by destroying our normal expectations and assumptions about pattern and order and neat categorization of experience, Truffaut has given us a means of apprehending the real world around us more intelligently and perceptively, for it is the real world he has shown us.

There are some occasions in *Shoot the Piano Player,* particularly in the love scenes, where the camera is allowed to take on the kind of creative function characteristic of *Jules and Jim.* In the early scene between Charlie and Clarisse (the prostitute) a mood of purely sensuous and physical pleasure predominates, an atmosphere of almost routine yet still enjoyable behavior. There is something ritualistic about the spatial detachment and separation of the lovers: Charlie lies in bed watching Clarisse undress and, despite (or perhaps because of) their obvious long familiarity with each other, she feels the need to titillate and stimulate him with a kind of striptease performance, hiding behind a screen and displaying piece by piece each segment of her seductive black underwear. (Characteristically for this film, having waved her black panties at him, she proceeds to emerge unexpectedly wearing her slip.) The sense of voyeurism is heightened by the way in which the camera pans to follow her, as though through Charlie's eyes, as she moves about the room. Finally she emerges nude (the uncut version of the film pokes fun at both the censor and the voyeuristic instincts of the audience by including a shot in which she is allowed to expose her breasts and Charlie immediately covers them with a sheet, telling her that the censor wouldn't approve). With an expression of comical lust on his face Charlie proceeds to wind up his alarm clock, put out the light, and dive under the sheets with her, to the accompaniment of muffled squeals on her part. The effect of the whole scene is external, detached; there is a sense of welcome physical enjoyment but little or no emotional commitment—the impression of a performance or a routine (heightened by brief shots of Charlie's metronome and by the reference to the censor) is strong. . . .

The two flashback love scenes between Charlie and his wife have a quality of tension and false reconciliation. In the quarrel scene, as Thérésa tries to tell him how much he has changed, the camera pans to and fro angrily with Charlie; then a close-up of his face turns out disconcertingly to be a mirror shot; the camera moves to bring her "real" presence into frame while he remains a reflection; finally both become briefly "real" as reconciliation is reached and a gentle pan accompanies them as they relax onto the bed. The fragility and misunderstandings of the relationship are conveyed vividly through the camera movements and the framing. In the later scene in which Thérésa confesses her affair with the impresario Schmeel, the camera follows her as she wanders round the room desperately trying to explain, close-ups of her face against a blank white background emphasize her isolation, and a close-up catches Charlie's indecision as he tells himself to go to her and help her but inevitably makes the wrong decision and leaves.

In contrast to the scenes with Clarisse and Thérésa, the one physical and detached, the camera content merely to observe, the other emotional and involving as the camera forces us into proximity with the characters, the love scene with Léna is both remote and immediate, serene and unsettling. After the flashback to Charlie's earlier career, the camera returns to the poster of him as Edouard Saroyan the pianist on Léna's bedroom wall, then pans slowly round the room taking in furniture, ornaments, discarded clothing; a close-up of Léna and Charlie kissing is superimposed on this, then vanishes as the shot ends on the two of them in bed. Léna is talking to him; he is passive, perhaps not even listening; brief dissolves to shots of the lovers together at earlier or later stages of the night punctuate her speech, revealing a wonderfully beautiful rhythm in themselves, but also creating a sense of fragmentation and separateness, a fragile and lovely harmony, never staying constant for long and always on the brink of disruption. The essential isolation of the lovers, the inability of the one truly to reach the other, is ironically counterpointed in the scene of Léna's death at the end of the film, as she slides in a breathtakingly beautiful sweep down a bank of snow and Charlie and Fido stumble toward her body. All Charlie can do on reaching her is brush the snow and blood from her face; a zoom into her now totally alien and unreachable beauty underlines his loss, yet a dissolve to the face of the new barmaid as he returns to work prepares us for the beginning of a new cycle of hesitation, commitment too late, destruction, and loss.

The film is also full of visual devices and jokes, some of them bringing dead metaphors unexpectedly to life: the "two-faced" barman is shown betraying Charlie and Léna in a split-screen shot that catches him in three different postures; one of the gangsters pleads for his mother to drop dead if he is lying and, framed in an antique oval design, an old lady clutches her heart and falls flat on her back, large, clumping boots rising and subsiding as her body hits the floor. The arbitrariness of normal screen conventions and continuity is indicated as Léna holds up a mirror to show Charlie the gangsters following several yards behind them in the street—and their faces loom huge and overwhelming on the screen. Throughout *Shoot the Piano Player* Truffaut presents us with a constant tension between spontaneity and stylization, between what we expect and what we actually see on the screen; and the incongruous rhythms and bizarre juxtapositions force a continual process of readjustment on the viewer as he watches, yet leave him at the end free to make his own application of what he has experienced. . . .

The world of the "present tense" of the film creates a closed environment from which Charlie has to escape physically if he is to redeem himself. At first sight the world created in the flashback seems to offer a deliberate contrast in sophistication and glamour, yet visually the two settings have a great deal in common. Charlie's world of fame and fortune is constricting and enclosed; it has an almost unreal quality about it, created largely through the lighting. Almost all the scenes in this section of the film are interiors—café, hotel room, audition, concert hall, press conference, the office where Lars Schmeel the impresario talks to Charlie/Edouard about his future (the lighting in this scene making the city seen through the office window look totally unreal). The implication rises inevitably from this that even in his "good" times Charlie moves in a world of his own and never really relates to other people. Even as a successful pianist he uses the piano as a barrier behind which he shelters or hides—an idea vividly conveyed in a shot that has the piano cover two-thirds of the screen with Charlie's expressionless face squeezed into the triangle left in the top right-hand corner.

The use of corridors in the flashback sequence increases the sense of unease that the other elements of this part of the film convey, and intensifies the feeling of a closed environment with no discernible exit for the characters. The most effective scene in this respect shows Charlie on his way to his audition, moving uneasily along a seemingly endless corridor. He walks in a jerky, hunched-up, almost uncoordinated way, wearing a coat much too large for him into which we feel he will vanish the moment things begin to get difficult and he needs to escape. He looks pathetic, comic, and vulnerable, all at once, and the hand-held camera that tracks back in front of him, tilting and rocking the frame slightly as it moves, crystallizes these essential elements in him. When he at last summons up enough courage to ring the bell and enters the room he is replaced by a girl carrying a violin who begins to walk away from the door down the corridor. The camera unexpectedly chooses to follow her rather than Charlie; it tracks smoothly away in front of her and we hear Charlie strike the first few confident notes on the piano. Still we accompany the girl, however; her face is tense and strained, she clutches her violin tightly and awkwardly, and a sense of unease and puzzlement is created at the time we should be sharing Charlie's apparent triumph. There is a cut; we expect at last to join Charlie, but instead we see the girl again, crossing a courtyard with buildings surrounding her on all sides. She stops and looks upwards as, totally unnaturalistically, the sound of Charlie's playing swells louder around her. By filming the turning point of Charlie's career in this way, Truffaut creates a vivid sense of how fragile and temporary the *façade* that he is creating will turn out to be. . . .

The city in *Shoot the Piano Player* is balanced by nature to some extent at the end, but here too Truffaut refuses to romanticize the countryside. Nature is cold and neutral, the cottage the Saroyans are hiding in is squatly and almost absurdly isolated. The approach to the hideout is shot so that the countryside itself is rarely seen: with the two gangsters focus is placed almost entirely on the interior of the car and their conversation with Fido; with Charlie and Léna, Truffaut and Raoul Coutard create an almost abstract pattern of streetlights and then falling snow on the smeared windshield. Nature of course provides no escape: Léna is shot and left to die in the snow; Charlie reaches her too late and can do nothing except brush blood and clinging snow from her face. The two sets of crooks exit in a farcical chase to continue their meaningless and absurd hostility, and Charlie is left back almost exactly where he started. . . .

Though I personally find the music of *The 400 Blows* satisfactory in its creation of a sense of lyricism in the grubby back streets of Paris and its involvement of the audience in Antoine's experiences, it is possible for an unsympathetic viewer to find it closer to the traditional emotional conditioning of the audience than that of any other of Truffaut's films. Jean Constantin's* music for *Shoot the Piano Player,* however, is required to serve totally different purposes and the result is a score almost as subtle and as essential to the final impact of the film as that of *Jules and Jim.* Much of the sound in the film is "natural," in the sense that it consists of music played by Charlie as part of his daily work (this device is used in *Love at Twenty,* in which virtually all the music consists of the classical music Antoine hears at concerts, plays in the record shop he works in, or listens to on his record player). Charlie is identified from the beginning with one particular tune, one he knows so well that he can play it without thinking, just as he tries to lead a life so centered round routine and mechanical repetition of the same experiences that he will no longer need to think or feel about anything. In the scenes in the bar at the beginning of the film we see other ways in which music can be used to deaden, avoid, or smooth over unexpected emotional eruptions. After the fracas with the gangsters and their pursuit of Chico, the waiter's song immediately establishes order and routine and the customers forget the incident at once, while throughout these scenes the incessant slickness of the dance music provides a background to an astonishing variety of sexual advances—which, because of the background, are taken for granted and not resented.

The first "unnatural" music in the film establishes the basic love theme as Charlie and Léna walk home from the bar, but background music as such is relatively sparse. The love theme, generally restrained and subdued like that of *The Soft Skin,* undergoes the same kind of process as the closing music of *The 400 Blows,* rising to a note of anguished finality and abruptness as the camera zooms in on Léna's face as she lies dead in the snow. Elsewhere music is used for scenes of violent activity like Charlie's fight with the barman and the final shoot-out at the farm, for moments of suspense and waiting, to cover transitions, and in the major love scenes—with Clarisse, the sound of a radio from next door (suggesting perhaps the mechanical nature of the relationship); with Thérésa, "their" love theme; with Léna, Charlie's piano tune orchestrated so that it is both different and recognizable, just as his love for Léna has only superficially affected his general outlook on life. But the main originality of the music rests in the way in which the virtual identity of Charlie and his piano is conveyed throughout. The flashback to

*Actually Georges Delerue replaced Constantin before work on the film music began.

his days as a concert pianist is introduced by the normal piano theme modulating into a piece of classical music; it ends with Charlie's circling round the piano in the bar, sitting down, and striking a few resounding concertlike blows while a dissolve covers an almost automatic and inevitable drift into the tune that is to provide his identity, his shell, and his armor for the rest of his life. Later, as Léna and the barman quarrel, he wanders over to the piano and tinkles a few notes on it before making his one belated and disastrous attempt to become involved with something outside himself. And at the end he briefly tries out a new tune before slipping, unconsciously and inexorably, into the routine he can never again escape from. . . .[1]

In *Shoot the Piano Player* the two songs heard in the bar at the beginning of the film both deal with sex as a crudely pleasurable physical activity in much the same way as most of the conversations and actions in the first half of the film do, and as Charlie would like to be able to and thus avoid the complications of giving himself emotionally. The second song in particular, with its breathless succession of apparent nonsense words (flashed out on the screen even in the French version to reassure audiences that they are hearing what they think they are) catches perfectly the tone and mood of the visual side of the film, with, in both cases, serious implications hidden underneath. Later in the film, the song Charlie and Léna hear on the car radio as they drive to the farm (the words continuous over a series of dissolves in space and time) takes up the themes of loyalty, betrayal, and emotional honesty that are on the point of working themselves out. . . .

Charlie Kohler's series of interior monologues in *Shoot the Piano Player* has something of the effect of a narrator explaining his thoughts, but it is really much closer to the kind of incessant inner conversation that we all carry on with ourselves almost every waking minute. It expresses very forcefully the essential conflict between the two aspects of Charlie's personality, summing up his fears, hopes, regrets, desires, and good intentions, together with his inability to do anything about them at the right time. He is constantly addressing himself in questions or imperatives, asking what he should do or desperately trying to order himself into action. There is only one occasion where the promptings of his actual behavior coincide: after Chico has fled from the bar pursued by the gangsters, Charlie tells himself not to get involved and simply "say good luck to him," following this with a muttered "Bonne chance!" aloud. But where the inner voice recommends involvement Charlie does his best not to listen and, if he does act, does so halfheartedly and too late. The result is not always as tragic as when he tells himself to forgive and comfort his wife when she confesses her infidelity, but yields instead to jealousy and inertia, leaves, changes his mind, and returns to find her dead. Walking along the street with Léna he holds an anguished debate as to

---

1. Some North American prints of the film crudely overemphasize Charlie's impasse by a voiceover repetition here of the barman's earlier "Music is what we need, man!" which is not in the original French prints.

whether to try to hold her hand, attempts fumblingly to do so and is repulsed, then rehearses various elegant and sophisticated ways of asking her to have a drink with him before blurting out "D'ya want a drink?" only to find that she has vanished (a scene that reminds me irresistibly of Charlie Brown trying to think of the right words with which to present his valentine to the little red-haired girl and doing so finally with a confident "Happy Christmas!"; both Charlies possess a common inability to make their inner and outer worlds coincide or even come within touching distance). The final metamorphosis of the inner voice ironically reverses the normal process as Charlie sits at his piano during the quarrel in the bar telling himself to stay out of it and suddenly finds himself taking part after all.

The dualities of Charlie's nature and of the world he moves in are echoed in the dialogue elsewhere in the film. The language of most of the characters is extremely slangy, down-to-earth, full of sexual jokes and innuendoes, reflecting Charlie's desire to punish himself by forcing himself into as sordid an environment as he can stand and systematically debasing or ignoring the values he had lived by previously. Conversations are short and terse, and Charlie himself speaks as little and as briefly as possible. He chooses to be in this environment but can never be fully part of it, as we see in the conversation in the car with the gangster, where Léna's smile becomes more and more knowing as the coarseness of the conversation becomes more explicit, till she finally takes an active part in it, while Charlie sits rather bewildered in the back seat and finally ventures as his contribution his father's remark that once you've seen one woman you've seen them all. The characters of this milieu are constantly attempting to explain and define themselves, but have neither the verbal nor the intellectual sophistication to succeed, though their very attempts are enough to give us insight into them. The flashback shows us a different world, where people talk more fluently and coherently, but where Charlie is equally ill at ease and uncomfortable. He can adjust fully to neither world, verbally, emotionally, or morally, and the result is the insecurity that plagues him throughout.

Charlie Kohler of *Shoot the Piano Player* attempts like the trio of *Jules and Jim* to live apart from society, but instead of moving into a wider, freer, more vital world, he retreats into one that is even more enclosed and restricted than that of normal experience. He makes more of a conscious choice than Pierre [the hero of *The Soft Skin*] does, but is equally unable to commit himself firmly to one course of action. Having failed his wife in a moment of extreme crisis, he wishes to avoid hurting himself or others in the future, but chooses a method that ensures that he will go on repeating his earlier mistake rather than correcting it. He tries to withdraw from social and personal relationships as far as possible and maintains a façade of aloofness and impassivity. Yet at the same time he continues to make himself available to others by living and working in their world, assuming that they will recognize and accept the dissociation he himself makes between his private, mental world and that in which he earns his bread. (It is also perhaps a subconscious acceptance of his real need of others.) But this doesn't work; others are fascinated, puzzled, or antagonized by him and attempt to draw him out, either for their own advantage, as Chico and his brothers do, or with the aim of helping him, as Léna does. Family loyalty, gratitude, love, guilt, all of them emotions he had thought he had suppressed, combine to make him respond to their promptings, but his refusal to acknowledge the effect of these emotions on him till too late insures that he never makes the right decision at the right time. He allows others to take the initiative for him and tries to opt out of responsibility until circumstances drag him in at a stage when he has no control over the course of events and can do nothing to prevent disaster. At the end of the film the introduction of a new barmaid and the sight of the impassive Charlie playing the same tune he has played throughout indicate that nothing has really changed for him and he will slip inexorably back into the old pattern. He shares with Jules, Jim, and Catherine the assumption that his telling himself that he no longer has certain emotions will automatically dispel them, and with Pierre the belief that if he sits tight and does nothing, things will somehow work themselves out. The result is an impasse in which commitment leads inexorably to disaster and lack of commitment proves impossible.

Despite Charlie's obvious weaknesses and self-deception, and the sordid surroundings, people, and conversation in which he chooses to move, it is impossible for us either to judge him or to dissociate ourselves from him. The style of the film disorients in a way that makes us ready to look at things with a fresh eye, and mingled with the shabbiness and weariness of the characters are humor and insight; people come vividly alive with very human weaknesses, needs, disappointments, self-protective deceptions, and *façades* that in the long run don't fool anyone, least of all themselves. Charlie's mask of world-heavy impassivity is constantly being knocked aside by the interior monologue that reveals his fundamental insecurity and vulnerability. His solution to the risks of life and involvement with other people is to make himself "smaller and smaller," to retreat into a "little circle" that shuts off the outside world as far as possible. As the other characters show, this is a not uncommon device, yet it is his failure to succeed with it, his acceptance of his need and responsibility for others that, paradoxically, humanizes him, and an ability to take Charlie into the worlds we ourselves have created and to accept our affinity with him can humanize us.

Truffaut, incidentally, follows the events and characterization of David Goodis's taut and atmospheric thriller *Down There* remarkably closely throughout, changing very little in terms of action and personality. The changes he does make, however, are in the direction of humanizing Charlie, making him more vulnerable and innocent, and also more comic, than he is in the novel (a process that takes in most of the other characters as well), and the shifts of tone and the bizarre juxtapositions that give the film its unique flavor have no counterpart in the book. . . .

Even the gangsters of *Shoot the Piano Player* with their jerky, automatonlike movements, their vague sense of better days and lost opportunities, their ineffectual imitation of actions and gestures from faintly recollected B movies, and their attempts to impress others with the need to take them seriously, have a humanity that somehow coexists with the fact that they end by killing Léna. (In all these respects they differ markedly from the tough, efficient killers of the book.)

Through the Looking Glass
Roger Greenspun

*Uneven, mangled, wobbly melodrama about barroom pianist who gets involved
with hoodlums. Satire and spoofs never quite come off.*

Capsule review of *Shoot the Piano Player* almost any week in *Cue*

*If there is any unifying tone in the film it is an existential irrelevance, coupled
with a shrug from Charles Aznavour, a masterful actor, which asks, What did
you expect? Existence is a succession of dirty jokes: nothing lasts, struggle is
futile, hope is obscene. (The title* Shoot the Piano Player *refers to a barroom
sign in old Westerns—"Don't Shoot the Piano Player"—but Truffaut's film
might as easily be called* Why Not Shoot the Piano Player?*)*

Judith Shatnoff in *Film Quarterly,* Spring 1963

*And Truffaut himself is so completely engaged in life that he pleads for the piano
player's right to be left alone, to live in his withdrawn state, to be out of it.
Truffaut's plea is, of course, "Don't shoot the piano player."*

Pauline Kael in *Film Culture* no. 27

*But Turley banged his hands against his knees. "Why ain't you there?"
"Because I'm here," Eddie said. "I can't be two places at once."*

David Goodis, *Down There*

Areturn to *Shoot the Piano Player* now, long after the impact of its initial
showing and, I hope, long before its enshrinement as a classic, requires
some explanation. *Shoot the Piano Player* has enjoyed exceptional popular
success, bucking Bosley Crowther in the art circuits and at least in New York
filtering down to some neighborhood houses; it has excited everybody worth
exciting; but among critics it seems to have inspired more enthusiasm for its
moods than understanding of its meaning. That it makes some kind of meaning,
despite Truffaut's own not very helpful postmortem comment that although a lot
goes on in his film there is no theme you can put your finger on,[1] and that such
meaning has to do with matters other than whether or not to shoot the piano player,
a question obviously designed to be let go begging, is the underlying point to these
remarks.

---

1. In an interview analyzing audience reaction in *Cahiers du Cinéma,* No. 138. Excerpts are translated
in *Film Quarterly,* Fall 1963.

From *Moviegoer* 1 (Winter 1964).

What I have to say will owe something to the most suggestive single commentary on Truffaut I know, Michel Delahaye's fine review of *Jules and Jim* in *Cahiers du Cinéma*, No. 129. *Shoot the Piano Player* embraces a phenomenology of extraordinary proportions: when a man's inner withdrawal creates a void in nature into which his wife then actually falls, theme and event become effectively indistinguishable, and my notions of how to account for the connections between them derive partly from Delahaye's insights into Truffaut's exploitation of visual-verbal puns and inversions.

I

So much happens in the Truffaut films that it is difficult even for a moment to draw back from their engrossing busyness and fix upon a single image in any one of them for a long close look. But it is a useful thing to do if you wish to isolate a revealing characteristic, and conveniently each of the three features gives us such an image at its very end. One remembers Antoine alone at the water's edge, caught in a still photograph with nowhere further to run, at the end of *The 400 Blows;* or Jules, his back to the camera, striding alone down the path of the cemetery where he has just interred his wife and his best friend; or the noncommittal face of Charlie Kohler, almost filling half the screen, appearing at the end of *Shoot the Piano Player* over the same honky-tonk tune with which the film had opened.

The first of these scenes reduces its film to stasis, the second prefigures escape, and the third suggests that everything moves around in a circle to come back pretty much to where it began. The music of Albert's ballad behind the retreating figure of Jules; Charlie's picking up the piano tune once again—by signaling an end to eventful progression both function in a way analogous to Antoine's stopping the movie. And each of the scenes contains a single character, not the suggestive grouping of even two characters in significant relation, so that we are left not with the figurative resolution of a drama but rather with just one figure, a man central to his world (as I think Jules rather than Catherine is for *Jules and Jim*) but bereft of that world's potential for sustaining and varying events. That each of these characters in certain particulars reproduces Antoine, desperately childlike in his need for the motherly attention of the woman who has for some reason been denied him, is thematically interesting for Truffaut's work so far. But perhaps *as* interesting is the final emphasis upon the man himself rather than upon any conclusive configuration to an action. I think it is fair to say that the Truffaut films develop activity rather than an Aristotelian "action," that they are concerned with making things happen rather than with the disposing of events in a dramatic structure, that by their own inner necessity they must at last center upon the actor—he who acts, or causes things to happen—and that they do not so much end as run down, or run on in what is pretty clearly to be mere repetition.

Like *Jules and Jim, Shoot the Piano Player* includes the telling of many stories: the normal happy life account of the man with the flowers, Chico's hard luck story in the café, the central flashback story of Edouard and Thérésa, Thérésa's own story of her shame, the crooks' crazy stories to Charlie and Léna and later to Fido, the story of the whole clan of the ill-fated Saroyans—going back generations, Charlie supposes, before one can discover the root of their curse. And, as in *Jules and Jim,* such an abundance of narratives seems partly to free the film as a whole from dependency upon any one story as basic structure, and to work for the suspension of "narrative," among other elements, within some different kind of form.

The problem is to describe the form, and here Michel Delahaye offers a clue in a few brilliant demonstrations. He notices, for example, that when Fido drops his milk bomb upon the hood of Ernest and Momo's car, they are obliged to turn on the windshield wipers to combat "l'opacité de cette blancheur qui risque de faire obstacle à leurs noirs desseins" [the opacity of this whiteness that stands in the way of their black designs]. Thus Delahaye assumes not only that whiteness darkens, but also that between the *visible* whiteness of the milk-spattered windshield and the conventional *ideas* of "black designs" there is a viable punning relation. The virtuosity of Delahaye's formulation is immediately matched and deepened by the movie, for not only are Ernest and Momo literally rendered light to make them no more than silhouettes, but their own evil "blackness" is within minutes made bright by their lively talking with Charlie and Léna in the initial kidnapping. Thus white opposes black, but white also makes black; and white and black are relative not only to one another but also within themselves—each showing a range of highlights and shadows once it is opened to close inspection. The enabling principle here is not the moral collapsing of black in white—which shades too readily in the minds of some critics to a gray acceptance of all conduct—but rather the fruitful notion of division into opposites itself, a multiplying of distinctions between and within spheres, of which black and white is only one manifestation, although a significant one for a film *in* black and white with the piano keyboard as one of its operative images.

Elsewhere I have attempted to identify abstract figures in *Jules and Jim*[2] and I have suggested that for that film, moving broadly through historic time, the circle ultimately is the lively restful figure containing and supporting the abundance of life that everyone has seen somehow as its central value. But *Shoot the Piano Player* is antihistorical, destroying time in the mirror image of its long flashback, moving in all directions through space, and finding its impetus to movement in the idea of cutting things up—dividing them so as to set part against part in a series of gestures that literally split the screen. *Shoot the Piano Player* is also full of circles: but notice that each of them, whether in the actual insets of the triple-faced Plyne,

2. In *Sight and Sound,* Spring 1963.

Ernest's mother dropping dead, or suave Lars Schmeel ominously fading out between Edouard and Thérésa in bed—or in the lyrical slow pan of Léna's room that shares the screen with a stationary shot showing Charlie and Léna kissing beneath an inverted horseshoe[3]—promotes a consciousness of discreet visual elements.

II

The catastrophes that invariably attend Charlie's major withdrawals—according to the principle of multiple relations I have borrowed from Delahaye, by which ideas, things, and images enjoy equality as phenomena—demonstrate the law that nature abhors a vacuum, at the same time that they enforce a plunge into the midst of events once again, restarting the round of activity in which the film lives. Quite simply: Edouard runs out on Thérésa after her eloquent admission of emptiness, and her body tumbles into the void he might have filled; Charlie splits from Léna at a crucial juncture, and her rush to mend the break ends with her sliding dead down a snowy hillside; even Plyne sinks into the circle of his own crushing embrace after Charlie tries calling it quits.

On the level of human motivation Charlie's fatal attractiveness to women relates to the need everybody in the film seems to feel for somebody else. The easy and real contact made and broken between Chico and the man who helps him at the beginning, Ernest and Momo's need not just to kidnap people but to make friends with them, the brute expression of Plyne's lonely frustration, even the ironic pathos with which Edouard looks for the real pianist in a bedroom mirror—all catch some aspect of a drive toward completion not in self-sufficiency but in personal contact. The amount of self-expression granted Clarisse, Plyne, the brothers, and so many others has more to it than an undeniable delight in character for its own sake; it is also a bid for bridging a gap that always threatens to appear beneath a surface that must be kept full and close if it is not to fail. When Charlie asks Léna for what reason she wants to back him in a return to the concert stage, she answers, not "pourquoi" but "pour qui. Pour moi et pour vous, pour nous deux."

Charlie's fatal attractiveness has its dark and unique underside as fate—in every woman who advances his career, from the old lady who used to drive him to his piano lessons and away from his brothers, to the mysterious girl with the violin who opens the door to Lars Schmeel's office for him when he is just about to back away—but it is not otherwise so very different from the mutual attractiveness of one for another that permeates the movie, and that finds its typical expression in

3. For the record, there is another bad luck sign, a cracked mirror in the Saroyans' country kitchen. Charlie comes upon it as his brothers joyfully confirm his membership in the clan.

everyone's telling somebody else part of a life story. Only Charlie clams up, and then people obligingly either tell him his own story (Léna), or make up stories for him (Lars Schmeel), or give him advice on how to improve his story (Schmeel and Plyne). But his own rich life is inward; his deepest dialogues are with himself. In response to Thérésa's moving and articulate confession he can only rush out of the room. While he lies in Léna's arms—by the cutting that alternates two time sequences in the course of their lovemaking—he is in fact already turning away from her while she recounts the history of her attempts to move toward him.

The headlong falls on the way to Charlie that occur in *Shoot the Piano Player* climax this preoccupation, and equalize planes of expression that in most films have at best no more than a metaphoric relation. Here every gesture takes place in space, or, better, makes the space in which and by which subsequent acts exist. There is no saying that character and situation influence one another; they *are* one another. It is therefore with the authority of image raised to the power of theme, and theme raised to the power of image, that the principle of division vitalizes and ultimately threatens this world. Split into a series of more or less precise oppositions, the strange career of Charlie/Edouard shuttles on, potentially into an infinity of mutually reflecting mirror images.

III

Thérésa falls from a very great height. She leaps from the pinnacle to which she has been instrumental in raising her husband (the later parts of their story are largely seen in sequences of walking up and down stairs) both into the void she finds within herself and into the gap he has made in their perfect union, where they were so many things to each other—husband and wife, student and teacher, waitress and customer—in a life game in which, as Schmeel neatly observes, everybody is a winner. Edouard turned Charlie completes her fall, descending down beneath the dark roadway where she dies to the absolute blackness of the cellar he is hidden in after killing Plyne. Together with Léna he ascends again, up into the bright sunlight and snow of the mountains, only to witness another fall beginning his own second descent.

The stories' similarity in spatial outline is completed by various complementary or opposing details: the two impresarios, Plyne and Schmeel, both sure they know what's wrong with Charlie and both after his women; Edouard's desertion of Thérésa because she is sullied, and Charlie's defense of Léna after Plyne brands *her* as sullied; Thérésa's loss of identity after Schmeel's attack, and Plyne's insistence that a Léna who speaks foul language is not a woman; a blond waitress in one story and a dark one in the other, but a dark death for the blond and a snowy white one for the brunette; a romantic tale of dedicated love and brilliant success supported by a grimy business deal, and an obscure and sordid life briefly illumined by a recklessly romantic dream.

Two stories, two parts of a life divided up to escape itself, so ingeniously reproducing one another, do more than give the film the air of fatality that persistently dogs Charlie and that finds general expressive outlet in virtually everything from the tough-luck café ballad on up. A major part of their function is realized in the very creation of a pair of reflecting surfaces, which, by their extensive relations to one another, enclose the *Piano Player* world within an apparently hermetic seal of correspondences. Within this enclosure it is hopeless to look for resolution. Charlie necessarily seeks his way through and out, and his famous withdrawal tendencies owe as much to the kind of space he occupies as to any quirk in his own character. Getting a real grip on Charlie is no easy task, as Plyne, Schmeel, Ernest and Momo, and any number of film critics all demonstrate—and as the piano player discovers for himself.

Who *is* Charlie Kohler? He is Edouard Saroyan. Who is Edouard Saroyan? A brilliant concert pianist. Is he? Edouard himself asks the question—of the critics, of Hemingway (does he collect my records?), of the janitor, of himself as he stands before a mirror hoping to catch an image of the real thing but seeing only the face that asks the question thrown back at him. Schmeel says that at last he "has" Edouard when he has a portrait painted, the dark figure of a pathetic man against a dark background. But just as Schmeel makes his boast the portrait is totally obscured, not by a deeper darkness but by brilliant flashes of light from news photographers—so that it too becomes a reflecting surface, revealing nothing at all. The problem of identity, the reliable place of a man among the things and events of his world, remains unsolved, but it remains the major problem in the film.

During the sequence with Schmeel and the portrait, Edouard does something typical: he moves from in front of the photographers' flashbulbs (*they* don't catch him; they catch a pose imitated from the man in the poster who has ideally conquered timidity) to the darkest recess of Schmeel's office, which is itself an arrangement in sharp intervals of bright windows and dark interstices—like the piano keyboard, like the double life, an alternation of black and white. *All* Charlie/Edouard's movements are between these extremes. To attempt making some controlled associations for black and white is to begin seeing the inclusive mode of *Shoot the Piano Player,* and in determining the potential for characterization of that mode, to work toward the conditions for life it fosters.

IV

Edouard and Charlie, Thérésa and Léna, Schmeel and Plyne, wealth and poverty, success and failure, light and darkness—these mirror one another, touch, interpenetrate, but never enter into solution. Simply to look at *Shoot the Piano Player* is to exercise a heightened awareness of contrast, beginning with a single spotlight cutting through a field of black, reaching a climax in the breathtakingly beautiful ride from Paris to the mountains—highway lights in the darkness, reflections off the windshield of Léna's car, brilliant sunlight on a high snowy landscape—and ending in the screen's strict vertical division into black and white.

To the extent that the *idea* of black and white hovers over the film, available for any new improvisation, it engenders and supports all activity, but actually explains none of it. It is pattern, and not morality or psychology or antipsychology, though it may lend itself to any of these for the time it takes to complete a gesture or establish an attitude. But this impartial vituosity exacts a toll upon the characters whose lives it activates but whose human responses it does not quite account for. There is a tension in the film that exceeds the potential of the brilliant determinism I have been describing, and that derives from a feeling but utterly unsentimental understanding of the complexities of lives that are caught in the proliferation of mutually exclusive terms their world offers. Everybody in *Shoot the Piano Player* is an articulate spokesman for a way of life, but almost everybody understands life as a selection from among absolute commitments. Charlie accepts Clarisse for bed and board but completely rejects her for anything else, Plyne knows exactly what is and what is not a woman, Schmeel divides and conquers—and so on through a range of demonstration that finds in the making of distinctions one of the film's crucial preoccupations. The corollary of so much picking of sides is a special kind of picking apart; the end of sharp distinctions is finally disintegration. And this is the burden of a speech given a moment before death, Thérésa's set confession, structurally at the center of the film, movingly describing a failure in personal integration that many people at one time or another feel but that only she totally articulates.

With perfect instinct, Truffaut has utilized most of the events in David Goodis's miserable novel, merely moving them from New York and Philadelphia to Paris, while rejecting almost all its interpretations of them. The one great exception is Thérésa's confession, where he has retained and elaborated upon a body of dialogue that remains isolated as pathos in the novel[4] but meaningfully connects with everything in the film. Thérésa describes Schmeel's precisely calculated method of attack, and the change, the loss of the old Thérésa, it has made in her. Schmeel has taken her body and discarded her heart; Schmeel slides out as efficiently as he slides in, and there have been no complications. But in the midst of a gleaming world—white sports car, white apartment, bright lights, shining blond girl—she discovers darkness and filth. A few scenes before, Edouard had looked in the mirror to find himself, and now she reveals that she has looked too—but there is no Thérésa anywhere, only a used-up dirty old rag. Schmeel has come and gone, but for her what she did yesterday is part of what she is today. "Yesterday" is her mirror, and it is different in quality from anybody else's. She looks specifically for an emotional continuity to life, and her way of describing the destruction of that continuity—the dissolution of bright surfaces and an awareness

---

4. Pages 80–82 in the Grove Press Black Cat edition.

of encroaching night—provides something very like a point of moral reference for the film's methods. Every death in *Shoot the Piano Player* follows an analogous pattern, but only Thérésa's is self-willed, a conscious recognition of the despair that accompanies the pattern, finding between its sharp distinctions the crack that opens to the abyss of total nonbeing, personal annihilation.

In this complex of surfaces any face is a mask, and every mask presupposes a secret life behind it. Charlie's two secret lives, the one he's leading and the one he's keeping secret, are of course the film's central stories; but other lives and stories have their place. (There are even fleeting suggestions of potential integration—in the late-discovered love and growing family of the stranger who helps Chico up after his collision with a lamppost, the first tumble in the movie and visually, with its dark night and flowers as against morning light and snow, an inverted counterpart of the last; or in the enthusiastic acceptance with which the other Saroyan brothers, great antidivisionists on principle, welcome back Edouard even with the cops probably on his tail, now that he has killed a man and is one of them.) But when the stories are over and the secret lives have mostly been exposed into obscurity, some faces still remain. As Chico tells Plyne very early, you don't get any information without paying for it; and if one of Charlie's women describes the apprehension of death for her world, the other dies to give it its image—in a terrifying slow dissolve that superimposes the dead face of Léna upon the movie's closing sequence. What we feel at this moment is not so much the pathos of Léna's pointless killing as the authority of death itself. The face that looks back at us from the snow, an inverted image to be sure, conceals no secret at all. What you can see is all there is to it, and that is quite enough. Léna's perfect containment, like Thérésa's total emptiness, is a cipher—but one or the other is all there is to discover when the running, fighting, loving, playing, remembering stop.

People have been so busy admiring Truffaut's marvelous inventiveness and vitality that they have ignored the fact that each of his films, beginning with the initiation to manhood through contact with death in *Les Mistons,* is finally about the failure, the turning stale, of inventiveness and vitality. The three features seal this point by turning their child-man protagonists into emblems of life possibilities exhausted; and especially in *Shoot the Piano Player* the emblem is fully, schematically developed. A wide screen divided down the middle into white and black, the line of the piano top across the bottom, Charlie's impassive face against the dark—the resources of film itself, the terms of this film's life, the man positioned to one side, and the machine for banging out the tune spanning both sides, holding the world together, keeping things going for the time being.

The Technique of *Shoot the Piano Player*
Karel Reisz and Gavin Millar

T ruffaut has said in an interview that what he is aiming at is "un éclatement de genres par un mélange de genres"—"an explosion of genres by a mixture of genres." He always tries, he says, to confound his audiences' expectations, to keep them constantly surprised. When the film seems to be going in one direction he likes to turn it round and send it off in another. He thinks of his films as circus shows with a dazzling variety of turns, and likes at the end to take the audience out into the country or to some idyllic scene—snow or the sea—as a reward for being cooped up in the dark for nearly two hours.

It should not be thought that Truffaut is being simply frivolous in saying this. In the first place his films bear out the thesis: each of them[1] does flick from moods of despair to exhilaration and does contain scenes of black comedy alternating with scenes of real tragedy or simply good-hearted unaffected joy. As for locations: the last scene of *The 400 Blows* has the boy hero running to the sea; the last [*sic:* it is the penultimate] scene of *Shoot the Piano Player* takes place in a snowstorm by a mountain chalet of fairy-tale improbability. *Jules and Jim* is such a lyrical medley of sea, river, alp, and forest that few spectators can surely have suffered from being cooped up with it. *Fahrenheit 451* ends in a snowstorm, in a forest.

Nor are Truffaut's aims the result of simple contrariness. They are the reflection of his philosophy. It is clear from his films that he celebrates what Rhode and Pearson call "the philosophy of discontinuity."

The swift changes of mood and pace that characterize his films are an attempt to match his form more nearly to the way life usually develops. We don't live life according to "genres." Nor is life, according to the way we think today, a taut unbroken chain of significant purposeful acts, linked by logic, as it is sometimes made to appear according to the editing pattern and plot development of the traditional cinema. Indeed, plot often disappears, as it virtually does in *The 400 Blows*. Antoine's life is described not so much by a series of dramatic events as by a string of nonevents: roaming the streets, playing truant, visiting the fairground, mooning about the flat, avoiding doing his homework.

The action is handled in long unbroken medium shots lasting as long as physically possible. The cuts come when they're unavoidable: when a character

---

1. *The 400 Blows, Shoot the Piano Player, Jules and Jim, The Soft Skin, Fahrenheit 451.*

From *The Technique of Film Editing* by Karel Reisz and Gavin Millar, 2nd rev. ed. (London: Focal Press, 1968), pp. 330–344.

leaves the room or goes out of sight down the stairs. It is clear to see from *The 400 Blows* that Truffaut is a pupil of André Bazin. When the shot lasts too long for comfort, but Truffaut wants to use the beginning and the end, he is not above chopping a bit out of the middle. In one scene involving Antoine's friend and the friend's father, the father goes out of sight through a doorway on his way to the kitchen. He soon reappears in the kitchen, some way away at the end of a dark passage. But between leaving this room and reappearing in the other one there has been a longer time lag than we are led to believe. A cat lazing on a shelf in the top left-hand corner of the frame makes a sudden "jump" to a slightly different position and betrays that there is footage missing. Or it could be that the camera was stopped and locked off in the end position in the first half of the shot and picked up again when the father had had time to get into position for the continuation of the shot. The point is that rather than cut to a new setup, Truffaut tries to preserve the sense of continuity. Similar examples occur elsewhere in *Shoot the Piano Player*. Truffaut disguises a jump cut between two different takes by joining the shots when Fido, the kid brother, realizes he is being shadowed by the "crooks" in their big American car. Again, in Thérésa's long, apparently one-shot, confession to Charlie/Edouard in their flat just before she commits suicide, Truffaut has very skillfully disguised the fact that he has used the first half of one take and the second half of another by finding a cutting point where the images are almost identical for a moment. The question of intention arises. Truffaut confesses that "he saves all his films in the cutting room." It isn't that these things had never been done before. But the New Wave directors take more risks, do them more frequently and with more boldness, and more often than not demonstrate that only if the audience is already confused will it be further confused by unconventional technique.

But in *The 400 Blows* the mysterious interview with the psychiatric social worker is a classic case of how not to do it, in traditional terms. During the interview the boy's answers are joined by dissolves and we never see the interviewer at all. As a "dramatic" scene, or as a treatment of social problems, the scene is a failure. But of course that isn't its purpose. The real subject is internal and that is what the method is designed to deal with. The subject is the boy's own internal world. He takes no interest in the interviewer. We don't see her because, for him, she hardly exists.

At the end of the film Antoine escapes from the detention center where he has been sent for stealing a typewriter. He runs to the sea, which he has never seen. The action is chiefly described in a very few, very long tracking shots taken from a car while the boy runs alongside. The sequence lasts several minutes. It is not so much an event as a state of mind of which the form of the shot is an apt expression. We feel the freedom of his flight as a great release after the various sorts of imprisonment, mental and physical, which he has suffered in the course of the film. In this example, and in that of the dissolves, too, the form of the shots has been as much a part of the meaning as any content they have "described."

More so than *The 400 Blows, Shoot the Piano Player* extends the vocabulary of the New Cinema in interesting ways. The story concerns a concert pianist, Edouard Saroyan, who discovers that his career really began when his wife slept with his impresario, Schmeel. She begs his forgiveness, but momentarily he turns from her in disgust. She commits suicide. He retires from society, changes his name to Charlie Kohler, and becomes a café player. He has a liaison with a new girl but is once more, after a series of adventures, indirectly the cause of his girl's death.

Charlie goes to Schmeel's flat for an audition. While he is waiting outside the door, he hesitates before pressing Schmeel's bell. He puts out a finger to it, and stops. There then follow two or three bigger and bigger close-ups of his finger and the bell button getting closer. The shots provoke a whole string of reactions: (1) They are funny. (2) They are menacing, as all moments are when the action slows up, or the cutting begins to go into a great deal of detail. So they should be, in view of what we later know is happening (but we don't know it then). (3) They are psychologically accurate since they represent his timidity. (4) They draw attention to a notorious *temps-mort,* that time that we all spend standing outside doors that won't open, or waiting for lifts that won't come. At those moments the universe shrinks to the dimensions of a doorbell that seems for a time to have more reality than oneself. And here we reach perhaps the most central consideration of all. (5) Charlie is a protagonist who embodies the philosophy of discontinuity. His life is a search for wholeness: the wholeness of success, the wholeness of an ideology, of a successful love affair, of a scale of values he can believe in. He looks for confidence and for trust. He doesn't succeed. The representation of his failure is carried in a sequence of images of increasing fragmentation. He is constantly seen reflected in a mirror that hangs over his piano in the café. We are introduced to him in the café's Gents, where he is knotting his tie and looking into the mirror. At the end of the film in the mountain chalet, sheltering from the police after he had accidentally killed a man, he stares into a little cracked shaving mirror and repeats to himself the words of his criminal brother: "Now you are one of us." His relinquishing of himself to Schmeel, the impresario, is marked by the completion of a portrait of him of which Schmeel says, "Thanks to this painting, I can look at you every day." Charlie's wife also speaks of being cut in two by the spider, Schmeel. In the context of this abounding fragmentation, it is not difficult to see the finger-on-bell shots as an indication that for Charlie the universe, the world of objects, is irretrievably breaking up beyond his power to control it. . . .

Let us look at a sequence from *Shoot the Piano Player* that is typical of Truffaut's work in its range of moods and technical dexterity.

	Ft.	Fr.

1. *A newspaper front page that announces the suicide of Thérésa, Charlie's wife. This is superimposed on a barely discernible view of a scrapyard across which the camera begins to pan right immediately. (The newspaper shot has been superimposed on the previous shot of Thérésa lying in the road, dead.) The paper fades and the pan reveals now cars in the junkyard, now a roadway, now a café exterior in a poor quarter.*

Newspaper reads: "Wife of noted pianist throws herself from fifth floor." Charlie's characteristic piano music starts.   29

L É N A ' S   V O I C E : You disappeared. You began a new life. Edouard Saroyan became Charlie Kohler. You visited your brothers in the snow and asked them to let Fido live with you. One day you found yourself at Plyne's. *The piano music stops.*

2. M L S : *Interior café by day. Plyne is mending a table. Charlie is sweeping the floor.*

   Charlie opens the keyboard.

You must have swept that floor a thousand times. There was a little upright battered piano in a corner. *A distant engine hoot.* You spent all your time—   48   6
—looking at it, walking all round it, looking at it again. One day you asked Plyne:
C H A R L I E : Can I play a bit?
P L Y N E : Eh?
C H A R L I E : I think I know how.
P L Y N E : Go ahead then. Just get it to make some music.

   [A woman] enters and picks up Charlie's cleaning utensils and walks toward camera. Charlie sits at piano.

3. B C U : *Full face of Charlie, left profile, seated at piano. He looks down at keyboard, serious, then begins to play.*
   The camera slowly swings right and pans left and tilts down his arms and on to the keyboard. Then it tilts up on to the hammers, seen clearly through the open front of the piano.
   M I X   T O

Classical piano music begins.   43   4

Music mixes to Charlie's café tune.

4. M S : *Interior of café. Nighttime. In a rectangular mirror above the piano Charlie is seen playing. Camera pans down left on to Charlie. He is enjoying himself.*

L É N A ' S   V O I C E : Who is Charlie Kohler? Little known. He's a pianist. He looks after his little brother. Above all, he wants no trouble.   16

5. M L S : *Charlie and two other musicians on the stand. People are dancing.*

Thanks to you, the local people started coming every evening to dance, and it got to be quite a place. Plyne took on extra staff, and some musicians.   10   8

		Ft.	Fr.
6. M C S : *Victor the drummer.*	Victor the drummer, who was always laughing without knowing why.	4	8
7. M C S : *François the bass player*	And his brother François the bass player—	3	4
8. C S : *François's hands on the bass.*	—with his long hairy hands.	4	2
9. M S : *Exterior of the café. Night. The camera begins a long tracking shot from left to right along the pavement outside the café, looking in. It passes over, after a while, the poster on the outside wall advertising "Charlie Koller." M I X , starting at about 24 ft. and clear in shot 10 at about 30 ft. from the beginning of shot 9.*	And then there was me—whom you looked at all the time without ever seeing. *The jaunty music of the café piano gradually mixes to a quieter, more dreamlike theme.*	27	
10. M S : *Interior of bedroom (Léna's). 9 is still panning when 10 begins. 10 too begins with a pan which continues through the shot, a full 360 degrees. But this pan is in the opposite direction, i.e., from right to left. The shot begins on a poster on the wall announcing a concert to be given by Edouard Saroyan. After 5 ft. of this pan, a close-up of Léna and Charlie kissing each other gently is superimposed and held through the shot until, at 54½ ft. in, it starts to disappear. The objects that the pan reveals on its course round the bedroom are in turn, the door, a radio, a window, a bowl of goldfish, a bust (i.e., a piece of sculpture), a bra and other clothes on a chair, and finally the bed with Charlie and Léna in it. The superimposed close-up of them fades completely just before the pan reaches the bed.*		64	
11. C S : *Charlie and Léna in bed.*	LÉNA'S VOICE: On my birthday, when I kissed everybody, it was just so that I could kiss you, you know. Then I saw you looking at me, and I looked at you, too.	22	
M I X *lasting ½ second.*			
12. M S : *Charlie and Léna in bed, moving in their sleep. The image is clear for little more than a foot. M I X lasting ½ second.*		2	44
13. *As 11.*	What were you thinking about when we were walking together in the street last night?	7	8

Ft.   Fr.

14. M S : *as in 12, same lengths of*
dissolve out of 13 and into 15. Clear
image for 2 ft. 12 frs.
M I X *to*

15. C S : *as in 13.*   Did you like me right away? Do you   11
                                         remember the evening you said to me—

16. *As 14 exactly in lengths.*
M I X *to*

17. *As 15.*   When I took your arm I was afraid you'd   9   12
                                         be shocked.

18. *As 16. Clear for 2 ft. 8 frs.*
M I X *to*

19. *As 17.*   I wanted you so badly to take mine.   7   8
M I X *to*

20. *As 18.*
M I X *to*

21. C U : *Léna in bed.*   10

The most interesting thing about this extract is that, although it employs a great diversity of styles and tones, it has, on the screen, a surprising homogeneity. This is only partly because of the unity brought to it by the narrator's voice.

In *1–4* we have moved from Thérésa's suicide to Charlie's new life as the café pianist. In that time we have also established the locale and tone of the café and learned a little about its people. We have learned especially about Léna's early feeling for Charlie. All the four shots seem leisurely. Shots *1* and *3* especially have a strong lyrical feeling in them. But they still perform a valuable function in conveying information and drawing character.

Shot *1* associates the sadness and squalor of Thérésa's death (she had thrown herself from a window) with the junkyard of old cars, by having the newspaper superimposed over both shots. The junkyard suggests the spiritual depths to which Charlie has been plunged by his wife's suicide. It also tells us, of course, what sort of area he has chosen to bury himself in order to get away from the bright lights and all his former friends. Léna's affectionate regard comes through in the commentary (especially in the description of Charlie's fascination by the piano), but the lightness of tone is not allowed to detract from the seriousness with which we are to treat Charlie. In the next shot his excellence as a pianist is brought to our attention by the intensity of the moving close-up, which seems to give him dignity. In no way does this cast any reflection on Léna's slight playfulness about him. It is this constant delicacy in balancing tones of feeling, in commentary/dialogue and image, that gives Truffaut's film the curious flavor of sadness and joy that it has.

In the next section the jokes are about, but not at the expense of, Victor and François. Charlie, in *4* and *5,* is happily jogging in time to the music. But they are not just jokes. Léna is talking about the three of them, and so we see Charlie at the piano, then the three on the stand, then Victor, then François, and François's hairy hands. But when she mentions herself it seems to be her characteristic modesty that prevents her from appearing when we should most expect it. Instead of her we see the exterior of the café, and in a long tracking shot past the windows, watch the happy couples inside. It is almost as though Léna is silently telling us that she feels she is shut out from this happiness. We know that that is how Charlie feels about his own life. A link between them is tacitly suggested, almost entirely by the absence of an expected shot, and the form of another.

But the exterior tracking shot is not simply a metaphorical device. The shot continues until we pan across a poster announcing the attraction of "Charlie Koller" playing at the café. With perfect logic this suggests the poster of Edouard Saroyan that we know is hanging in Léna's bedroom. In a curious dissolve the poster of Saroyan, with something of a metaphorical force, since it represents as it were the wishes of Léna, appears to displace the stand-in, Charlie Kohler. So we see, too, that the movement of the camera along the pavement and away from the café was a way of expressing the movement of Léna's mind away from the café and toward her own bedroom where she lies now with Charlie.

The dissolve is curious because, breaking all the rules, it not only begins at the end of *9* on movement, not only continues in *10* on movement, but the movements are in opposite directions. The effect mixes the images in such a way as to suggest pleasant reverie, though it doesn't pretend that it is a picture of what Léna herself is seeing.

The pan from the poster of Saroyan on the bedroom wall is the longest shot in the sequence. Because of the close-up of Charlie and Léna superimposed over it, the underlying images of the bedroom are hard to discern. This is what makes the moment when the goldfish bowl swims into view particularly delicate. For a few seconds as the camera pans over them, the four goldfish are seen, in long shot, nibbling the surface of the water in exactly the same way as the lovers are nuzzling each other's faces. The superimposition disappears just before the pan completes its circle and we come back to the bed again. The next eleven shots are a most unusual device. The short alternate shots into and out of which we dissolve so quickly show the lovers stirring vaguely in the abandoned attitudes of sleep. They take liberties with our conventional idea of the time scale, and they work, literally, like a charm.

 **Filmography and Bibliography**

Truffaut Filmography, 1954–1983

1954   *Une Visite (A Visit,* short subject)

1958   *Les Mistons (The Mischief-Makers,* short subject)

1958   *Une Histoire d'eau (A Story about Water,* short subject)
Directed with Jean-Luc Godard.

1959   *Les 400 Coups (The 400 Blows)*
Screenplay by Truffaut, dialogue by Truffaut and Marcel Moussy.

1960   *Tirez sur le pianiste (Shoot the Piano Player; Shoot the Pianist* [U.K.])
Screenplay by Truffaut and Marcel Moussy, adapted from the novel *Down There* by David Goodis.

1962   *Jules et Jim (Jules and Jim)*
Screenplay by Truffaut and Jean Gruault, adapted from the novel *Jules et Jim* by Henri-Pierre Roché.

1962   *L'Amour a vingt ans (Love at Twenty)*
Episode film by Truffaut (whose episode was titled "Antoine et Colette") and four other directors:

Renzo Rossellini, Marcel Ophuls, Andrzej Wajda, and Ishihara Shintaro.

1964   *La Peau douce (The Soft Skin; Silken Skin* [U.K.])
Screenplay by Truffaut and Jean-Louis Richard

1966   *Fahrenheit 451*
Screenplay by Truffaut and Jean-Louis Richard, adapted from the novel of the same name by Ray Bradbury.

1968   *La Mariée était en noir (The Bride Wore Black)*
Screenplay by Truffaut and Jean-Louis Richard, adapted from the novel *The Bride Wore Black* by William Irish (Cornell Woolrich).

1968   *Baisers volés (Stolen Kisses)*
Screenplay by Truffaut, Claude de Givray, and Bernard Revon.

1969   *La Sirène du Mississippi (Mississippi Mermaid)*
Screenplay by Truffaut, adapted from the novel *Waltz into Darkness* by William Irish (Cornell Woolrich).

1970 *L'Enfant sauvage* (*The Wild Child*)
Screenplay by Truffaut and Jean Gruault, based on the 1806 book *Mémoire et rapport sur Victor de l'Aveyron* by Jean Itard.

1970 *Domicile conjugal* (*Bed and Board*)
Screenplay by Truffaut, Claude de Givray, and Bernard Revon.

1971 *Les Deux Anglaises* (original title *Les Deux Anglaises et le continent*) (*Two English Girls; Anne and Muriel* [U.K.])
Screenplay by Truffaut and Jean Gruault, adapted from the novel *Deux Anglaises et le continent* by Henri-Pierre Roché.

1972 *Une Belle Fille comme moi* (*Such a Gorgeous Kid Like Me; A Gorgeous Bird Like Me* [U.K.])
Screenplay by Truffaut and Jean-Loup Dabadie, adapted from the novel *Such a Gorgeous Kid Like Me* by Henry Farrell.

1973 *La Nuit américaine* (*Day for Night*)
Screenplay by Truffaut, Jean-Louis Richard, and Suzanne Schiffman.

1975 *L'Histoire d'Adèle H.* (*The Story of Adèle H.*)
Screenplay by Truffaut and Jean Gruault, adapted from the book *Le journal d'Adèle Hugo* by Frances V. Guille.

1976 *L'Argent de poche* (*Small Change*)
Screenplay by Truffaut and Suzanne Schiffman.

1977 *L'Homme qui aimait les femmes* (*The Man Who Loved Women*)
Screenplay by Truffaut, Michel Fermaud, and Suzanne Schiffman.

1978 *La Chambre verte* (*The Green Room*)
Screenplay by Truffaut and Jean Gruault, based on several short stories by Henry James, including "The Altar of the Dead" and "The Beast in the Jungle."

1979 *L'Amour en fuite* (*Love on the Run*)
Screenplay by Truffaut, Marie-France Pisier, Jean Aurel, and Suzanne Schiffman.

1980 *Le Dernier Métro* (*The Last Metro*)
Screenplay by Truffaut and Suzanne Schiffman.

1981 *La Femme d'à coté* (*The Woman Next Door*)
Screenplay by Truffaut, Suzanne Schiffman, and Jean Aurel.

1983 *Vivement Dimanche!* (*Confidentially Yours; Finally Sunday* [U.K.])
Screenplay by Truffaut, Suzanne Schiffman, and Jean Aurel, adapted from the novel *The Long Saturday Night* by Charles Williams.

Selected Bibliography

Allen, Don. *Finally Truffaut.* New York: Beaufort Books, 1985. An updated version of *Truffaut,* published in 1974.

Braudy, Leo, ed. *Focus on "Shoot the Piano Player."* Englewood Cliffs, N.J.: Prentice-Hall, 1972.

Collet, Jean. *Le Cinéma de François Truffaut.* Paris: Pierre Lherminier, 1985.

Crisp, C. G. *François Truffaut.* New York: Praeger, 1972.

Fanne, Dominque. *L'Univers de François Truffaut.* Paris: Editions du Cerf, 1972.

Fox, Joan. "The New Wave." In *The Film,* ed. Andrew Sarris, pp. 39–44. Indianapolis, Ind.: Bobbs-Merrill, 1968.

Insdorf, Annette. *François Truffaut.* Revised edition. New York: Simon & Schuster, 1989.

Kinder, Marsha, and Beverle Houston. "Truffaut's Gorgeous Killers," *Film Quarterly* 27, no. 2 (Winter 1973–1974): 2–10.

Monaco, James. *The New Wave: Truffaut, Godard, Chabrol, Rohmer, Rivette.* New York: Oxford University Press, 1976.

Petrie, Graham. *The Cinema of François Truffaut.* New York: A. S. Barnes, 1970.

Truffaut, François. *Hitchcock.* New York: Simon & Schuster, 1967.

———. *The Films of My Life.* New York: Simon & Schuster, 1978. Originally published as *Les Films de ma vie* (Paris: Flammarion, 1975).

———. *Correspondence 1945–1984,* ed. Gilles Jacob and Claude de Givray; trans. Gilbert Adair. New York: Farrar, Straus & Giroux, 1990.

———. *Hitchcock.* New York: Simon & Schuster, 1967.

Walz, Eugene P. *François Truffaut: Guide to References and Resources.* New York: G. K. Hall, 1982.